DILEMMAS OF SCHOOLING

DILEMMAS OF

SCHOOLING

TEACHING AND SOCIAL CHANGE

ANN & HAROLD BERLAK

METHUEN
LONDON AND NEW YORK

First published in 1981 by
Methuen & Co. Ltd
11 New Fetter Lane, London EC4P 4EE

Published in the USA by
Methuen & Co.
in association with Methuen, Inc.
733 Third Avenue, New York, NY 10017

Typeset by Inforum Ltd, Portsmouth
Printed in the United States of America

British Library Cataloguing in Publication Data

Berlak, Ann
Dilemmas of schooling.
1. Elementary schools – Great Britain – Social aspects
I. Title   II. Berlak, Harold
373.941   LB1567.G7
ISBN 0-416-74140-1
ISBN 0-416-74110-X Pbk

Science is to lighten the toil
of human existence

There is joy in doubting
I wonder why

Can society stand on doubt
Rather than Faith?

Brecht, *Galileo*

For our children, Lev, Mariam and Rachel, who enrich our lives, struggle with us, and often remind us how little we understand of children's views of the world.

In memory of Dina and William who showed us the meaning of justice and love.

CONTENTS

PREFACE AND ACKNOWLEDGEMENTS

This book is our effort to make sense of our experience as teachers, teachers of teachers, schooling researchers, parents of three children, and citizens. We address not only our academic colleagues, educationalists, sociologists, and curriculum researchers, but the entire community of teachers and non-teachers, who as citizens of constitutional democracies have the right and responsibility to see to it that the nation's schools operate in their and their children's best interests.

Our contribution to a more active exercise of this right and responsibility is a 'language of schooling' intended to help surmount the obstructions to communication between and among academic experts, practising educators, and citizens. The terms of the language are sixteen dilemmas that will, hopefully, be useful for guiding teachers' and non-teachers' collaborative, critical inquiries into the schooling process, illuminating the relationship of everyday school events to broader social, economic, and political issues, and the alternative possibilities for action.

In an effort to speak to three audiences we have necessarily slighted many of the significant problems and issues of concern to each. Academic readers may find underdeveloped our treatment of the theoretical underpinnings, and disconcerting our choice to confine largely to a single chapter and to the end notes our discussions of other critical and interpretative social scientists who have been working on similar problsms. On the other hand, some general readers might have preferred fewer forays into social and political philosophy and a more systematic clarification of the educational policy issues of the 1980s. Practising educators, particularly teachers, are likely to find thin our discussions of the many practical pedagogical, curriculum and evaluation questions we raise and only briefly address. If our book has merit, it is not its great depth of treatment of any subject but its breadth; its effort to join the theoretical with the practical in one domain of human activity, schooling.

There are many friends and colleagues who have contributed to the writing of this book, and we can acknowledge only a few of them by name.

First, the teachers and head teachers, particularly those in the three schools we describe and analyse in some detail. They allowed us to intrude upon their and their students' lives, and added immeasurably to our knowledge and understanding of children, teaching and learning. We hope we have not violated their trust.

Naida Tushnet Bagenstos, and Edward R. Mikel, both longtime friends and colleagues. They began with us in 1973 this effort to develop a language of schooling cast as a set of dilemmas. Their contributions to this work were enormous and selfless.

Marilyn Cohn and Vivian Gellman. They worked with Harold during the years we were writing this book, developing an elementary teacher education program at Washington University that bridged the gap between theory and practice. They brought a vision of the practical possibilities, and knowledge of the complexities, of relating knowing and doing.

Rita Roth, Rebecca Glenn, David Dodge, Timothy Tomlinson, friends and colleagues, we have been privileged to work with over the years, whose ideas greatly extended and clarified our own.

Martyn Hammersley, John Naylor, and Ian Westbury. They were able to see what we were trying to do, often before we understood it ourselves. Their encouragement and trenchant criticisms were invaluable.

Andy Hargreaves, Harold Silver, Sara Delamont, and an official in the local educational authority where we conducted our observations. Their careful, sympathetic reading of the manuscript helped us to shape it into its present form.

Finally, we thank some old and more recent friends: Judson T. Shaplin, at one time Associate Dean at Harvard Graduate School of Education and later Director of the Graduate Institute of Education at Washington University (retired). He made it possible for us – and many others – to pursue careers as scholar/practitioners. Donald W. Oliver, Professor of Education at Harvard, who years ago sowed the seeds of the idea of a critical analysis of the problematics of social life in terms of a set of dilemmas. Finally, Barry A. and Gail M. Kaufman, colleagues, dear friends and intellectual compatriots who sustained us during the difficult times.

Ann and Harold Berlak
St Louis, Missouri, USA
January 1981

PART ONE
CONTROVERSIES AND CONTEXT

INTRODUCTION

The eighth decade of the twentieth century opens with the world's first and largest capitalist nations in economic eclipse. The prognosis holds little or no hope for return to the post Second World War years of economic expansion coupled with rapid growth of the welfare state.[1] The economies of Britain and the United States stagnate; unemployment is high, inflation that reduced the buying power of the pound and dollar by more than half over the preceding decade continues. People worry increasingly about their own and their children's fates, and schooling issues are deeply implicated in their concerns.

The idea of the common school, a cornerstone of constitutional democracy and of democratic socialism, is once more under attack in both countries. People ask more insistently whether it is possible for a single system of tax-supported schools to provide all youth — regardless of social class, cultural and racial origin, history of oppression or privilege — with the skills and knowledge required to succeed in the intense competition for employment or entry into favored universities, professional and technical schools.[2] On both sides of the Atlantic skepticism is expressed by more intense public pressure for separation of the exceptionally talented, creative and/or dim, uninterested or troublesome students into different classes, programs or schools. Questions are raised whether laws should compel adolescents who show no aptitude for or interest in school to remain. In Britain the Conservative government's proposal to underwrite private or independent schools by providing direct grants or 'vouchers' to students undercuts the present policy formulated in the 1960s and 1970s to create a single system of comprehensive secondary schools. Articles in newspapers and popular periodicals in

1

the UK, the US and Canada question whether young children are being taught what they need to know to survive during the difficult years ahead. The debate over 'progressive' v. 'traditional' methods has virtually disappeared in Britain and North America; lines are now drawn over how far 'back to the basics' to go. And the issue of accountability – often cast as who is to blame for the failures of schools – children, teachers, parents, educationalists, school administrators, government officials – is a nasty undercurrent in all these controversies.

On the shop floor, in the schools, teachers and school head teachers are, as usual, preoccupied, often in isolation, sometimes with others, about the decline in standards, whether more or less discipline is the best response to hostile or indifferent learners, how to provide for the more able or for those who lag behind, how much to yield to individual or organized public pressure for relatively greater curriculum emphasis and expenditures, on development of basic reading skills, mathematical skills, and vocational training at the expense of the humanities, arts, social studies, music, dramatics and other aspects of the curriculum that have little or no market value. In some states and local school districts in the US the very real fear of loss of voter support for school tax levies and bond issues pushes directly on local school officials and teachers to respond to these widely advertised concerns.

Many of the problems that face parents, academic educationalists, teachers, heads and other school administrators are at their root the same, yet people rarely help one another clarify the practical issues each confronts and explore policy alternatives. Just as with great economic and social issues of the day, people talk by one another, rarely expecting to persuade or be persuaded. Schooling profession-als rarely invite citizens or parents to help them formulate the issues. In the US particularly, many parents, community groups and school governing boards have become impatient with, if not distrustful of, professional promises and ask for, sometimes demand, an objective monitoring of children's, teachers', school heads' and, occasionally, other administrators' performance; while in Britain it is no longer so certain that parents are content to leave schooling matters to the professionals. Attitudes of the public and teachers toward the role of educational scientists remain mixed as publicly expressed skepticism increases. Some maintain the hope that the scientists will penetrate our educational confusions and uncertainties. Yet the scientific work that reaches the public, for the most part, is used not to illuminate the issues but to lend authority to the preferred policies of those who

2

presently govern the schools, or as missiles in the continuing battle of words between left and right, scientific rationalizations of social and economic interests and values of the protagonists.[3]

It is difficult to assess the conflicting diagnoses, to formulate alternative solutions, or merely to find words that are mutually accepted and understood. C. Wright Mills's words of twenty years ago are as apt today:

[O]rdinary men, when they are in trouble or when they sense that they are up against issues, cannot get clear targets for thought and for action; they cannot determine what it is that imperils the values they vaguely discern as theirs. . . . In due course (the individual) . . . does not seek a way out; he adapts. . . . This adaptation . . . results not only in the loss of his chance, and, in due course, of his capacity and will to reason; it also affects his chances and his capacity to act as a free man.[4]

We offer in this book a modest contribution to the solution of these problems. We provide a general orientation for examining schooling practices and a set of terms, sixteen 'dilemmas', that relate the daily problems of schooling to the social and political problems of the society at large. This approach and the concept of 'dilemmas' are intended to be useful to citizens, researchers, parents and professionals for clarifying differences over schooling practices, and for engaging in collaborative inquiries into the origins and consequences of present patterns of schooling and the possibilities and desirability of change. To borrow from C. Wright Mills, ours is an effort to formulate 'private troubles as public issues', to illuminate in one form of institutional life, schooling, 'the intricate connections between everyday behavior and the course of history';[5] the relationship of the mundane, the ordinary – and sometimes unusual – events of everyday school life to the significant broader concerns of social and economic justice, and the quality of life.

This relationship of social life in the particular to larger social questions is often cast in the argot of Anglo-American social science as the relation of 'micro' to 'macro'. When stated in such grand terms, it is often seen as a problem for a particular class of experts – social scientists, philosophers and other university academicians – who generally have no continuing first-hand experience in the realities of daily school life. The details of the 'micro', the everyday events in the classroom and school, are ordinarily left to the educationalists – teachers, teachers of teachers, state and local educational authorities and classroom or pedagogical researchers. Our effort is to cast these two concerns as one – to provide a language for examining the macro in the micro, the larger issues that are embedded in the particulars of the everyday schooling experience.[6]

In the remainder of Part One we first provide an overview of the contemporary controversies concerning economic and political priorities and policies and their connection to schooling questions; second, attempt to locate ourselves within the current traditions of social research; and finally, give a brief account of the history of our study and an explanation of the organization of the book.

I PUBLIC ISSUES AND
SCHOOLING CONTROVERSIES

SOCIAL, ECONOMIC AND SCHOOLING SHIFTS

We began the work that led to the publication of this book almost a decade ago, in 1972, in the closing years of an era when there was, if not a universal, a widely held conviction among middle-of-the-road and left-leaning political leaders and intellectuals that social injustice and poverty could be overcome; that equal opportunity, material plenty and a high quality of life could and would be extended to all through or with the aid of governmental policies and programs, with schools playing a significant role in the gradual change to a more progressive social order.

In Britain, in the late 1960s and early 1970s, with the stimulus of the Plowden Report,[1] informal methods associated with infant schools were extended more broadly and upwards to the junior schools, and 'positive discrimination', intended to dissolve the legacy of the class society, became government policy. Educational Priority Areas (EPAs) were established 'to make the schools in deprived areas as good as the best in the country'.[2] Numerous curriculum development and educational research projects were funded by the Department of Education and Science, the Schools' Council, the Nuffield and Ford Foundations, and the Social Science Research Council. And as we indicated perhaps most significant was national policy that supported dissolution of the dual system of secondary modern and grammar schools, and their replacement with a unitary comprehensive system.[3]

In the US at this time Research and Development Centers were established at several major universities, Regional Educational Laboratories and collaborative school/university projects aimed at solving a variety of educational problems. Federal dollars were provided to encourage reform of teacher education and the development of innovative training programs for educational professionals, experienced teachers and researchers. Numerous projects were funded by the Federal government and private foundations to develop new curricula, utilize new technologies, and help children from 'culturally deprived' or 'socially different' homes who were seen as victims of prejudice or of social and economic oppression.[4]

Portrayals of the 1960s and early 1970s as times of great progressive advance and public optimism are surely overstated.[5] Nevertheless, there is an unmistakable shift in mood as we enter the 1980s. Today it is difficult to find many who express confidence in the ability of our institutions, including schools, to fulfill their promises.[6] Economic, social and schooling policies and priorities in both nations have also changed. Though liberals, conservatives and radicals disagree between and among themselves over whose interests the newer policies serve and over their prospect for success, there is no quarrel over their general outlines. Labeled by proponents and critics as 'neo-conservative',[7] their central tenet is that governments cannot manage economic and social affairs as effectively and efficiently as free markets. What follows from this policy premise is reducing to a minimum government spending and lowering the priority for government programs that extend equality of opportunity, improve the quality of life, raise standards of safety, health and environmental pollution and provide services – medical care, housing, recreation and cultural activities.

However uncertain the commitment to progressive educational policies of both nations during the last two decades may have been, the conservative schooling policies are now often endorsed – or at least tolerated – as the only reasonable alternative, not only by avowed conservatives, but by people at all social levels and of many shades of political opinion. Radicals, liberals and organized groups that presume to speak for the interests of the poor and the oppressed minorities argue not only that schools have failed to bring about equal opportunity but that they have not even delivered the least one should expect – minimal competency in reading, writing and arithmetic.[8] 'Back to basics' is also endorsed by members of the more privileged classes, including many university-educated liberals of the 1960s, who see schools as having sacrificed the minds of the best and finest in the pursuit of what are now taken to be unrealizable egalitarian ideals.[9] Schools are seen also as having failed the children of the 'silent majority' – those in the US and Britain who see themselves as the exploited middle and working classes who bring up their families, pay taxes, keep their homes in good repair, live by the rules, yet have had their economic position and prospects eroded in recent years. Many see themselves and their children as victimized by favoritism ('positive discrimination' or 'affirmative action') granted to oppressed groups (immigrants, urban poor, blacks, women) whose exploitation they may or may not grant but for which they feel they have no historic responsibility. Many students demonstrate their doubts about the value of schooling by attending only sporadically, particularly as they approach school-leaving age. In some areas vandalism and violence in the schools are frequent,[10] and many students, particularly in the secondary schools, have abandoned any pretense of learning useful skills let alone pursuing an understanding of themselves and their culture more generally.

These doubts and criticisms of public schooling, coupled with the prevailing economic conditions and political climate, play themselves out in the curtailing of public funds for education generally, and for equalizing policies in particular.[11] Rather than using declining enrollments as an opportunity for broadening opportunities for those at the bottom of the social and economic ladder, reducing class size, exploring ways of making schools more effective, or finding alternatives to the present institutionalization of the schooling process, teachers are sacked, art, music and recreational budgets are reduced, school counseling and special service programs are dismantled or curtailed.

Shifts in primary schooling policies

Effects of the shifting political mood and economic priorities on daily life in primary schools are evident in both countries, but in our view are more striking in the US. Where informal education has had strong roots in Britain it appears to continue, though hampered by adjustments in budgets and personnel priorities.[12] In the US, however, during the eight years since we began our work, the 'open education' movement which in large measure drew its inspiration from British informal methods is moribund.[13] Why informal primary schooling remains firmly rooted in Britain can only be understood in terms of differences in the histories and structures of primary schooling of the two nations.

First, in the US, in contrast to Britain, 'open' or informal education was a top—down movement, originating with middle-of-the-road liberal school reformers and intellectuals, and its influence never penetrated very deeply into classroom practice. Second, the administrative structure of schools buffered and nurtured informal

7

approaches in Britain while in the US it hastened their demise. British school head teachers and other administrators are not as easily affected by local economic fortunes or by shifts in political winds as their American counterparts. Though they may be on occasion called to account by school governing boards, in Britain school head-teachers' positions are secure. American principals, on the other hand, are easily fired or demoted, and hence are vulnerable to the pressures that are brought directly to bear on American superinten-dents. Organized, public-spirited (and not so public-spirited) interest groups can influence a superintendent or LEA governing boards, and these pressures are quickly passed through to principals and on to teachers.[14] Finally, 'objective' testing has long played a far stronger role in American education, including elementary schools. For many years standardized tests have been administered to every student yearly, sometimes bi-yearly, and the scores are prominently dis-played in children's permanent records which follow them through-out their careers. Since such tests rarely reveal consistent advantages for informal methods, their use contributed to the easy abandon-ment of whatever inroads the open education movement made in the late 1960s and 1970s.

Informal methods have not, of course, escaped public criticism in Britain. The Black Papers, published from 1969, condemned pro-gressive methods and policies, but it was not until the middle of the 1970s that such arguments gathered political force. The national furore that was precipitated over the internal policies of William Tyndale Junior School in London added fuel to the developing national debate over primary-school methods.[15] What, in a different political climate, might have remained a local dispute among staff, school managers and parents, escalated into a national media event with charges and counter-charges over excesses of progressive edu-cational ideology and methods. The dispute and the subsequent official inquiry made news repeatedly over a three-year period and contributed to the initiation in 1976 of the 'Great Debate' by the Prime Minister, James Callaghan. Though perhaps more a public relations campaign than a debate it did raise to the status of a national issue the future of progressive educational policies at all levels.

Social and educational problems remain and divisions over policies will likely become more rancorous if economic conditions do not improve markedly. In both nations there is a contradiction in the theories and programs propounded by neo-conservative intellectuals and political leaders, and the realities of the economic and social policies they pursue. Though their argument is that governments should avoid using public funds and institutions to further social and political ends, there appears to be little reticence to pursue or advocate governmental policies and programs that serve the national interest as they define it. The most striking examples are the governmental policies in both countries of providing tax incentives for large corporate and individual investors and, in the US, of underwriting loans for failing national industries. In the arena of schooling policy conservatives press for 'back to basics' as they define it, for policies, often including costly testing programs, that hold schools and teachers accountable, and for various forms of public subsidy of 'private' or 'independent' schools.[16] The policies they promote are designed to confront a limited range of problems that in their view can and should be solved through the schools. The issue once again is not whether there shall be national and local priorities in schooling policy, but whose interests they will serve.

It is our hope that the dilemma language will be useful in clarifying for professionals and the public some of the debates over schooling practices and their relationship to the major political and economic questions of the day, and for helping to identify alternative possibilities for making schooling a richer, more engaging and challenging intellectual, cultural and social experience for all students.

II THEORETICAL CONTEXT

VENERATION OF SCIENCE

We live in a scientific age. Final arbiter of our fates is not priest, prophet or prince, but the penetrating eye of the scientist who transcends personal preferences, parochial interests and prevailing social and cultural norms to reveal the world as it is. The ideals of liberal constitutional democracy are freedom and equality – with science providing minister and citizen with the means of establishing what has been and what is, in order to make the best estimate of what is possible.[1] The penchant to look to science and scientific technology to undergird and justify social policy can be seen in the recurring controversies over schooling policies and priorities over the last fifty years. Not only has social science served to justify and legitimate structural changes in schools, and to set policy; it has also shaped the way educational professionals and laypersons think about human learning and the educative process.

Until the 1970s, virtually all the sociological studies that received public notice were used to support the need for progressive education policies.[2] In the UK the writing of R.H. Tawney (1926), and the empirical sociological studies of Jean Floud, A.H. Halsey, F.M. Martin (1956) and others, both galvanized political opinion and legitimated efforts to terminate the 'hereditary curse upon English education'[3] by eliminating the dual, class-based structure of secondary schooling. Similar arguments by psychologist Kenneth Clark (1953), sociologist James Coleman (1966), and others hastened the demise of legalized racial segregation in schools in the US.[4]

Less than a decade later, another Coleman study was used, along with the writings of socialists Christopher Jencks, Samuel Bowles, Herbert Gintis, and genetic élitists Arthur Jensen and Richard Herrnstein to buttress the case *against* efforts to equalize opportunities for historically oppressed peoples and races by changing the structures of schools.[5] These studies added the weight of social science to the common wisdom that the governmental programs of the 1960s and early 1970s with this aim had no detectable effects, were therefore an inefficient use of tax money and human effort. Government efforts to equalize opportunities were unjustifiable not only on moral grounds, as conservatives had long argued, but also on practical grounds. Using the same forms of logic and methods of social research, they turned the earlier argument of sociologists – that equalizing opportunity through schooling was both just and efficient – on its head.[6]

The form of social science technology used in these studies, the psychometric and sociometric methods, served not only as scientific tools used in the equal opportunity–social selection studies cited above, but have been used more directly in the conduct of schooling – for sorting students according to levels of ability, intelligence, creativity, aptitude and achievement; for identifying emotional, perceptual–motor and other learning problems/deficiencies of young persons.[7] Tests were and continue to be used to demonstrate the natural inferiority of the non-white races,[8] and in the US, the test technology made possible the rapid proliferation of state 'minimal competency' and 'accountability' programs.

Test technology is not only integral to the decision-making apparatus at all levels, but influences much of our thinking (or consciousness) about educational matters. For example, teachers, parents, even those who are skeptical of tests, often take as self-evident, or as a scientific fact, the assumption that human capacities – intellectual and/or creative abilities, etc. – are normally distributed by nature in the form of a bell-shaped curve. The assumption, that it is not culture, society or man, but nature that distributes human talents with a few at the very top and very bottom and most in the middle, is taken as given in virtually all 'objective' psychological and educational tests, and underlies most of the statistical operations used to draw comparisons among persons and groups. Though assumed as scientific fact, the notion that human talents and achievements are so distributed is at best problematical.

This same scientific logic and the same techniques also underlie the great volume of classroom, pedagogical (or 'micro') research that has filled educational research journals and kept educational researchers gainfully employed over the decades. While most commentators on educational practice might agree that such research has never commanded the respect of teachers and school administrators,

11

it has continued to define the terms in which many curriculum and pedagogical issues are raised and argued.

GROWING SKEPTICISM OF PREVAILING FORMS OF SOCIAL RESEARCH – THE SEARCH FOR ALTERNATIVES

Paradoxically, over the preceding decade, there was increasing use and vigorous defense of psychometric and sociometric technology at the same time as their claims to scientific status and objectivity, and their promise of value-free social science as arbiter of conflicting claims, were becoming vigorously disputed in the academy and in the popular press.[9] Criticism of 'objective' tests and methods was not unknown a decade ago. (Indeed, cogent criticisms were made of such methods, including tests, in the 1920s.) What is new is that profound doubts about these technologies and the social science assumptions that undergird them are expressed not only in the fringes, left and right, but in the most respectable places.[10] For example, Fred Hechinger, an education writer for the *New York Times*, wrote at the end of 1979 in an editorial titled 'Frail sociology':

The Surgeon General should consider labeling all sociological studies: Keep out of reach of politicians and judges. Indiscriminate use of these suggestive works can be dangerous to the nation's health.[11]

After reflecting upon studies by James Coleman (1966 and 1975) and Christopher Jencks (1972 and 1979), Mr Hechinger notes how the shifting winds of sociological interpretation have corresponded so nicely with the changing political climate over the decade, and he concludes:

However unintentional, this convergence of the views of the sociological left and the intentions of an ungenerous right obstructs school reform. And it demoralizes people who believe, often for overpoweringly good reasons, that great efforts in the classroom *can* help children succeed. In the matter of social policy, doing the right thing – integrating schools, aiding poor pupils – should come from a clear sense that special help can bring special rewards. There is no need to wait for the next interesting, but frail, study.

Gabriel Chanan of the National Foundation for Educational Research, writing in *The Times Educational Supplement* (London) in 1976 of Neville Bennett's book, *Teaching Styles and Pupil Progress*, put it more directly: 'Social research must be understood as primarily an ideological rather than a scientific phenomena.'[12]

It is hardly a ringing endorsement of the usefulness of social science for practical policy when doing the right thing is exalted over the scientific rules of logic and evidence. Indeed, Mr Hechinger and Mr Chanan are not only dismissing the claims to objectivity by the prevailing forms of social science, but seem to be rejecting the premise of social science altogether. More guarded and subtle, but essentially similar, criticisms have been made in the professional scholarly literature over the preceding decade. The dramatic disclosures of the deceit of Cyril Burt, upon whose work much of the confidence in IQ testing rested, was a significant contribution to the developing skepticism.[13]

The growth of criticism of prevailing forms of social research among sociologists and psychologists has at its root a debate over 'positivism', the set of assumptions about persons and society that underlies the psychometric and sociometric technology, and has been the dominant perspective of social research in the twentieth century. In the US what was, a decade ago, a debate in the rarified reaches of academic epistemology and among social theorists has penetrated into virtually all of the sub-specialties of the social and psychological sciences and into university departments and schools devoted to training persons for the social service professions (social work, education, public administration). In Britain the intellectual debate, peaking earlier, has subsided, but the political questions it raised in and outside the academy remain unresolved.

The term positivism, itself an intellectual booby trap, has received a number of first-rate dissections over the preceding decade.[14] We will not recapitulate the arguments here. In most general terms, positivism denotes an orientation to doing social science wherein the differences between scientific work in the social and physical worlds are assumed not to be fundamental. The approaches of positivist social science have in common a press toward precise specification of 'independent' and 'dependent variables'. This most often takes the form of focusing on external observable factors that are capable of being converted into a set of numbers. The intention is to bypass the complexities, difficulties and bias that are considered unavoidable in interpretative inquiries into the relationship of social context to human consciousness.

The debates surrounding the Jencks, Coleman and Bennett studies, which prompted Messrs Hechinger's and Chanan's despair over the role of social research, are not only disagreements over the use and interpretations of a few numbers, but represent profound differences between positivists and their increasingly respectable detractors. Part of the disagreement is rooted in the centuries-old debate over

13

free will and determinism – in its contemporary dress, whether it is possible to do social research and/or build a corpus of scientific knowledge and theory based on an assumption that persons are hapless objects, buffeted and shaped by culture and society (and, for social biologists, by nature itself). Critics of positivism – including several varieties of interpretive and critical sociologists – take as a starting place a view of persons as beings with the capacity to create culture and transform the conditions of their own living, and a *reflexive* conception of human consciousness and social context (i.e., human consciousness and behavior shape and are shaped by culture and history).

Criticism of the failure of research in the positivist tradition to study *everyday socializing and educative processes* as they occur in schools, including teachers' and students' awareness of their experience and their continuous reflexive adaptation to one another, has been made by many critics.[15] Schooling research that claims to evaluate the relative merits of method A v. method B, or to discover the relationship of schooling processes to social change, by examining inputs and outputs – but not the process itself – is sometimes called derisively 'black box' research. The general criticism of such research is that any study of persons or society is partial if it attempts to draw conclusions about the consequences of social life upon persons and collectives without inquiring into the complex, dynamic connections between inside and outside forces – how consciousness and action shape society and culture. From this perspective it is impossible to know the effects of schooling, individual, social or economic, without direct study of how human thought and behavior both affect and are affected by social process and structures. It is the argument of some critical and interpretive social scientists that only by studying how schooling experience affects and is affected by the lives and consciousness of the participants in the process, can one draw any conclusions about what schooling contributes to social stability and change.

About a decade ago a number of British researchers, drawing on a variety of social theoretical traditions – North American and European – and doing 'close in' studies of schooling processes, found common commitment not only in the need for direct observation and analysis of the schooling process, but also in a conception of persons and society that denied positivist assumptions.[16] They stressed the more active, creative aspect of persons, their capacity to give and share meaning and to exercise control. (This emphasis should be distinguished from the resurgence of so-called 'participant observa-

14

tion' or 'qualitative' research in schools in the US in the early years of the 1970s.[17] Much of this latter work rejected 'positivist' methods, argued for direct study of classrooms, but did not question the positivist conception of scientific laws and explanations.)

This diverse group of British researchers, sometimes classed (uneasily) together as the 'New Sociologists', though they did not deny the significance of political and social forces outside the classroom, often did not directly confront in their analyses the connection of the daily events of classroom life to culture and to the social and political life of the society.[18] Many succeeded, nevertheless, in explicitly confronting the positivistic value-free claims by looking critically at the implicit definitions of knowledge teachers transmitted in classrooms. Instead of accepting as given the school's notion of what it means to be 'educated' and studying how it is that students differentially achieved that designation (the preoccupation of many sociologists of prior decades), they took as problematic the school's definition of the educated person.[19] Some identified themselves with the developing field of the sociology of knowledge,[20] thus setting the stage for studies that could link classroom teaching and learning experiences to broader social and political questions. As Brian Davies remarks (commenting upon these issues), every sociological approach must 'strike a more or less complex balance between the priority of the individual or society'.[21] One major criticism of some of the 'New Sociologists' is that in their attempts to study classrooms in ways that do not portray persons as entirely controlled by outside forces, they have overestimated the capacity of persons to act freely and have often ignored the powerful constraints that bear upon them. A related criticism is that they rely so heavily on the 'insider's' or actor's perspective and become so immersed in the minutiae of daily life, that they rarely attend to how societal forces and power relationships affect classroom structures and processes, and persons' perceptions and behavior.[22]

Over the decade there has also been a resurgence of interest in schooling research in various Marxist traditions. Two individuals, the British researcher Basil Bernstein and the Frenchman Pierre Bourdieu, who share some assumptions with the 'New Sociologists' and with Critical Marxists, must be mentioned to complete this brief review of the context of contemporary schooling research. Both attempt to clarify how the social inequalities of British and French societies respectively are recreated by the structures and processes of schooling. Central to Bourdieu's analysis is *cultural capital*; a concept that refers to high status knowledge, dispositions and skills, which are acquired and/or reinforced within the institutions of society, particularly schools. At the level of the individual, cultural capital refers to the inherited or acquired linguistic and cultural competence that facilitates achievement in school[23] and provides access to prestigious and economically rewarding positions in society. Bourdieu's analyses of the role educational institutions play in recreating existing social inequalities in French society are provocative, and have stimulated the thinking of a number of Anglo-American researchers including Basil Bernstein.

Professor Bernstein's work is distinguished by his long-standing effort to link the processes and structures of curriculum (the how and what of knowledge transmissions in school) to the inequalities of the British social class structure.[24] He analyzes schools as agencies of cultural transmission by constructing 'a typology of "educational codes" . . . whose abstract and formal rules . . . generate the form and content of valid knowledge as well as the structure of relations between teacher and pupil. . . . [These codes] govern the production, transmission, and reproduction of systems of messages and underlie curriculum, pedagogy and evaluation.' [25] To connect the highly abstract notions of 'codes' to curriculum, pedagogy and evaluation, Bernstein postulates what are his most widely known concepts for analyzing classroom processes: *classification* and *framing* which are intended to hold together 'structural and inter-actional [that is, macro and micro] levels'.[26] Bernstein's ultimate intention is to develop a theory that integrates linguistic codes,[27] educational transmission and social class[28] in a way that would allow for 'responsiveness to and change in structures but would also indicate that there was at any one time a limit to negotiation'.[29] Though, as he acknowledges, his work has not always succeeded in drawing these links – it is constantly undergoing revision and development – in recent years he is unquestionably the most significant figure among Anglo-American social scientists engaged in the quest for understanding the role of educational processes in social transmission and change.

Both Bernstein and Bourdieu have been criticized for excluding from analysis significant aspects of the cultural, political and social contexts of schooling.[30] They have also been criticized for paying insufficient attention to the schooling process as it is lived by teachers and students – the everyday realities to which their theorizing refers[31] – and for formulating concepts at a level of abstraction well removed from the language and experience of schooling.[32] As a consequence, their work has been described as difficult to understand.[33] Both, but

16

Bourdieu in particular, have also been criticized as being over-determined, that is, not allowing for the possibilities of human control of the processes they describe,[34] and therefore, in their present forms, able to make only limited contributions to the clarification of action alternatives open to teachers in classrooms.

We think that much of the criticism of the New Sociologists and of Bernstein's and Bourdieu's work is misdirected.[35] However, it is clear that at present the works of Bernstein and Bourdieu do not represent the lived experience of schooling; thus, their efforts to theorize about connections of micro to macro, though suggestive, are inadequate. The New Sociologists, on the other hand, though they more often attend to the nuances of the schooling experience and the meanings taken by its participants, have not yet succeeded in relating their empirical work to social–political theory and educational practice. It is within the context of the struggles of these several traditions of schooling research to illuminate the relationship between everyday schooling activity and economic, social and cultural change that we place our own efforts.[36]

Schooling research and educational policy

Research on schooling at the present is in ferment in Britain and, as of late, in North America as well. The underlying politics of positivist methodology is far more widely acknowledged than a decade ago. But in spite of the growing legitimacy of newer approaches to the study of the relationship of schooling to society, it is still positivist social science that draws headlines and most heavily influences public political debates. Although these newer forms of sociological research have made major inroads in the academic world of the UK and North America over the decade, their political influence on practical policy appears minimal. In Britain, for example, at the height of the 'Great Debate' over 'progressive methods', despite the strong tradition of 'interpretive' research, it was Neville Bennett's *Teaching Styles and Pupil Progress* that made the headlines.[37] That the study made a number of the more familiar grievous errors committed by classroom researchers over the years was overlooked (for example, reducing 'teaching style' to three types along a single dimension, progressive, traditional and mixed, a version of a long discredited democratic authoritarian dichotomy of an earlier era). In the political battles the focus was on attacking and defending the allegedly statistically significant superior achievements of children taught by 'traditional' methods as measured by objective tests. Similarly, although IQ as a measure of genetic endowment or ability has increasingly been shown by a number of critics as problematical[38] if not untenable, its use in schools as an approximation of a child's 'ability' or potential has not greatly diminished, and standardized tests, despite their generally acknowledged limitations, increasingly dominate public attention as measures of educational productivity.

III A BRIEF HISTORY AND
OVERVIEW OF THE BOOK

We went to England at the height of the open education movement in North America; a time when many professional educators, intellectuals, and political leaders of diverse persuasion appeared to be united in a belief that schools could promote humane values and social justice – and be places where children learn to read, write, do mathematics to a high standard without sacrificing other areas of intellectual, social, moral and aesthetic growth, nor the joys of childhood. Books by John Holt, Paul Goodman, Jonathan Kozol, George Dennison, Herbert Kohl and others,[1] portraying the absurdities and horrors of American public schooling, were widely read and generally warmly received by middle-of-the-road liberal and left-leaning journals of opinion.[2] Educational reform was a hot item. 'Alternative schools' were being created in store fronts and within the existing systems. In many locations 'teachers' centers' based on the English experience were struggling to become established with the assistance of foundation and federal grants. Teacher-education programs normally populated by compliant young women were drawing politically active admirers of Herbert Marcuse and/or Charles Reich's *Consciousness III*.[3] 'Open' and 'humanistic' education sessions and workshops were everywhere, even at the national conventions of the staid professional education associations.

Many of those who argued for school reforms at the time used the English informal primary schools as a model of what was possible, basing their judgment on what they had seen, read about or heard of these schools. In retrospect, what was interesting about those more active days of the American open education movement was the number of persons of differing political persuasions who viewed reform as desirable *and possible*. The dormant progressive education movement at its height in the 1930s probably could never claim such

19

widespread interest in the reform of schools. A good deal of John Dewey's influence on American schools was confined to those shepherded by enthusiastic and committed social visionaries. We were led to believe from much of what we read that humane and liberating schools were flowering in England, the oldest and first developed of capitalist countries, not only in quiet villages but in slums and suburbs of the cities. Charles Silberman, whose influential study was funded by the Carnegie Foundation and whose book, *Crisis in the Classroom*,[4] published in the US in 1970, was widely read, posed the question in a form that apparently resonated in the minds and hearts of practically minded reformers. 'What is, is possible.' The implication was that if it could happen in Britain, then why not in capitalist America. Indeed, why not?

We spent six months working and observing full time in English primary schools, four to six weeks in each of three schools and one, two or three days in sixteen others. After a short period of observation in several schools we realized that, though the schools we were seeing were different in many respects from the ones we had known, they were not strange, but familiar. With notable exceptions, most of the British and American literature on 'open' or 'informal' education had created an image of informal English primary schooling that was different from what we were experiencing.[5] We asked several helpful and widely respected local advisors, many teachers, and several head teachers whom we knew, whether we had selected the wrong schools. We took time from the schools we were studying intensively, and visited several they suggested, including six that had the distinction of having been mentioned or featured in one or another North American or British publication. After we found that these schools looked to be variations of the ones we were studying, we pursued for a time not well-known schools, but well-known head teachers, who had written or had been written about in the open education literature. We finally were persuaded that we had, indeed, seen 'it' – the schools we had chosen to study in depth, if not typical, were certainly not atypical of informal primary schools, at least in this area of England.

We realized that despite the sobering words and cautions of Joseph Featherstone and Lillian Weber, and despite our skepticism, we, too, had been misled by the images of freedom and self-motivation in the 'open' and 'informal' education literature. We did find that many of the schooling events portrayed were indeed common in the schools we visited. But behind these images we observed various forms of direct and strong intervention by teachers, and became increasingly aware of the broader context of these events, and the complexity of the dynamics underlying the behavior patterns. Eventually, we were able to identify variations in overall patterns of classroom organization and teacher control reasonably quickly in each new situation we visited. By the time we had completed our stay, we felt we had a deeper understanding of the richness, variety and complexity of life in these schools than we had of the several we had taught in or had experienced first-hand over the years – probably because in the English schools we had for the first time the opportunity to be outsiders, observing and analyzing, as well as participants in the situation. It also became clear that many of the efforts of its proponents on both sides of the Atlantic to account for open or informal education in terms of a static set of principles, beliefs or commitments – most notably the Plowden Report, and in the US Roland Barth, Charles Rathbone, Anne M. Bussis, Edward A. Chittenden and Marianne Amarel – were inadequate.[6] Whatever the thinking and personal commitments that underlay the informal educational practices we observed, there was a far greater complexity in the schooling process and in the way that teachers and heads talked and thought about the process than was revealed in most of the popular and professional literature that attempted to portray and/or persuade others of its merits.

After our return we found it extremely difficult to characterize the beliefs and behaviors of teachers in the schools we had observed, and we became far more tolerant of others' attempts to say something about them. When pressed by university and public-school colleagues to say how the things we had seen and experienced in the English schools compared to the American counterparts, we could say with conviction that sixteen of the nineteen (these sixteen include the three we studied in depth) were, according to our own values and beliefs, superior in most respects to schools we knew in the United States, and among the sixteen were several of the best schools we had ever seen, and one school was among the worst. We would add that the schools were by no means utopias; many of the junior schools, particularly at the upper ends, were quite ordinary. In addition, in none of the schools could we say there was a direct challenge to the political values and attitudes of British society; thus, those who see American society as unjust and/or corrupt and see the American school system as witting or unwitting accomplices in perpetuating injustices, would undoubtedly find fault with these schools on the same grounds. However, given important similarities in the social, political and economic systems of Britain and the US, and given that both have mass compulsory education, there was little question in our minds that the English schools we had seen were in general better institutions for young children to spend their days and, in our view, were far less damaging to children

Upon our return we were confronted with the problem of finding language to characterize our observations in abstract and general terms. We were asked whether the classrooms were more 'teacher centered', 'democratic', dependent upon children's rather than adults' standards; whether teachers and administrators were more sensitive to children's needs and emotions, more concerned with mastery of the 3 Rs or with 'self-motivation' than their American counterparts. We could not easily formulate answers that represented our observations. Although we often would say 'yes' and 'no', and document both statements, this did not capture the reality we experienced. Clearly such claims as 'open classroom teachers believe children have the right and competence to make learning decisions'[7] missed the mark. There was a sense in which such generalizations were true and not true. Standing alone such statements were serious distortions of the informal schooling process we had come to know. Our effort to describe and understand our recorded experiences led us by increments to develop a language, a set of concepts that would more adequately represent the complexity we had experienced. With the collaboration of Naida Tushnet Bagenstos and Edward R. Mikel we developed, in the year following our return, a set of what we came to call 'dilemmas' that appeared to us to have great promise for representing the complexity of the phenomena without overlying our own educational or political preferences on our descriptions.

The terms of the language are as follows (the division into three sets will be explained in Part Three):

Control set:

1. 'Whole' child v. child as student — (realms)
2. Teacher v. child control — (time)
3. Teacher v. child control — (operations)
4. Teacher v. child control — (standards)

Curriculum set:

5. Personal knowledge v. public knowledge
6. Knowledge as content v. knowledge as process
7. Knowledge as given v. knowledge as problematical
8. Learning is holistic v. learning is molecular
9. Intrinsic v. extrinsic motivation

10. Each child unique v. children have shared characteristics
11. Learning is individual v. learning is social
12. Child as person v. child as client

Societal set:

13. Childhood continuous v. childhood unique (childhood)
14. Equal allocation of resources v. differential allocation (allocation)
15. Equal justice under law v. *ad hoc* application of rules (deviance)
16. Common culture v. sub-group consciousness

As we continued to work on this language we became increasingly aware of the background assumptions, the underlying views of human thinking, culture, society and social change that were implicit in our conception of dilemma. Our effort to articulate these assumptions as we worked on the clarification of the dilemmas led to the writing of this book.

BACKGROUND ASSUMPTIONS – ORGANIZATION OF THE BOOK

The concept 'background assumptions' we borrow from Alvin Gouldner. He calls them background assumptions because they provide the background

out of which the postulations in part emerge and, on the other hand, not being expressly formulated, they remain in the background of the theorist's attention. . . . Background assumptions are embedded in a theory's postulations. Operating within and alongside of them, they are as it were 'silent partners' in the theoretical enterprise. Background assumptions provide some of the bases for choice and the invisible cement for linking together postulations. From beginning to end, they influence a theory's formulation and the researchers [*sic*] to which it leads.[8]

If one were fully to articulate and rationalize one's background assumptions, they would constitute a coherent social theory. We offer no social theory, but we will lay out in some detail the theoretical conceptions underlying the dilemma language. Here we state our background assumptions briefly in order to make clear to readers our personal and social commitments.

We do not claim to have transcended these assumptions. Rather, we hope to demonstrate the *positive* contribution these assumptions can make in the analysis of classrooms and schooling processes, and in portraying differences among them without overlying the particu-

23

lar political preferences of the observer, and for guiding inquiry into the relationship of everyday schooling decisions to one's own personal choices, and to the broader social and political policy issues. We see ourselves as making four related assumptions.

1. Schooling has as its primary function transmitting the culture and the society to the young. The responsibility of teachers, the reasons they are hired and paid, is to exert control over students' lives. Teachers as agents of society insure the continuity of the society and culture, by imprinting on children views which are taken for granted and which were imprinted upon them through schooling and other social institutions. This is what could be called the *person as object* assumption – persons' lives are shaped by their experience in the institutions of their society.

2. Teachers, head teachers and students are not merely passive objects; they have the capacity to become self-conscious of the structures and forces that have shaped and continue to shape the views that they take for granted, and they have the capacity to act differently on the basis of these reflections. This is what we call the *human consciousness* assumption, and it carries with it the idea that persons can, to some degree, transform or change the social world. Assumptions one and two taken together are another way of saying that *all schooling activity* is *cultural, economic* and *political activity* in the sense that in every acting moment external forces are within teachers and in their situation (whether they are aware of them or not), and in the sense that teachers as agents of the society create a social, political and cultural environment for children which is in some measure under their conscious control. From these situations, meanings are taken and transformed as all participants, including children, continue to live and grow in years and experience. Schooling activity can, therefore, be simultaneously liberating and constraining, and teachers and children are both subjects and objects.

3. The third assumption is derived from the previous two – that schooling activity cannot be explained, understood or adequately described without taking into account the subjective experiences of teachers, *and* the social, cultural and political forces and structures that are omnipresent in all social situations.

4. All social scientists' work has embedded in it a view of how their theories and findings are related to practical action.

Though the scope of the book is wide, its contribution is limited to explicating sixteen dilemmas of schooling, making explicit the assumptions underlying them, and demonstrating their usefulness to teachers, other educational professionals, scholars who conduct theoretical and empirical studies on schooling, and citizens and parents who are often caught in the cross-currents of competing arguments of government officials and professionals. We see our language as making a useful but modest contribution to the understanding of the relationship of macro to micro, of everyday school life to social change, a problem that remains inadequately conceptualized in spite of a number of significant contributions over the last several years.

In Part Two we present a literary portrait of the schools, what interpretive researchers often call an 'ethnography'. It is intended to provide a common experience which we use in subsequent parts of the book to exemplify the theoretical arguments and the use of the dilemmas for analyzing the schooling process. It was written independently of the subsequent analyses, but our background assumptions undoubtedly influenced our portrayals. Part Three, 'Towards a theory and language of schooling', has two chapters. In the first, we attempt to articulate the social theoretical conceptions that underlie the dilemma language, drawing heavily upon George Herbert Mead and several critical social scientists. Second, we describe each of the sixteen dilemmas with illustrations drawn from the narrative. Readers who prefer to begin with the concrete, may wish to invert the order of their reading of these two chapters. Part Four, 'Interpretations of the schools', also includes two chapters. In the first, we show how the dilemma language may be used to portray differences among teachers and schools, using as points of reference the portraits we have painted of the schools and our own personal experience in elementary and secondary schools in the US; in the second, we explore the uses of the dilemma for analyzing the origins and consequences of schooling patterns, thus the contribution of schooling to social continuity and change. In Part Five, the final chapter of the book, we illustrate how the dilemmas may be used by citizens, educational practitioners and educational researchers for engaging in critical inquiry into the nature of the schooling experience and the possibilities and desirability of making changes in classrooms and schools.

NOTES TO PART ONE

Introduction

1 See, for example, 'The threatening economy', *New York Times Magazine* (30 December 1979) for comments by twenty leading economists representing a wide spectrum of political perspectives.

2 See Edgar Litt and Michael Parkinson, *US and UK Educational Policy* (New York: Praeger, 1978) for a statement of the growing concern in both countries that 'neighborhood-based comprehensive schools . . . may have the adverse and unintended consequence of discriminating against working class children'. They state, 'the growth and success of the comprehensive . . . school remains as much a matter of controversy in Britain as in America' (p. 107). Our review was written prior to our notice of this book, yet there are some striking similarities in our views.

3 See the discussion of Neville Bennett's *Teaching Styles and Pupil Progress* (London: Open Books, 1976; also Cambridge, Mass.: Harvard University Press, 1976) below, p.17. More recently, Michael Rutter *et al.*'s *Fifteen Thousand Hours* (Cambridge, Mass.: Harvard University Press, 1979; London: Open Books) has received wide notice in Britain.

4 C.W. Mills, *The Sociological Imagination* (London: Oxford University Press, 1959), pp. 169–70. Christopher Lasch places this malaise in a historical and psychological perspective in *The Culture of Narcissism* (New York: Warner Books, 1979).

5 Mills, op. cit. In *The Sociological Imagination* Mills eloquently and clearly sets out what he takes to be the promise of social science and the task of the social scientist. Our own views are close to and have been influenced by his.

6 See Basil Bernstein, *Class, Codes and Control (Vol. 3) Towards a Theory of Educational Transmissions* (2nd edn) (London: Routledge & Kegan Paul, 1975), 23, for a statement of the origins of the macro–micro dichotomy, and of the problems that result from it. Robert Heilbroner – in a review of *A Guide to Post Keynesian Economics*, a book edited by Alfred S. Eichner, *New York Review of Books* (21 February 1980), 19–22 – makes a similar point concerning the relationship of macro to micro in economics. He states: 'The division of the study of economics into macro and micro approaches seems on the surface like a very convenient way of examining the economy from two different vantage points, micro yielding to a worm's eye view, macro yielding to a bird's eye view. But what is strange is that there is no way of going from one view to the other. . . . Thus macro and micro are not complementary sides of a stereopticon giving us a single complete picture from two incomplete ones. They are, rather, two quite different pictures that cannot be combined' (p. 19). We return to this issue in Chapter II.

Chapter I

1 *Children and Their Primary Schools, A Report of the Central Advisory Council for Education* (the Plowden Report) (London: HMSO, 1967).

2 Ibid., 465.

3 See Adam Hopkins, *The School Debate* (Harmondsworth: Penguin, 1978); and W. Kenneth Richmond, *Education in Britain Since 1944* (London: Methuen, 1979). The policy on secondary education was initiated by the Labour government elected in 1964. Circular 10/65 requested local authorities to draw up a plan 'to eliminate separatism in secondary education'. Margaret Thatcher, as Conservative Secretary of Education, withdrew Circular 10/65 in 1970. See Harold Silver, 'Education and public opinion', *New Society* (7 December 1978), 576, for an account and discussion of this period. See also his introduction to *Equal Opportunity in Education* (London: Methuen, 1974), and his recent *Education and the Social Condition* (London: Methuen, 1980).

4 See Litt and Parkinson, *US and UK Educational Policy* (New York: Praeger, 1978), for a discussion of comparative educational policies in the US and Britain. See Joel Spring, *The Sorting Machine, National Education Policy Since 1945*

(New York: David McKay, 1976), for a review of educational policy in the US during this period.

5 Litt and Parkinson, op. cit., 111–23; Robert Thornbury, *The Changing Urban School* (London: Methuen, 1978), especially ch. 2, 'The EPA myth'; and *Children and Their Primary Schools*, op. cit.

6 Litt and Parkinson, op. cit., especially ch. 1.

7 This policy has been described in similar terms in *Time Magazine* (August 1979), 24 and by S.M. Miller, 'The recapitalization of capitalism' in *Social Policy*, 9:3 (1978). *Time* views these policies approvingly while Miller provides a critical perspective. See also Peter Steinfels 'What neo-conservatives believe', *Social Policy*, 10:1 (May/June 1979).

8 Many observers have noted that working-class persons generally favor strict discipline and focus on the 3 Rs. Though this has sometimes been seen by educational reformers as evidence of the illiberal, anti-progressivist stance of the working class, we see it as a rational response to the practical realities that face those of limited means who recognize their children's futures depend upon exhibiting such traits as obedience and willingness to subject oneself to external controls. This has long been the situation of the marginal working-class poor. See Samuel Bowles, 'Unequal education and the reproduction of the social division of labor' in M. Carnoy, *Schooling in a Corporate Society: The Political Economy of Education in America* (New York: David McKay, 1972), for a position that in some respect parallels the one we take here.

9 See, for example, Paul Copperman, *The Literacy Hoax* (New York: William Morrow, 1978) for a recent statement of this conservative humanist perspective; also see Thornbury, op. cit., ch. 13, 'Counter-reformation with inquisition' for an analysis of the 'conservative backlash' – the argument for self-discipline, social control, academic standards and rejection of the progressivists' argument for connections between personal experience and school learning as represented, for example, by John Dewey in *Experience and Education* (London and New York: Collier Macmillan, 1963).

10 For a discussion of the problems and causes of school violence see Hopkins, op. cit., 92; Thornbury, op. cit., 4–9. See also *Violent and Disruptive Behavior in Schools* (N.A.S., 1975); Rhodes Boyson, *The Crisis in Education* (London: Woburn Press, 1975); and an article in the *Wall Street Journal* (5 February 1980), entitled, 'Blackboard jungle. In inner-city schools getting an education is often a difficult job'. We are not claiming that disruptions in schools have greatly increased in recent years. They probably have but such claims are too facile for many of the same reasons that claims that crime rates have increased in recent years are problematic. National Institute of Education, *Violent Schools, Safe Schools: The Safe School Study Report* (Washington DC: US Department of Health, Education and Welfare, 1978). Violence and disruption in secondary schools are very serious problems and many observers (cf. Thornbury, op. cit., 4–9) would probably argue that our characterization of these problems is vastly understated.

11 See Litt and Parkinson, op. cit., 116; also Alan Walker, 'A right turn for the welfare state', *Social Policy*, 10:5 (March/April 1980), 49.

12 These subjective judgments are based on observations and conversations in 1979 with several persons associated with schools we studied in 1972 and with officials in the local education authorities (LEAs) in which these schools are located. Several outreach workshops and summer programs for teachers we were told had disappeared or had been greatly reduced despite widely held acclaim of their usefulness. It was reported to us that LEA-sponsored programs in the arts, humanities and environmental studies had lost ground in battles for diminishing

human and material resources. We sometimes heard great pessimism expressed, but not the deep despair we hear from the more progressive-oriented teachers and administrators in the US. Our observations are in part confirmed by Hopkins, op. cit. and Thornbury, op. cit. (though in our view these sources are as lacking in careful documentation as is ours).

13 There are networks of persons in the US who continue to work for progressive educational practices and policies. The North Dakota Study Group on Evaluation (University of North Dakota, Grand Forks, North Dakota) under the leadership of Vito Perrone has as its members persons in many parts of the country who continue to work, sometimes in relative isolation, sometimes with others, to strengthen progressivist educational practices. Among the more lively centers of activity are the TALC/Teacher Shelter, Oakland, California, Amity Buxton, Director; Prospect Center, North Bennington, Vermont, Patricia Carini, Director; Children's Thinking Seminars, Cambridge, Massachusetts, Bill and Sara Hull, leaders; Philadelphia Teachers' Learning Cooperatives, Philadelphia, Pennsylvania; Workshop Center for Open Education, City College of New York, Lillian Weber, Director. The North Dakota Study Group also publishes a monograph series which exerts influence far beyond its limited circulation. Many in the open education movement who have remained practicing educators now devote their political energies to combating the growing use of 'objective' tests for measuring educational productivity and for assigning students to special educational programs or 'treatments'. The North Dakota Study Group has contributed to the growth of the 'Truth in Testing' movement, and to efforts to use the courts as an arena for challenging state-mandated minimum competency testing.

14 Lillian Weber in her study discusses the differences at length in the *English Infant School and Informal Education* (New York: Prentice Hall, 1971), 232–51. Her book in our view remains the most dependable source of information on informal primary methods written for North Americans. She not only describes the primary and nursery schools, but traces some of the intellectual roots of the English progressive school practices.

The different traditions of professional training also appear to us to be quite significant, as documented by David Tyack and Elisabeth Hansot, 'From social movement to professional management: an inquiry into the changing character of leadership in public education', *American Educational Journal* (formerly the *School Review*), (1980). Also interesting are Raymond C. Callahan, *Education and the Cult of Efficiency* (Chicago: University of Chicago Press, 1962); and David Tyack, *The One Best System* (Cambridge, Mass.: Harvard University Press, 1974), ch. 23. In England the head teacher rises from the ranks rather than being selected from among those who possess administrative credentials. In the US a person who has virtually no experience in elementary-school teaching can be appointed as head of an elementary school. This represents differences in development of the profession of school administration as well as differences in patterns of local school governance and finance.

15 For a fuller discussion of the incident see Adam Hopkins, op. cit., and Robert Thornbury, op. cit. For two journalists' views see John Gretton and Mark Jackson, *William Tyndale: Collapse of a School or System?* (London: George Allen & Unwin, 1976). For the perspectives of several teachers and the head who were at Tyndale see *William Tyndale, The Teachers' Story* by Terry Ellis, Jackie McWhorter, Dorothy McColgan and Brian Haddow (London: Writers' and Readers' Cooperative, 1976).

16 This contradiction in the neo-conservative position has been noted by numerous 'left' critics. It was also pointed out by liberal Ralf Dahrendorf's sharply worded attack on the Thatcher government's policies in higher education in the *London*

Review of Books (1980). Also see Steinfels, op. cit., and J.K. Galbraith 'Oil' in *New York Review of Books* (27 September 1979).

Chapter II

1 Ironically, in 1972, Daniel Moynihan, White House Counselor and Nixon advisor, supported increased spending on educational research in order to demonstrate the futility of investing in education. Reported by Joel Spring, *The Sorting Machine, National Education Policy Since 1945* (New York: David McKay, 1976).

2 The introduction to Harold Silver's *Equal Opportunity in Education* (London: Methuen, 1973) was very helpful to us in writing this section. Also useful were the introductions to Karabel and Halsey's *Power and Ideology in Education* (New York: Oxford University Press, 1971); Brian Davies's *Social Control and Education* (London: Methuen, 1976); and ch. 7 in Basil Bernstein, *Class, Codes and Control (Vol. 3) Towards a Theory of Educational Transmissions* (2nd edn) (London: Routledge & Kegan Paul, 1975).

3 Quoted by Silver, 1973, op. cit., xii, from R.H. Tawney's *Equality* (London: Allen & Unwin, 1931), 142–4. In 1922 Tawney wrote *Secondary Education for All* for the Labour Party, and served on the Hadow Committee that produced in 1926 the politically and socially significant report, *The Education of the Adolescent*.

4 Kenneth Clark, 'Effects of prejudice and discrimination on personality development', prepared for the Mid-Century White House Conference on Children and Youth, 1950, was cited as n. 11 of the *Brown vs. The Board of Education* decision in which racial segregation in US schools was declared unconstitutional. Kenneth B. Clark, *Prejudice and Your Child* (Boston: Beacon, 1955), is a summary and revision of the manuscript. James Coleman *et al.*, *Equality of Educational Opportunity* (Washington, D.C.: US Government Printing Office, 1966). See also *Harvard Educational Review* (Winter 1968), a special issue expanded into the volume *Equal Educational Opportunity* (Cambridge, Mass.: Harvard University Press, 1969), for a compendium of responses to the Coleman Report.

5 The second Coleman study is James S. Coleman, Sara D. Kelley and John A. Moore, *Trends in School Segregation 1968–73* (Washington, D.C.: The Urban Institute, 1975).

Also see *Social Policy*, 6:4 (January/February 1976), which includes a critical appraisal of Coleman's revised position; Christopher Jencks *et al.*, *Inequality: A Reassessment of the Effects of Family and Schooling in America* (New York: Basic Books, 1972). Samuel Bowles and Herbert Gintis, *Schooling in Capitalist America* (New York: Basic Books, 1976); this book has been reviewed widely, see particularly Robert Heilbroner's review, in the *New York Review of Books* (15 April 1976), and Joseph Featherstone's in the *New Republic*, 174:22 (29 May 1976). The work of Bowles and Gintis has sometimes been cast as simple-minded mechanistic Marxism by their critics. For a corrective see Sherry Gorelick, 'Schooling problems in capitalist America', *Monthly Review*, 29:5 (1977); and Harvey Kantor, 'The great school warriors', a review of Diane Ravitch's *The Revisionists Revised* in *Social Policy*, 9:5 (March/April 1979). We do not claim that Professors Bowles and Gintis endorse the ways their work has been misinterpreted by liberals, conservatives or leftists.

Arthur Jensen: 'How much can we boost IQ and scholastic achievement', *Harvard Educational Review*, 39:2, (Winter 1969), 1–123; and *Genetics and Education* (New York: Harper & Row, 1972; London: Methuen, 1972). His newest book (see below, n. 8) once again implies a genetic basis for differential performance on IQ tests. Jensen has numerous critics. See Allen Gartner, Colin Greer and Frank Riessman (eds), *The New Assault on Equality* (New York and London: Harper & Row, 1974); Ken Richardson and David Spears (eds), *Race and Intelligence* (Harmondsworth, Middlesex: Penguin, 1972); Clarence J. Karier, *Shaping of the American Educational State* (New York: Free Press, 1975); Leon J. Kamin, *The Science and Policits of IQ* (New York: John Wiley, 1974); John Loehin, Gardner Linsey and J.N. Spuhler, *Race Differences in Intelligence* (San Francisco: W.H. Freeman, 1975); Samuel Bowles and Herbert Gintis, ' "IQ" in the United States class structure' in A. Gartner, C. Greer and F. Riessman (eds) op. cit. For a particularly cogent and technically thorough review see Daniel M. Kohl, 'The IQ game: bait and switch', *School Review*, 84:4 (1976). Herrnstein's widely quoted article is 'IQ', *Atlantic Monthly*, 22 (December 1971). (Herrnstein was featured in both *Time* and *Newsweek*'s edition, 23 August 1971.) We examine Jenck's *Inequality* again in Chapter XI.

6 See Silver, 1973, op. cit., xvi–xxix.

7 See Kamin, op. cit., particularly the historical chapters. He points out that the IQ test technology and its proponents contributed to passage of the discriminatory Immigration Act of 1924. The results of testing draftees during the First World War were interpreted to demonstrate the natural superiority of the 'Nordic' races. Respected practitioners of the new science of psychometrics concluded that 79 per cent of the Italians, 80 per cent of the Hungarians, 87 per cent of the Russians, and 83 per cent of the Jews tested at Ellis Island were feeble-minded. Karabel and Halsey, op. cit., and Brian Davies, op. cit., show how the methodological commitment to quantitative variables has repeatedly led to bypassing study of the schooling process.

8 See Arthur Jensen, *Bias in Mental Testing* (Glencoe: The Free Press, 1979); and also 'How much can we boost IQ and scholastic achievement?', *Harvard Educational Review*, 39:2, 1–123, 1969. For a review of Jensen's most recent book, see Stephen Jay Gould, 'Jensen's last stand' in *New York Review of Books* (1 May 1980). Articles which reported Jensen's new book and, as Gould points out, failed to ferret out the central fallacies of Jensen's argument, appeared in *Time* (24 September 1979), 49 and *Newsweek* (14 January 1980), 59.

9 Debates over the claims of objectivity, the relationship of values, social facts and theory, and the nature of explanation are commonplace among philosophers of science; for example, see May Brodbeck (ed.), *Readings in the Philosophy of the Social Sciences* (New York: Macmillan; London: Collier Macmillan, 1968). However, the respectability of positivist social science remained relatively undisturbed through the 1970s, despite indications that all was not well.

When Stanislaw Andreski published a biting and penetrating polemic, *Social Science as Sorcery* (New York: St Martin's Press, 1972), it received virtually no notice in academic journals. Yet many of the criticisms that he voiced are now regularly found within the journals of established social science disciplines. C. Wright Mills's *The Sociological Imagination* (London: Oxford University Press, 1959) also anticipated by more than twenty years many of the criticisms that until recently had not penetrated the mainline journals of educational research. We deal with the critiques of 'traditional' social science again in Chapters VI and XI.

10 Detailed criticism of tests and their use were made by Banesh Hoffman in his *Tyranny of Testing* (New York: Crowell Collier, 1962), though they were generally dismissed by professionals and the press as gross overstatements. The prevailing view of the times, which persists today though with less certainty, was expressed by Paul Woodring, 'Are intelligence tests unfair?', *Saturday Review* (16 April 1966). 'It seems obvious that a modern school system cannot operate

30

effectively without some sort of large-scale testing' (p. 80). What follows from such an assumption is that, though perhaps flawed, 'aptitude' and 'achievement' tests are the best we have and therefore must be used to assess educational productivity. This position has been questioned recently by numbers of persons and groups. In the US the critical literature on testing has become voluminous. Because of the widespread use of such tests across all areas and levels of education, many national organizations and scholarly associations have been drawn into the fray (the American Federation of Teachers, AFL–CIO, National Education Association, Association for Supervision and Curriculum Development, National Academy of Sciences, National Research Council, National Parent Teacher Associations, National Council of Teachers of English to mention but a few). In addition there are several special interest groups issuing pronouncements. Probably the most significant development in recent years is the establishment of the National Consortium on Testing, in Washington, D.C., to act as a public interest group that subjects to close scrutiny the claims of the test publishers, be they profit-making corporations, or public service non-profit corporations (for example, Educational Testing Service, Princeton, New Jersey).

11 Fred Hechinger, 'Frail sociology', *New York Times* (5 November 1979).
12 Gabriel Chanan, *The Times Educational Supplement* (14 May 1976).
13 See Jeffrey M. Blum's review of L.S. Hearnshaw's *Cyril Burt, Psychologist* (New York: Cornell University Press, 1979) in *Harvard Educational Review* 50:2 (May 1980), for an introduction to the issue and a bibliography.
14 A useful introduction to the issues is the *Ethnography and the Schools*, a part of the Open University Course, 'Schooling and society', Units 7–8, prepared by Martin Hammersley and Peter Woods (Milton Keynes: Open University Press, 1977). Two books we found particularly helpful are Brian Fay, *Social Theory and Political Practice* (London and Boston: Allen & Unwin, 1975), with a useful bibliography for the uninitiated; and Anthony Giddens, *New Rules of Sociological Method* (New York: Basic Books, 1976). See also Richard J. Bernstein, *The Restructuring of Social and Political Theory* (London: Methuen, 1979).
15 See, for example, Sara Delamont, *Interaction in the Classroom* (London: Methuen, 1976); Michael Stubbs, *Language, Schools and Classrooms* (London: Methuen, 1976); Robert Walker and Clem Adelman, 'Interaction analysis in informal classrooms; a critical comment on the Flanders system', *British Journal of Educational Psychology*, 45:1 (1971); Hammersley and Woods (eds.), 1977, op. cit.; and Caroline Hodges Persell's review of Rutter *et al.*, *Fifteen Thousand Hours* (Cambridge, Massachusetts: Harvard University Press, 1979; London: Open Books) in *Harvard Educational Review* (May 1980), with responses to her review in *Harvard Educational Review*, 50:4 (November 1980).
16 Among the persons whose work is associated with this general orientation are many of the contributors to the Open University reader, *The Process of Schooling*, edited by Martyn Hammersley and Peter Woods (London: Routledge & Kegan Paul, 1976), and to the volume also edited by Hammersley and Woods, *School Experience* (London: Croom Helm, 1977). Also see two collections of papers, Peter Woods (ed.), *Teacher Strategies* (London: Croom Helm, 1980); Peter Woods (ed.), *Pupil Strategies* (London: Croom Helm, 1980). Amont the earliest and best known works are David Hargreaves, *Social Relations in a Secondary School* (London: Routledge & Kegan Paul, 1967); and C. Lacey, *Hightown Grammar: The School as a Social System* (Manchester: Manchester University Press, 1970). For a critical appraisal see Karabel and Halsey, 1971, op. cit.; Brian Davies, op. cit.; Len Barton and Roland Meighan (eds.), *Sociological Interpretations of Schooling and Classrooms: A Reappraisal* (Nafferton, Driffield: Nafferton Books, 1978).

Chapter VI lays out the theory of George Herbert Mead that directly or indirectly influenced much of the work of the 'New Sociologists'.

17 There is a variety of persons and perspectives one could place within the tradition of work that is, on the one hand, akin to the atheoretical traditions of much of North American anthropology, and, on the other, to R.K. Merton's sociological orientation, for example, *Social Theory and Social Structure* (Glencoe, Illinois: Free Press, 1957). Some merely sought to describe social life allegedly free of preconception. Others were more committed to developing middle-range propositions; see H. Zetterberg, *On Theory and Verification in Sociology* (Totowa, New Jersey: Bedminster Press, 1965), and L.M. Smith's work (cited below), again, purportedly without imposing one's political and social values. See R. Bernstein (op. cit.) for an excellent analysis of Merton's position. Among the most influential works in this general tradition are: L.M. Smith and W. Geoffrey, *Complexities of an Urban Classroom* (New York: Holt, Rinehart & Winston, 1968); L.M. Smith and P. Keith, *Anatomy of Educational Innovation* (New York: Wiley, 1971). For L.M. Smith's more recent work, see 'Effective teaching: a qualitative inquiry in aesthetic education', *Anthropology and Education Quarterly*, 2 (1977), 127–39. Conversation and seminars with L.M. Smith and his students have been helpful in our efforts to clarify and justify our position.

18 See criticisms by Karabel and Halsey, op. cit., 44–61; Henry Giroux and Anthony N. Penna, 'Social education in the classroom: the dynamics of the hidden curriculum', *Theory and Research in Social Education*, VII:1 (Spring 1979); and Michael Apple, *Ideology and the Curriculum* (London and Boston: Routledge & Kegan Paul, 1979), especially pp. 139–40.

19 See Geoff Whitty, Block III Unit book, *School Knowledge and Social Control* (Milton Keynes: Open University Press, 1977).

20 See Michael F.D. Young (ed.), *Knowledge and Control*, op. cit.; Geoff Whitty and Michael Young, *Explorations in the Politics of School Knowledge* (Nafferton, Driffield: Nafferton Press, 1976); John Eggleston, *The Sociology of the School Curriculum* (London, Henley and Boston: Routledge & Kegan Paul, 1977). It is Karl Mannheim's work that is most often cited as having been the source of this strand of sociological study of knowledge in Britain. See K. Mannheim, *Ideology and Utopia: An Introduction to the Sociology of Knowledge* (London: Routledge & Kegan Paul, 1936).

During the closing years of the last decade the work of a number of American researchers with similar commitments received wider notice and the 'New Sociology' began to make its way across the Atlantic. These include Aaron V. Cicourel *et al.*, *Language Use and School Performance* (New York: Academic Press, 1974); Eleanor Burke Leacock, *Teaching and Learning in City Schools* (New York: Basic Books, 1969). More recent work includes: Frederick Erikson, 'On standards of descriptive validity in studies of classroom activity', paper delivered at AERA, Toronto, 1978; Hugh Mehan, *Learning Lessons: Social Organization in the Classroom* (Cambridge, Massachusetts: Harvard University Press, 1979).

Prior to 1978 there was little mention in the US of the work of the British 'New Sociology' except among a number of North American curriculum theorists, who until recently were not generally known to American classroom researchers. Christopher J. Hurn's essay review of Michael Flude and John Ahier's *Educability, Schools and Ideology* (New York: Halstead Press, 1974) and several of the Open University course books, 'Recent trends in the sociology of education', *Harvard Educational Review*, 46:1 (February 1976); Michael Apple's review of Gerald Bernbaum's *Knowledge and Ideology in the Sociology of Education* (London: Macmillan Press, 1977) and Peter Woods and Martyn Hammersley (eds.), *School Experience: Explorations in the Sociology of Education* (New

York: St Martin's Press, 1977), in *Harvard Educational Review*, 48:4 (November 1978), brought work which was known by a few to a wider audience of educational researchers. Elliot G. Mishler, in an article 'Meaning in context: is there any other kind?', *Harvard Educational Review*, 49:1 (February 1979), brought to the attention of North Americans alternative research approaches of ongoing work on both sides of the Atlantic, including the work of the American researcher Pat Carini, who had long taken a phenomenological approach to analyzing children's work; see P.F. Carini, *Observation and Description: An Alternative Methodology for Investigation of Human Phenomena* (North Dakota Study Group on Evaluation Monograph Series, Grand Forks: University of North Dakota Press, 1975).

In the last two years work of a larger number of North American curriculum theorists and researchers who depart from the narrower psychological tradition of American instructional research is becoming widely known. See M.W. Apple, 1979, op. cit.; Henry A. Giroux, 'Beyond the limits of radical education reform: toward a critical theory of education', *Journal of Curriculum Theorizing*, 2:1 (1979), and op. cit.; Thomas S. Popkewitz, 'Paradigms in educational science', *Journal of Education*, 192:1 (1980); Hugh Mehan, op. cit. By 1980 the index of the program book for the annual meeting of the American Educational Research Association (AERA) listed eight sessions under the entry 'Ethnography'; by contrast there was one entry for 'Educational objectives', four for 'Educational opportunity', three for 'Multivariate analysis'. Indeed, a recent volume of *Harvard Educational Review* (50:4; November 1980) indicates that alternative perspectives now have wide currency in some circles.

21 Davies, op. cit., 20.
22 This argument is made in general terms by Brian Fay, op. cit., 83 and Anthony Giddens, op. cit., 28–53. Such criticisms are directed specifically at the 'New Sociologists' of education by Karabel and Halsey, op. cit., and by Rachel Sharp and Anthony Green, *Education and Social Control: A Study in Progressive Primary Education* (London, Henley and Boston: Routledge & Kegan Paul, 1975), 1–35; Michael Apple, op. cit., and Henry Giroux, op. cit.
23 David Swartz, 'Pierre Bourdieu: the cultural transmission of social inequality', *Harvard Educational Review*, 47:4 (1977), 544.
24 Basil Bernstein, op. cit., 7. Our review of Bernstein's work is based primarily on Bernstein's own summary of the research he conducted most directly related to schooling during the decade 1966–75. This summary is the introduction to *Class, Codes and Control*, Vol. 3 (1975). See also a review of the 1978 edition of this book by Michael Apple, 'Curriculum and Reproduction', *Curriculum Inquiry*, 9:3 (Fall 1979).
25 These two codes, integrated and collection, underlie the forms of curricula, pedagogy and evaluations that occur in classrooms. See Mohamed Cherkaoui, 'Basil Bernstein and Emile Durkheim', *Harvard Educational Review*, 47:4 (November 1977), 558.
26 Bernstein, 1975, op. cit., 8. Bernstein explains the function of classification and framing as follows: '*Power and control are made substantive in the classification and framing which then generate distinctive forms of social relationships and thus communication, and through the pattern initially, but not necessarily finally, shape mental structures.*' [Bernstein, 1975, op. cit., 11, italics in original]
27 A major part of Bernstein's work does not focus on schools, but is devoted to examining how class regulates the structure of communication within the family and so the initial socio-linguistic coding orientation of children (what he labels as restricted or context specific v. elaborated or context free forms of language), ibid., 22. For details see *Class, Codes and Control, Vol. 1 Theoretical Studies Towards a Sociology of Language* (London: Routledge & Kegan Paul, 1973).

28 Bernstein, 1975, op. cit., 22.
29 Ibid., 8.
30 Ibid., 553; Sara Delamont, op. cit., 38.
31 Swartz, op. cit., 553; Davies's comment (op. cit., 124) is not really in the nature of criticism when he says that Bernstein's 'major working categories are in their nature immensely formal and in need of . . . modification which goes with the vitality of real world test'.
32 Compare, for example, Bernstein's portrayal (1975) of formal and informal classrooms in 'Class and pedagogies: visible and invisible' with our own.
33 Swartz, op. cit., 553; Michael Stubbs, op. cit., 36.
34 Davies, op. cit., 139 directs this criticism at Bourdieu. Apple, 1979, op. cit., says essentially the same of Bernstein's work.
35 See David Hargreaves, 'Whatever happened to symbolic interactionism?' in Barton and Meighan, op. cit. For brief evaluations of critiques of Bernstein's work, see O. Banks, 'School and society' in Barton and Meighan, op. cit.; and Davies, op. cit., 132–3.
36 The need to forge links between macro and micro studies has been voiced by numbers of researchers, for example, Karabel and Halsey, op. cit., 61. See Sara Delamont, 'Sociology in the classroom' in Barton and Meighan, op. cit., for a brief exploration of this problem. She argues that macro and micro perspectives cannot be recombined in a simple additive fashion, as if they were part of a construction kit (p. 69). Sharp and Green's work (op. cit.) is a well-known effort to connect macro and micro analyses. It has, however, been severely criticized for distorting classroom data in order to fit into the Marxian frame (see David Hargreaves in Barton and Meighan, op. cit), and for underestimating the autonomy that can characterize teacher actions (see Brian Davies, op. cit., 164). Paul Willis's *Learning to Labour* (Westmead: Saxon House, 1978), a study of the transition of working-class boys from school to work, is a most promising effort, though it attends little to classroom processes. Also see Andy Hargreaves, 'The significance of classroom coping strategies' in Barton and Meighan, op. cit.; and Ian Westbury, 'Schooling as an agency of education: some implications for curriculum theory' in W.B. Dockrell and David Hamilton (eds.), *Rethinking Educational Research* (London, Sydney, Auckland and Toronto: Hodder & Stoughton, 1979). More recently, in the US, Michael Apple (op. cit.) and Henry Giroux (op. cit.) have formulated this problem as a central task for educational research.
37 Neville Bennett, *Teaching Styles and Pupil Progress* (London: Open Books, 1976; also Cambridge, Mass.: Harvard University Press, 1976). Also see Thornbury, *The Changing Urban School* (London: Methuen, 1978), 160. He, as do many others, seems to accept Bennett's conclusions which are based entirely upon achievement test scores. We return to this issue in Chapter XI.
38 See nn. 7, 8 and 13, Chapter II for citations.

Chapter III

1 John Holt, *How Children Fail* (London: Pitman, 1965; Harmondsworth, Middlesex: Pelican Books, 1969), *The Underachieving School* (London: Pitman, 1970; Harmondsworth, Middlesex: Pelican, 1971); Jonathan Kozol, *Death at an Early Age* (New York: Houghton Mifflin, 1967); Paul Goodman, *Compulsory Miseducation* (New York: Random House, 1977); George Dennison, *The Lives of Children* (New York: Random House, 1969); Herbert Kohl, *36 Children* (New York: New American Library, 1967). Also Allen Graubard, *Free the Children* (New York: Vintage, 1972). The foregoing remain interesting and useful though they are rarely read today. We question the common wisdom that they are

'romantic' writers (that is, fuzzy and untrustworthy). They sometimes provide excellent accounts of school life and provide thoughtful and, in many cases, realistic possibilities for action.

2 For example, the *New York Review of Books*, the *New York Times, Saturday Review, Harpers Magazine, Atlantic Monthly, New Republic* and *Progressive*.

3 Herbert Marcuse, then a professor of politics and philosophy at Brandeis University, was one of the few voices of the left whose work was not considered narrowly ideological by respectable liberal and conservative academicians. Among his better known works are *One Dimensional Man* (Boston: Beacon Press, 1964); *Counterrevolution and Revolt* (Boston: Beacon Press, 1972). He became popularly referred to as the theoretician of the New Left, a designation which some likely took to mean (mistakenly) that he was an apologist for the New Left in the US in the late 1960s to early 1970s. His name was far more widely used than his books were read. Charles Reich in *Greening of America* (New York: Random House, 1970) apparently coined the term Consciousness III. Space prohibits discussion, but the term generally refers to the presumably new liberated consciousness that the New Left sometimes claimed was emerging in the 1960s and early 1970s. We feel incapable of summarizing the logic of Mr Reich's arguments; his book, which was taken seriously in its time, has since descended into a much deserved obscurity.

4 Charles Silberman, *Crisis in the Classroom* (New York: Random House, 1970).

5 The open education literature became voluminous between 1968 and 1972. Within the vast corpus of articles, books and pamphlets there was much excellent and useful writing, some of lasting interest, that was lost in the surfeit. Lillian Weber's the *English Infant School and Informal Education* (New York: Prentice–Hall, 1971) is as useful today as when it was written. It also contains a good bibliography. Also notable were the writings of Joseph Featherstone, a set of essays in the *New Republic*, that were collected and published under the title *Schools Where Children Learn* (New York: Liverwright, 1971), and his 'Report analysis: children and their primary schools', *Harvard Educational Review*, 38:2 (1963). Featherstone provided North American readers with a non-idealized picture of informal schooling and he also anticipated the attack on progressive education from the left. 'England remains', he wrote in the introduction, 'like America. A caste-ridden capitalist nation; the millenium is far away. Yet, a comparable change in our schools would mean a great deal for the quality of our children's lives' (1971, p. xii). Several booklets and pamphlets published by Educational Development Center are still useful and provacative, particularly W.P. Hull's 'Leicestershire revisited'. William Hull's reflections and analysis of the problems he saw in the directions that open education was taking in the early 1970s in the US are reported in a series of unpublished papers he wrote between March 1971 and October 1972 collected under the title 'The case for the experimental school'. Hull anticipated the backlash that the know-nothing open education enthusiasts helped to create. Published in Britain were John Blackie, *Inside the Primary School* (London: HMSO, 1967); Leonard Marsh, *Alongside the Child in the Primary School* (London: A. & C. Black, 1970).

6 For example, Charles Rathbone, one of the leading advocates for open education in America during this period, wrote 'Open education sees teaching more as a lateral interchange . . . between two persons of nearly equal status. . . . It is the student who is more often the initiator. . . . A teacher is in a sense a travel agent. He helps a child go where the child wants to go.' [C. Rathbone, 'The implicit rationale of the open education classroom' in C. Rathbone (ed.), *Open Education* (New York: Citation Press, 1971), 106–7] Roland Barth, describing 'the philosophical, personal and professional roots from which these open education

practices have sprung and upon which the open educators depend so completely for their success', argued that most open educators 'strongly agree' with statements such as the following: 'If a child is fully involved and having fun with an activity he is learning'; 'Children have the competence and right to make significant decisions concerning their own learning'; and 'Children are innately curious and will explore their environment without adult intervention'. ['So you want to change to an open classroom', *Phi Delta Kappan* (October 1971), 97–9] The ways in which these writers identified these beliefs raised doubts about whether they had in fact identified ideas that guided the teachers' action or instead had identified the educational creeds or philosophies of teachers, or, more likely, of educational and school advisors. See Ann and Harold Berlak, N.T. Bagenstos and E.R. Mikel, 'Teaching and learning in the English primary schools', *School Review*, 83:2 (1975); and Ann and Harold Berlak, 'On the uses of social psychological research on schooling', an essay review of *Beyond Surface Curriculum: An Interview Study of Teachers' Understandings* (Anne M. Bussis, Edward A. Chittenden, and Marianne Amarel; Boulder, Col.: Westview, 1976) in the *School Review*, 85:4 (August 1977) for critical reviews of the literature. Ronald King, in *All Things Bright and Beautiful* (New York: Wiley, 1978), apparently studied schools that were similar in many ways to those we studied, at approximately the same time. His conclusions about the ideologies that guide informal teachers' activities are similar to Barth's and Rathbone's. Like some of the earlier American studies, the framework or theory of teachers' 'ideologies' was drawn from analyses of head teachers' philosophies and from an analysis of the Plowden Report, with which the head teachers claimed to agree. King's support for his conclusions about the ideas that guide teachers' actions includes the following: 'I cannot say that all the teachers had read the [Plowden] report and agreed with it, but all three headmistresses had copies prominently displayed in their rooms. Two of them spoke of it most enthusiastically, one calling it her Bible. "And I agree with every word of it" ' (p. 11).

7 Barth, op. cit., 98.
8 Alvin W. Gouldner, *The Coming Crisis in Western Sociology* (New York: Equinox, 1970), 29.

PART TWO
THE SCHOOLS

INTRODUCTION

In Part Two we describe moments in the lives of children and teachers at the schools we visited in England over a six-month period. In Parts Three and Four, we look through the lenses of the sixteen dilemmas at these moments to illustrate the potential of the dilemma language for ordering the flux of classroom life, and placing the mundane events of daily school life in the perspectives of culture and time.

The schools we chose to study reflected our interest in understanding the range of schooling activities English teachers, heads and advisors labeled 'informal' primary education *as it was practiced* in schools serving children of differing social backgrounds. We made no effort to define a 'representative sample' of informal schools or teachers, first, because we had no basis for establishing in advance explicit criteria for judging degrees of informality. Second, since we were limited to six months in England we knew we would have time for three extended stays at most, and no sample of three, however chosen, could represent the variations in schooling patterns of a region let alone an entire nation. Our visits for one and on occasion two to four days in sixteen other schools in two local educational authorities provided us with some assurance that the three schools we had chosen to study in some depth were not atypical of schools in the region. We represented ourselves as we were, ex-teachers, teacher educators, who were interested in seeing and recording the differences between these primary schools and the elementary schools we knew first hand in the US, and in seeing for ourselves what 'informal methods', which had captured the interest of many North American school reformers, looked like in practice. We did not present ourselves nor did we think of ourselves primarily as social scientists.

Over the course of the six months we visited sixteen schools and somewhere in the vicinity of one hundred classrooms. Virtually all our time, however, was spent in the three schools we chose to study four to six weeks each, with return visits of several days before we left England. The catchment areas of the schools differed widely. The first school we studied, *Port Primary*, was in an area the locals called a village but was rapidly being transformed into a suburb of new modest homes a few miles from a small industrial and commercial town. The second, *Castlegate Infant*, was on the edge of the largest city in the area and served a large council housing estate, what we and our American readers would call a public housing project. The third, *Heathbrook Junior*, was in an older affluent suburb of homes perhaps 15 to 20 years old. In each school at least half the teachers were thought of as 'informal' by the head teacher. Port Primary was selected for us by a person in the local education authority whose name was given to us by an acquaintance. This school had, we were told, an 'informal' infant department and a junior department that was in the process of 'transition' under the leadership of Mr Nigel, the new head teacher. It was a felicitous choice, for in this one school we were able to see practices that, according to the head and an LEA advisor, represented a range of methods from 'informal' to 'formal'. Thus with Port Primary as our point of reference we were able to identify the other schools we wished to observe and study either briefly or in depth.

Our portrayal of the schools is drawn from field notes in which we recorded daily events, words of children and school staff, personal impressions, questions and judgments, and from transcribed tape-recorded interviews with ten school heads, eighteen teachers and twenty-seven children. The narrative is intended to suggest both the range and the complexity of daily life in classrooms that can be ordered by the dilemma language.

To show the fine-grained texture of classroom life that can be represented by the language we have chosen to describe in great detail one classroom, Mrs Martin's at Port. We counterpose to this portrayal scenes from other classrooms at Port, Heathbrook, Castlegate and several other schools in order to suggest the range of schooling patterns we observed within the three schools and among all nineteen.[1]

Table 1   Teachers and head teacher of the three schools studied in depth

Port Primary School

Mr Nigel	Head teacher
Mrs Martin	Reception class
Mrs Eden	Second-year Infants
Mrs Carpenter	Third-year Infants, Deputy Head teacher
Mr Edgar	Junior
Mrs Newhouse	Junior team

Castlegate Infant School

Mrs Hollins	Head teacher
Mrs Paynter	Second-year Infants
Mrs Lawton	Second-year Infants
Miss Gault	Third-year Infants

Heathbrook Junior School

Mr Bolton	Head teacher
Mr Scott	First-year Juniors, Deputy Head teacher
Mr Carlson	Third-year Juniors
Mrs Colton	Third-year Juniors

Note: We list only those teachers who are referred to by name in the narrative and subsequent analyses. All names and identifying details have been changed in order to protect the anonymity of staff and students.

Table 2   Teachers and head teachers of the other schools

Newton Infant

Mrs Willis	Head teacher

Highrock Junior

Mr Park	Head teacher
Mr Jerrid	Teacher

Other

Mr Sprinter	Teacher
Mrs Calthorpe	Head teacher

IV PORT PRIMARY

It is an English winter day: dark, cold and damp. With difficulty we have located Port Primary and are only ten minutes late. Ten days earlier, we had spoken to an official of the local education authority requesting his permission to visit primary schools, and asking that we begin in a school which was neither famous nor inundated with Americans. He had questioned us carefully. We told him we would welcome the opportunity to help out in the schools, and that except for occasional day-visits to other schools, we would spend every day in the same school for four or more weeks. He promised that within a few days he would find a school where we could begin our work and subsequently we could make our own arrangements, though he wished to be informed of our whereabouts. Six days later, he called to tell us that Mr Nigel, Head teacher at Port Primary School in the village of Port, was expecting us on the following Monday morning.

As we maneuver our aged Vauxhall through the twists and turns of School Street the first time, we fail to notice a break in the long brick wall, the open gate and the small black rectangular sign with gilded letters 'Port Primary School'. After being reassured by a bakery shop attendant that there was a school to be found in School Street, we find not a single building but a maze of interconnected red brick forms arranged helter-skelter, like children's blocks on an asphalt mat. Along one side of the asphalt there is a high brick wall; on the other, a waist-high cast-iron fence separating the school yard from an expanse of grass. In a far corner of the grass field, perhaps 400 yards from where we are standing, is a playground – slide, swings and a roundabout. The field, we learn later, is 'the Common' (though obviously it had been a very long time since animals grazed here). Surrounding the Common in the distance we see the remains of the roofline of an old village, dominated by a grey-stone church bell-tower, a scene completely hidden from view of the busy two-lane road that cuts through the village. Momentarily, in the quiet of the school yard, we are transported from the twentieth century.

We enter the green door to the right of the gate and are in a corridor, hardly wider than our outstretched arms; on both walls hang children's coats and cardigans. Sounds of children in class-rooms from behind closed doors are familiar. We take only a few steps and are greeted by a smiling man in his early thirties: 'You are the Berlaks?' 'I'm Jack . . . Jack Nigel.' He holds out his hand and shakes ours vigorously. We follow him, no more than a half-dozen steps to his office. As we enter he quickly removes several stacks of papers from the one extra chair, disappears, and a moment later is back with another. His office is a clutter of books, papers and boxes. Three empty terraria lie by his desk. It is an office that looks less like a work place than the way station of a man who spends most of his time elsewhere.

He begins by relating to us two histories: his personal story – of his own schooling and his experience as a student teacher in one of the schools praised by an American journalist, and as teacher and deputy headmaster at Heathbrook Junior School – and the history of Port School prior to his appointment late in the last school year. He tells us in some detail about the evolution of Heathbrook (a school we were to study later) and how the head, whom he greatly admires, and the teachers at Heathbrook were able over time to deal with 'kids that destroyed and interfered with others' activities', how these children were gradually given freedom as they learned to use their own time efficiently. On occasion he uses the words 'team teaching' or 'integrated day', 'informal' and 'informal'. Though we are uncertain of his meanings, we ask few questions. There will be time for clarification. For the most part, however, his language is descriptive and clear. Every few minutes he pauses and looks to see whether we share his intense interest in his subject. We do. He tells us that the school he inherited was a 'good and happy' school, with an excellent infant department but with many 'chalk and talk' junior teachers.[1] 'They did sums on the board.' He is planning, he tells us, to 'informalize' the junior teachers, moving carefully and slowly, 'doing one thing at a time'. He again uses his experience at Heathbrook as illustration, speaking with the energy and optimism of a man deeply committed to a new endeavor who has had few opportunities to share in much depth his interests, problems and concerns.

At 10.15 we walk several paces to the library that doubles as the teachers' tearoom. The entire space is little more than 15 feet square, 'created out of some dead space', Mr Nigel explains, 'and pro-visioned by some hardworking mothers'. As the teachers enter for morning tea, we are introduced as two Americans who will be visiting for a month, helping out and observing. We stand elbow-to-elbow drinking tea in this crowded room. With the exception of a young woman who is introduced to us as a teacher-in-practice, Mr Nigel is without doubt the youngest among us. The atmosphere is congenial. We receive several unsolicited invitations from teachers to visit their classrooms. They are interested in us, and we feel included. As we leave the room, the children crowd through the narrow passageway, returning from playtime. Mr Nigel exchanges friendly words with several. He beckons a little girl: 'Clara, Mrs Martin says you wanted to spend 25p on sweets; does your Mum know 'bout it?' The child smiles sheepishly. 'Perhaps we'll have a chat.'

As we tour the building, the relative locations of the classrooms are difficult to grasp, since rooms appear to have been patched to the original building over the years without overall plan. Most of the rooms open to the outside, several have doors that connect them to others. The sizes of the classrooms vary greatly. Two of the rooms are smaller than any classroom we have seen in the States. In each there is a free-standing gas fire ringed with a sturdy wire barrier. Our tour is brief, only a few minutes to glance in the door or walk through each classroom. Jack Nigel tells us we are now on our own. He is off to fetch the school's one TV set for a teacher.

MRS MARTIN'S CLASSROOM

The setting; the actors; first impressions[2]

I enter Mrs Martin's 'reception' class of $4\frac{1}{2}$ to $5\frac{1}{2}$ year olds. At first sight, it appears the virtual opposite of the first years of school I knew as a child. No rows of varnished pine and black cast-iron desks and chairs securely fastened to the floor. But the smell is familiar – musty wood mingled with the medicinal scent of disinfectant. In place of the symmetry, the military arrangement of people and physical space, the drab browns, grays and washed-out yellows, and silence broken by continuous droning of adult voices that I knew as a child, there is here asymmetry, irregularity in shape and form, continuous sounds of children's voices interfused with those of adults. Clusters of little people, not in military ranks, but standing or sitting here and there on floors, chairs or tables.

At first glance no simple pattern of activity is apparent. Two or

43

three in clusters playing with conkers,[3] some writing, several working puzzles, others engaged in vigorous, quiet (but not surreptitious) conversation. Several are reading to themselves, some appear to be working on arithmetic problems, two are at the easels. Mrs Martin smiles a pleasant greeting from her desk which, positioned on the perimeter, affords her a good view of the entire scene, then continues her talk with a small boy who stands beside her while four or five quietly chatting children wait their turn.

We eventually will decide to study this classroom in some detail. The participants are 29 children, Mrs Martin and, some time during the day, a teacher's aide (Mrs Maxim), the school secretary, the 'dinner ladies', Mr Nigel – and for six weeks, and at irregular intervals over a six-month period, one of the Berlaks.

Continual movement and bright colors – reds, blues, greens, yellows – everywhere, but not the feeling of disorder, tension and shrillness that we have ourselves seen and experienced as adults attempting to manage large numbers of children in limited space without imposing military discipline. The longer we observe, the more we will become aware of the complexity and variations. Even after we have become familiar with the basic routines, we will find nuances that indicate that events are not always what they seem. As the years pass and we examine our recorded observations and interviews, we will continue to discover complexities that increase our respect for Mrs Martin. What we will see on closer observation will not alter our initial impression that the children work and learn without the constant vigilant patrol of the teacher's eyes. In spite of the continuous movement, there is a sense of tranquillity and purposefulness. Whatever else we may find upon closer observation we consider this a significant achievement for any teacher of young children.

Children's handiwork is everywhere. Tempera paintings, three-dimensional paper productions, cut, arranged and pasted in ways only children's imaginations could devise. On shelves, on top of cabinets and tables there are papier mâché pussy-cats, creatures from outer space, cereal-box lorries, towers and prams, plasticine bowls, ray guns and whatnots in various states of incompletion. The teacher's contributions are also evident: a three-dimensional blue and yellow choo-choo train, a green bear and red monster amid trees with leaves of words, a bulletin board with a not-quite-complete display on Denmark. Chalk trays run the length of two walls which now serve as galleries of art, concealing their original use.

Emptied of its contents, the room is rectangular, not quite 20 feet wide, not quite 40 feet long. The walls are a disagreeable pink. Yellow incandescent globes of light hang from chains. Between the two windows on one long side of the rectangle stands the gas-fired heater, intruding three feet into the room, on the other long side, one window and a door that opens to the outside. Through the door, one sees a band of asphalt about 15 feet wide, the gated iron fence, and beyond, the 'Common'. To the right of the door, an upright piano, crackle brown with graying keys. On the short wall, a door leads to Mrs Eden's 'second year (or middle) infants' class to which Mrs Martin's children will pass after they have completed their stint in this, their reception, class. To the right of the door, situated so that it overlooks the entire classroom, is Mrs Martin's wooden desk. From this vantage point, the classroom appears as a clutter of old furniture and makeshift shelves and partitions. Closer inspection reveals that everything is sturdy, and the arrangement of the room obviously premeditated. Within the open shelves along the walls (painted royal blue, bright yellow or red), there are the tools of the infant teacher's trade: stacks of cards faced with transparent plastic, displays of books, boxes of educational games, crayons, plasticine; and what the teachers refer to generally as 'apparatus' – cubes of plastic that snap together, conkers, buttons, stacks of white plastic containers. In the cabinets or in small bins there are large wooden bricks, large and small 'Legos', collections of cereal boxes and a variety of cardboard spools and cones, undoubtedly waste from one of the factories in a nearby city, lying in wait for their transformation into *objets d'art*. Everything is orderly, but there is also clearly no compulsivity about details – a stack of books on a chair, an abandoned gerbil cage misplaced among the maths apparatus.

There are five child-sized tables in the shape of hexagons, each formed by pushing together two tables, and surrounded by five or six chairs. An open space at the left center of the floor is covered by an 8 foot by 10 foot rug of undistinguishable color that doubtless had a long career in someone's front parlor. On the other short wall, on the side of the room opposite Mrs Martin's desk, is a sand table covered with a heavy cloth. To the right, there are two art easels almost hidden from view by one of two new-looking factory-made pieces of school furniture in the room, a bank of drawers each displaying a child's name that serves as storage space for his/her papers, books and pencils. (The other is a cabinet holding a bank of gray plastic trays containing maths cards and 'apparatus'.) Occupying space along one wall is a play hospital, 'a child's paradise', the observer records – real salves and bandages, nurses' and doctors' costumes, a child's car fitted out as an ambulance.

This reception classroom setting is the workplace for children who are under six years of age. Here, the children are expected to begin to master the elements of what has become defined (in this setting at least) as literacy – the so-called 'basics' or '3Rs'. One distinction between this and adult workplaces is that here entry and exit depend largely upon age. Children enter the 'reception' class three times a year – September, January and April – when they are 'rising fives', or at the beginning of the terms in which they observe their fifth birthday. Approximately a third of the 'rising sixes' will pass through to Mrs Eden's class at the beginning of each term. Therefore, what is taken as normal is a continuously shifting membership and a process of continuous socialization of recent entrants.

Mrs Martin refers to those who are assigned to table numbers 4 and 5 as her 'newer ones'. Tracy, a friendly and garrulous occupant of table 3, refers to tables 1 and 2 as 'top', and to 4 and 5 as the 'lower' (three other children who overhear our conversation confirm her view). Samuel and Steven, who often sit side by side at table 4, call theirs 'the bottom' (both pronounce the word in two distinct, emphatic syllables). Lucille, a table 4 occupant overhears the conversation with Samuel and Steven and interrupts to say indignantly, 'Mrs Martin doesn't call it bottom.' (We too will never hear her call it 'bottom'.)

From an objective point of view, table 1 and 2 children are those who are expected to complete fewer but more complex tasks; as a group they are the oldest (rising sixes), and the ones who, if all goes as planned, are destined to move into Mrs Eden's class at the beginning of the following school term. The children who entered school most recently, those Mrs Martin calls 'newer ones' or 'first termers', sit at tables 4 and 5. Those who are neither first termers, nor ready for Mrs Eden, sit at tables 3 and 4. This stratification by table is by no means absolute since, of course, the age distribution will vary from term to term. And, children who, for one reason or another, do not proceed at normal pace will for an extra term or more sit at a higher-numbered table than their age warrants.

To speak of the children as assigned to tables gives a distorted impression. The children mix more than our description implies. Children usually are permitted to sit in any empty seat they wish, though the majority, when they sit, choose their assigned table.

The contents of the bank of drawers (see Z on floor plan) are of some significance, the variations corresponding in general to the table status of the children. In addition to one or two pencils, a

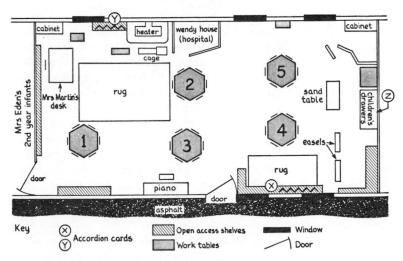

Figure 1 Floor plan of Mrs Martin's classroom

rubber, and some odd personal belongings (for example, a small doll, a cache of candy or toy motor car), the majority of children have a 'normal reader' (a paperback book that is part of a commercially produced series of readers) out of which protrudes a white bookmark with page numbers recorded in the teacher's hand, and a library (that is, non text) book. Each child has two to four LEA-issue blue-backed composition books, each with twenty-four sheets of paper. The narrowest of these, in the shape of a grocery list, is the 'dictionary', each page headed by a letter of the alphabet. Recorded on each page are words written in the teacher's hand, that are used by the children in writing the 'news'. The second, about $6\frac{1}{2} \times 8$ in., is called the 'number' or 'sums' book where children record their mathematics work. A third, the 'writing' or 'copy' book, is used to record a range of writing activities described in a subsequent section. The largest book, approximately 10×15 in., is the 'news'; on each page the children draw a picture with crayon or pencil and write one, two or three sentences underneath. The 'news' can vary greatly in average number of handwritten lines. Three or four have a far greater proportion of written matter to picture. Most have one or two written lines per picture.

The drawers of children who reside at tables 3, 4 and 5 (those who are the 'newer ones' as well as those who are 'not ready to advance') have fewer and somewhat different contents. For some table 4 and 5 children the 'news' is written lightly in the teacher's hand and traced by the child. At the time of our earliest observations most of the drawers of table 5 children contained no reader since it was too early in the term for most of them to have mastered the 'sight' vocabulary Mrs Martin considers the prerequisite to receiving a copy of the 'normal reader'. At the beginning of the term only a few children at tables 4 and 5 have a 'dictionary' – those whom Mrs Martin judges are able to write all the upper- and lower-case letters. (By mid-term all have 'dictionaries'.) Also, at the start of the term, only table 1 and 2 occupants have a number book – those who, according to Mrs Martin, have developed a concept of numbers, can without difficulty add and subtract using mathematics 'apparatus', and can write all the digits 0–9 on paper.

A day in Mrs Martin's classroom

It is a cold morning in February. The asphalt just outside Mrs Martin's and Mrs Eden's classrooms teems with children, dressed to resist the frosty air. On the perimeter, fifteen women stand dispersed in groups of two or three, some chat, at least half with a hand on a pram or a push chair. Mrs Martin in a dark coat emerges from the wing of the building that houses the library tea room where the teachers gather each morning before dispersing to their classrooms. She crosses in front of the mums, 'good mornings' are exchanged; the tone is pleasant, each woman addressing the others as 'Mrs'. Mrs Martin pauses and speaks to one parent, 'Jason wasn't at all tired yesterday afternoon.' Jason was ill last week and Mrs Martin, as we see on other occasions also, takes it as her responsibility to reassure a concerned parent. Most of the women, Mrs Martin tells us later, are mums of the first termers, and their numbers will shrink as the term progresses and the children become accustomed to daily school attendance.

A few moments after nine o'clock the asphalt is deserted. The children are in their classrooms. As they enter Mrs Martin's room, they hang their coats, mufflers and hats on a set of hooks by the door which, on this cold morning, do not quite accommodate the load. The children disperse. Many go to the new cabinet, slide out a drawer which carries their name and holds their school books and pencils. Some fetch their readers; others one or more of their blue-backed books. A few go directly to one of the shelves and carry to their place at the table or on the rug some of the 'maths apparatus', cards or jigsaw puzzles.

The day is composed of a three-hour morning session that begins at nine o'clock, and an afternoon session that runs from half past one to half past three. These two sessions are quite distinctive, but with considerable variations within each. A distinction is made between morning and afternoon sessions by both teachers and children, but they do not always use the same words to describe the differences. Some children refer to the morning activities as 'work' and the afternoon activities as 'choosing'. The 'timetable' given by each teacher to Mr Nigel labels the morning hours 'individual desk work, reading, arithmetic, etc.', and the afternoon as 'choice activity, reading'. Sometimes teachers and more often children speak of the morning activities as 'work' and the afternoons as 'play'. Mrs Martin herself tells me she does not like to distinguish work and play. This uncertainty over language, as we will argue later, turns out to be of some significance.

In ten minutes, the general shape of life in this classroom from nine to twelve o'clock Monday to Friday may be seen. At any given time, one generally finds a third of the children sitting at the tables, six to eight others sitting or partially prone on one of the rugs, an equal number are in transit – to and from Mrs Martin's desk, fetching or returning materials from the open shelves or their personal drawers. The remainder, fidgeting, shuffling a bit, talking softly, wait their turn curled in a queue around Mrs Martin's desk. She generally deals with a single child at a time, the average encounter taking perhaps 40 to 50 seconds, varying from a nod of approval that takes but a moment to several minutes while she listens to a child read two or three pages from a reader and makes a few notations.

There are scheduled departures from this pattern – on Mondays, as many as fifteen minutes are devoted to a collection of 'dinner' money and book-keeping. 'Prayers' interrupt the morning session for twenty minutes every day, usually at 9.30. From 10.40 to 11.00 is playtime (or recess), followed by milk-drinking time during which teachers have their morning tea. Twenty minutes are taken out on Wednesday and Thursday for 'P.E.' and dance respectively. At 11.45 on Thursday is a fifteen-minute television program on 'phonics'. Except for these periods of time, Mrs Martin sits at her desk or makes unscheduled circuits of the room at regular intervals to observe the children (for a few moments, or as many as five minutes) and emergency forays to deal with an ill or misbehaving child. Occasionally, she will read a story before 'dinner time' if the mood of the class or teacher seems to warrant, or, as was the case one day while we were there, the room was too dark to work because of the

49

rationing of electricity due to a coal miners' strike.

How do the children know what to do during the morning hours? On the top of the cabinets (marked X and Y on the floor plan) are two sets of free-standing rigid cards, each set taped together accordion-fashion, made by Mrs Martin, one for tables 4, 5 and some at 3, and the other for the other table 3 children, and for tables 1 and 2. Each set indicates which tasks the children must complete each morning. The tasks include writing news, doing a jigsaw puzzle, completing maths, money (shopping), clock, and 'writing readiness' cards of various levels of difficulty, browsing a book. Readers will find some additional details of the morning tasks, and the sequence of activities in reading and maths in the notes for this chapter.[5]

From 1.30 to 2.40, during the afternoon session, children generally choose two activities, though the expectation is not explicit. There is always a role-play area; usually this is the Wendy house, but during the time of our extended visit it had become the kitchen of 'Port Hospital'. There is always one table set aside for writing, and the reading shelf provisioned with children's literature (as opposed to 'readers'). There is also one 'art and crafts' table, set up by Mrs Martin, during the lunch hour, every day, sometimes with the aide's help. The activity could be pasting, linoleum block printing, Easter bunny or spring flower making. Brick (block), Lego, plasticine (or 'modeling clay'), and the sand table are almost always available. The latter three are, on occasion, withdrawn 'so they [the children] will not lose interest'.

Between 2.40 and 3.10 is playtime and clean up, and at 3.15, a sit down – always a story; on occasion a brief lecture, a discussion, or a time to show the group a notable achievement by a child – a painting or a craft. Every Thursday Mrs Martin and Mrs Eden read a story in each other's classroom. This practice we are told by both teachers is a way for the reception children to become acquainted with their next teacher. As in the morning, there are scheduled interludes; singing on Tuesday from 1.45 to 2.15, and on some weeks, a television program from 2.22 to 2.33 on Wednesday.

A morning in detail

Every workplace, factory floor and executive office has implicit and explicit routines and norms for entering and leaving, moving to and fro, addressing authorities and underlings, taking breaks from assigned or chosen tasks, giving and receiving evaluation of performance. In order to discover how these routines and norms are patterned, we believe it is necessary to look more closely at the daily flux of life in this classroom; not only at what persons do, but what they say about what they do.

Infant prayers

Mrs Eden's classroom next door. The morning work period is in full swing. Mrs Eden glances at the clock – 9.28 – claps her hands and calls out, 'in a line'. Even before her cue, a two-by-two line had begun to form by the door that leads into Mrs Martin's room. First in line are Julia and Lois, holding hands and swinging their arms with great enthusiasm as they converse. In the other arm Julia cradles a basket. Though I hear no directives, two partly-assembled jigsaw puzzles that lay by my feet a moment ago have disappeared, packed away on the shelf. Mrs Eden walks towards the door. 'I see some bits and bobs in the Wendy house.' Now she stands by the door at the head of the line and observes the scene. She says in a voice just loud enough to be heard by all, 'When it's prayer time, you must stand quietly.' Julia's and Lois's arms come to a virtual standstill. There is a sudden hush, but 'small voice' talking and whispering persist. 'That is *clever*', she says to Maria who has rushed forward to show her completed 'news'. 'I'll have another look after prayers.'

There is little pushing or posturing for positions at the head of the line, only an elbow here and there; the few hostile grimaces dissolve quickly. In the minute since Mrs Eden clapped her hands, the children have put their work materials in their proper places and lined up in pairs. Nearly half hold hands, both boys and girls. All except one couple are of the same sex. (During the work period the sexes looked well integrated.)

Piano music from next door; an unfamiliar melody but a familiar cadence – we recognize kindergarten struttin' music. Julia, on cue from Mrs Martin, opens the door. Mrs Eden takes her place at the center of the semicircle of children who sit on the rug, on chairs, or on the edge of one of the work tables. One or two children cross over to the territory occupied by the other class to find a place near their siblings. There is a bit of shuffling, but surprisingly no lost tempers, as more than fifty children fit themselves on or around the rug and face the piano. Three boys from Mrs Eden's room jockey for position in the back row. The observer, who is the last to enter, notices that two children sit in Mrs Eden's room. One is Samuel from Mrs Martin's class. Unnoticed by the observer he must have wriggled his way through the crowd as Mrs Eden's children were entering. These children, we are informed later, are Jehovah's Witnesses.

51

Mrs Martin stops playing. Mrs Eden's (followed by several children's) eyes turn towards two boys at the back of the assembly. The boys shrink quickly into seats on the edge of the semicircle of children.

'Prayers' or 'assembly' begins. It is a ritual we see repeated with various degrees of secularization in many schools during our six-month stay. 'Whom shall we say a special prayer for today?' Two, three, four hands shoot up before Mrs Martin has completed her question. 'Ooh-ooh', 'yes', 'yes' accompany the more enthusiastic hand-wavers. Two or three cannot resist calling aloud . . . 'Mrs Martin' . . . Mrs Eden puts a finger to her lips. The more boisterous responses diminish. She nods and smiles at a child who has taken a pose of studied silence and whose hand is stretched high overhead. 'A prayer for old people', the child responds. 'Yes', Mrs Eden's eyes acknowledge, 'particularly now during the blackout' . . . 'What way can we help old people?' 'Oooh' 'Oooh' 'Oooh' arms wave. An unrelenting arm-popper is recognized. The first few words are missed. '. . . they have to have candles.' 'She's been a very clever girl today', Mrs Eden says to Mrs Martin. 'Mm, yes'. 'And grown-ups should see that they have candles', another child volunteers. Another adds. 'Old people get confused. If they have candles, they might start a fire.' 'Where did you hear that?' Mrs Eden asks. 'Wireless', is the response. 'Yes', a nod by the teacher. 'They feel colder than we. Yes, it is very sad.' Mrs Martin adds that some may not have help and may be cold. 'It is important that old people have everything ready for the blackout. Remind Mummy to go see older people.'

Six more children make contributions. One tells about an old person who fell downstairs. Another embellishes the tragedy.

Mrs Martin plays a line of music. It is a cue that the discussion is over. Hands are withdrawn. (Every child who vied for attention was recognized to speak at least once.) Mrs Martin repeats the musical phrase on the piano. 'Who knows . . .' The end of the question is drowned in several 'oohs'. A child is recognized and offers the name of the hymn: 'I must try to be loving and kind'. The group sings in unison. The children look attentive – most know the hymn. Several mouth the words, trailing behind the others, only occasionally uttering any intelligible sound. A few, perhaps four or five, do not sing at all. Immediately after, Mrs Martin plays several bars of the introduction to 'Twinkle twinkle little star'. Now all sing with considerable spirit as Mrs Eden leads hand clapping in cadence with the music.

The song ends. A child exits to Mrs Eden's room. In a moment the two Jehovah's Witnesses enter and take a place on the floor. Julia, eyes glistening, now stands in the center. Mrs Eden seats herself on a child's chair and holds Julia by the shoulder giving her an affectionate squeeze. The noise level is higher now, and I miss the words said to the child. Julia points and Lois, smiling, comes forward and both girls stand holding hands.

'Julia is six', Mrs Eden announces. 'One, two, three, four, five, six.' Children clap and chant 'one, two, three . . . six' in unison. 'Jolly good.' Mrs Martin plays 'Happy birthday' as children sing.

'And what do we have here?', Mrs Eden looks at the basket Julia has been holding. The teacher's hand pauses, a finger is poised on the basket. Children crane their necks to see what is about to appear. Mrs Eden, with the master timing of an experienced performer, pulls out and holds an object up for all to see. 'A dot to dot' [book]. 'It's from Althea', Julia informs the group. The teacher reaches into the basket again and pulls out a box of crayons; the ritual continues. No matter how modest the present, there is, before each display, a hush and expectant eyes. 'Doll clothes' are announced and shown to the group. 'And what is this? Goodness knows what . . . a costume. And who made this?' 'Gail did.' 'Oh, what a very clever sister you have.'

The two women banter with each other and the birthday child. Julia reads a birthday rhyme from one of the cards. Mrs Martin to Mrs Eden, 'Are you pleased with Julia?' Mrs Eden responds 'Yes, very pleased. . . . *Carol!*' (A noticeable change in tone.) Mrs Eden shoots a stern glance to her left then smiles and continues, 'Look at this pussy cat.' (Holding up a birthday card.) Children laugh (the picture is a caricature). Mrs Martin, 'Did you write that [the inscription on the card], Christine?' Christine nods. Mrs Eden, 'Oh, Mrs Martin, I thought her mummy had written it.' Mrs Martin gives Julia and Lois each a sweetie. (A week later it is Samuel's birthday. He chooses no partner, smiles but says not a word during the ceremony. He shows no presents or cards and receives a shiny tuppence from the teacher.)

9.43: Children are a bit restless. A chord and the familiar struttin' music. Mrs Eden's class, with little confusion, begin to exit more or less in the inverse order they had arrived. A child in hasty pursuit of another is slowed by Mrs Eden's firm fingers on his shoulder.

The desk

Before the last of Mrs Eden's class is through the door, the queue has begun to appear by Mrs Martin's desk. Mrs Eden, who departed with her class, reappears at the doorway and she and Mrs Martin discuss the problem of heating water for tea before the electricity is turned off (due to the coal strike). The conversation ends in a few moments, but in this time the queue has swelled to no less than fifteen children who wait on both sides of her desk. Mrs Martin walks the few steps from the doorway to her desk. By the time she has settled in her chair, the number of children who wait is reduced to seven. She accomplishes this feat while in transit. Making eye-to-eye contact, she nods at three children who have completed jigsaws and sends them on their way. 'Have you finished your writing?', she asks one – 'Yes, 'm' is the reply. 'Get your reader then' . . . 'Good Maris', she touches the child's hair. A touch on the shoulder and a nod for Jeanne, a smile and a tap for Peter, both of whom hold rigid cards on which they have correctly matched a number symbol to an array of plastic objects. 'Do one more', she says to Jeanne. All this takes less than thirty seconds. She has dealt with the children in order of complexity of problem, violating her convention of dealing with them in the order in which they arrive at the desk.

Within the next few minutes, Mrs Martin has seen all who had been waiting but others, or the same children, reappear to take their place. The children from tables 4 and 5 return most frequently. Mrs Martin explains, 'the young ones need my constant attention in the beginning of the term'.

Elaine from 'top table' is next. (Over the next twenty-five minutes, she returns three times.) Mrs Martin regularly takes her eyes from her work at the desk and looks over the classroom. Her eyes stop frequently in the vicinity of table 4, on the opposite side of the room, but in her direct line of sight. She watches Samuel and Steven both playing with toy motor cars. She pauses a moment. 'Samuel and Steven are wasting time.'

The scene at Mrs Martin's desk continues; three, four, five, six children are always waiting. As she deals with a child, the others generally attend to what she says and does, thus the desk encounters are not completely individual. Occasionally she will enlist the aid of another child standing nearby whom she thinks may be able to help. (At Mrs Martin's request, Janet spells 'penny' for Matthew and he writes it in his 'dictionary'.) Periodically she looks up: 'Samuel, get on with it.'

Elaine is back and her picture is approved. She announced she will be writing a long story today and will be using the two remaining pages in her 'news'. Mrs Martin tells her that this afternoon she will receive another 'news'. Elaine is pleased. The receipt of a new book is for her a special occasion.

Angela, who was sitting at table 4, marches towards the desk and, without waiting her turn and in a controlled but annoyed tone, announces that 'Steven is under the table'. By the time Mrs Martin lifts her eyes, Steven, aware that a report was imminent, is now matching cards with color names to circles of color.

Jeanette, from table 2, is next. Her dictionary is open at 'P'. 'Please Mrs Martin, pinched.' At this same time Robert is reading haltingly, 'Janet and John went . . .' After Robert completes the page, Mrs Martin writes the page number on the white bookmark, makes a tick and writes a sentence in a book which serves as part of the record-keeping system for her reading 'scheme'.

David places his 'news' before Mrs Martin. It is a jumble of lines of pencil and black crayon, nothing distinguishable. David watches Mrs Martin's eyes. She makes a small tick on the page, and in a gentle voice says, 'David, you can do better.' David purses his lips. She draws a line at the bottom of the page. 'A bee stung a boy', he says, which Mrs Martin writes lightly with a pencil in well-formed, teacher script. David returns to the chair he was occupying and begins to trace over the letters of the sentence – but backwards, beginning at the end of the sentence. Elaine is wandering, offering tutelage to any taker.

Mrs Martin rises from her desk and completes a wide circuit through the room. She nods approvingly at Andrew at table 1 who looks up and smiles as she passes. She pauses for a moment near the center of the room; 'Duncan'. She stoops down; he is on the rug, a scatter of conkers, but no other work. 'Have you done your "news" or jigsaw?' 'Yes, Mrs Martin.' 'Do a number card then.' He goes off. I, in response to Mrs Martin's request, sit on a child's chair near table 1 listening to children from the 'top' tables read. I follow as closely as I can the procedure I have seen Mrs Martin use. I listen to several children read, recording the pages on their white bookmarks as they finish. For a child who repeatedly mispronounces 'oo', I write on the reverse side of the bookmark 'oo' and underneath 'look, book, took'. Simultaneously as I listen to children read, I write words in 'dictionaries' as they are requested by the children from their 'news'. Elaine holds her 'dictionary' open at 'P'; 'plimsolls'. She tells me, 'I have a new book. I've done my clocks and when I come back [from playtime] I will do my "shopping".'

Mrs Martin, on her most recent walkabout, has picked two boxes of cards from a shelf and put them on table 2. She explains later that 'lotto' – which she makes available only to the top groups – will 'turn them off so I can give the new ones the attention they require . . . particularly early in the term'.

Mrs Martin is again stationed at her desk. She has invited Samuel, who stands by her, and Steven, who waits behind, to the desk.

Samuel: 'I can't do it.' (News picture.)
Mrs M: 'Sure you can. Do you have a pencil?'
Samuel: (Nods no.)

Simultaneously she approves with a nod Susan's picture and offers her a tissue for her runny nose. She then writes 'Samuel' in his copy book in pencil and he retreats to his table.

Mrs Martin is standing. 'If you've finished, you may choose.' (It is a comment she repeats several times, more frequently during the last hour of the morning.) At the desk, Cheryl reads her 'news' to Mrs Martin. Mrs Martin then holds up about a dozen cards, one at a time, one word on each, 'house', 'this', 'there', 'dog'. 'Good Cheryl, I think you are ready for your *Janet and John* [her first 'normal reader'].' After tea time I wander in Cheryl's direction. She proudly announces she knows her words and now she can read on her own. She offers me the cards so she can demonstrate her newly acquired proficiency.

Elaine is at the desk asking for 'jealous'. Brian, who was having trouble copying a line of '8s' earlier and received a few moments of instruction, has also returned. (Earlier Mrs Martin held his hand lightly, guiding him through two '8s'.) He has made several fine '8s'. 'Good, Brian.' Without saying a word further, in black felt-tip pen she completes the loops on two that look more like wiggly '0s' than '8s'. 'A few more', she adds, touching the top of his shoulder. Off he goes.

'Have you finished Linsley – because you are doing plenty of talking?' 'Good Andrea.' She has completed a card with 6 multiplication problems (the lower numbers in the $2\times$ and $3\times$ multiplication tables). A tick is placed in the corner of her maths book. She asks her to 'work out' a problem by pointing to '$3 \times 3 = $' on the card. The child, using a can of conkers that Mrs Martin retrieves from a drawer in the desk, ponders a moment. Mrs Martin is silent. Andrea makes three groups of three. Mrs Martin offers and she happily accepts a sweetie.

Tracy, our self-selected informant from table 3, is next in line. She holds a card on which she has finished matching spools to circles on the card. Mrs Martin points to the first set on the card as the child touches each spool and counts aloud. 'One, two, three . . . eight.' The child writes the numeral '8' in her maths book, 'one . . . two'. Mrs Martin points to the place and the child begins to write a 2, not quite underneath the 8. The teacher nudges her hand just slightly and the child forms a 2 so that it is precisely under the 8. Mrs Martin: . . . 'together eight plus two?' She writes plus sign in a black felt-tip pen and draws a line under the 2. Tracy counts, subaudibly to ten. 'Ten', she says and writes. A smile and the child leaves. Without being told she goes to the shelf and takes a second card of the same type. (The observer sees no indication made to Tracy that she is to do another card, the cue, we infer from subsequent observation, is Mrs Martin's failure to put a tick at the corner of the page.)

'Samuel.' He comes forward with his 'news', pencil in hand. (I look below me on the floor and see that the boy sitting next to Brian has made four quite passable '8s' in Brian's book thus completing his assignment for him.) To Samuel at the desk: 'You said you couldn't do it . . . that's *fine*, Samuel.' She finds him an empty page in his 'news' book. It is a few minutes to playtime and tea. Some children have begun picking up the materials. 'Samuel why don't you do a picture of your daddy coming for you?'

It is 10.40. 'You may leave your work on the floor, but tidy up a bit.' She asks a child to pick up a set of cards that have been left scattered on the floor, making no effort to find the culprit. A child picks up stray 'unit cubes'. There is a light drizzle outside. Most children are in wraps waiting to go out. Mrs Martin untwists sleeves in a child's cardigan. 'Thank you', he says. 'Don't run', she admonishes one of the newer ones, a straggler, who has been so engrossed in her work that she has missed the cues for playtime. Mrs Martin pauses to comfort a child who has lost 2p for 'lunch' (snack). She says, 'It will be found.' We go to morning tea.

Dinner at Port

At twelve o'clock approximately two-fifths of the children who attend Port walk home for their midday meal. The remaining eat school 'dinners'; the juniors in a nearby secondary school, the infants in Mrs Eden's room — the food having been brought in insulated containers. There are two sets of impressions that stand out in our notes and our memories of dinner at Port: how the food is served and the role the adults take in the process. The juniors sit at tables with an adult, a teacher or a school visitor, sitting at the head. (Where there are not enough adults to go around a 'top' junior presides.) The 'dinner ladies' bring the food and the person at the head serves or oversees serving. Before eating, all participants ceremoniously mumble a prayer.

In Mrs Eden's room the 'dinner ladies' serve each infant and teacher personally. Before a child is excused to go outside, he or she holds up a hand, a teacher inspects the plate from a distance, and nods or indicates with a movement of her hand that a few more carrots must be eaten. The dining ritual, for both infants and juniors orderly and relaxed, bears a closer resemblance to an extended family Sunday dinner scene than to the scene in an American elementary-school cafeteria. The midday break lasted one and a half hours, a pleasant change from the 20 – 25 minute hurried lunch-time we had become accustomed to in American schools.

An afternoon

The afternoon begins as does the morning; the children play outside, but fewer mums wait nearby. One of the dinner ladies supervises the children as the teachers finish a cup of tea. At half past one, the outside is again deserted. Childhood shrieks of joy and agony come to an abrupt end. School begins again.

Mrs Martin's classroom at 1.30. The classroom seems different. The actual changes are minimal, the child-high partition that served as the Wendy house (now the hospital–kitchen) has been moved to center floor as have the ambulance and two cots. Two silver-painted corrugated boxes with 'X-ray' written in black have appeared. Table number 4 has been moved and converted to an arts and crafts table on which has been set carefully three stacks of square paper – white, black and gray; six pairs of scissors; several rulers; a box of small geometric figures – diamonds and triangles cut from stiff cardboard; five cups of white school paste; several sharpened pencils. Table number 5 is rimmed with several rectangles of brown fiberboard, in the center several cans filled with colored plasticine. Fresh white paper has been tacked to the easels; yellow, orange and red tempera paints have been placed in the trays beneath. The maroon cloth has been withdrawn from the sand table.

The room invites children's attention. They enter with great energy, taking seats in chairs, on tables or on the rug. Mrs Martin stands near the center of the rug by the hospital.

'How many do we have today for the hospital?' she asks. The children appear to talk freely but she does not need to strain to be heard.

From nine or ten children waving hands eagerly, some accompanied with 'oohs', and 'Mrs Martin, please', she chooses six. Mary, who has been sitting immobile and silent, lower lip curled, is approached by Mrs Martin. A few words too low for me to overhear and Mary, her face cheered, joins the others in the hospital. Within a few minutes, the children are dispersed throughout the room.

Mrs Martin steps 'into' the hospital and helps several of the children into nurse and doctor uniforms that hang on a hook. The hospital, complete with kitchen, cots, an ambulance, X-ray, stethoscopes, salves, bandages and a nursery for the newborn, grew out of Mrs Martin's response to a child's interest. It continued to be elaborated throughout our stay. (When we returned at the end of the next term the hospital space had yielded to a Viking ship.) Mrs Martin's version of the hospital's origin:

Mrs M: Well, it . . . started because one of the children had a nurse's outfit and she came in it and the next day someone else brought hers and they said we'll play at hospital. I said you can use Father Christmas' cave as a hospital if you like. Well it was Father Christmas' cave, so I ripped everything off and just put white paper and big crosses. It is marvelous, you see . . . it gained momentum and more and more and more wanted to join in. I thought it's time to develop. I ripped all that down and made it more permanent – and then we added a piece on and they're still fascinated by it.

Ann: They are!

Mrs M: Well, I made dressings you see and then the X-ray and the maternity. They're making the ambulance now.

Ann: So, it came out of the children's interests?

Mrs M: Entirely the children's interests, entirely.

Ann: And you just brought it along. But you added the X-ray machine and things like that – you made their play easier.

Mrs M: The reason I wanted to do it was the fact that a lot of the children are frightened so much of doctors and nurses and they sort of dissolve into tears as soon as they see white coats you see and I thought, well some of them will probably have to go into hospitals to see the doctor, you know. Most of them have, at some stage, so here's another good reason for having the hospital to get rid of this fear, you see, so it becomes a familiar thing.

Time: 1.37. Mrs Martin stands by the easels. Five children wish to paint, there are places for four. She leads Robert to a shelf where he picks up a number game. There is no protest. She asides, 'I like number games, they have to count and ask a friend to play.'

The observer looks about the room to locate children who are not gainfully employed. There are two, one of the 'top' girls and Jeremy. When I glance around a moment later I see that Robert has found Jeremy and they have settled on the rug with a maths game that requires throwing dice and doing addition and subtraction.

1.38. Mrs Martin, 'Don't stand on the bed'; her voice is raised but pleasant. She is now seated in a child's chair at the arts and crafts table with five children who have distributed scissors among themselves and are waiting. Mrs Martin is demonstrating. She pastes cut-out pieces of white on black backgrounds creating snowflakes. 'Everyone can be different', encouraging children not to duplicate the ones she has begun. The children begin working busily. She watches for a moment, then moves her chair next to Brian (the boy who had his troubles with lines of '8s' and enlisted his friend's aid). He is struggling with the scissors and she guides his hand as he completes cutting a rounded and jagged triangle. She helps him hold the triangle template as he traces in pencil. When the template is removed he looks at his triangle and is pleased at the vast improvement over his first effort. 'Nice', Mrs Martin remarks. She looks across the table. 'I like that', she says to Samuel who has cut several free-hand triangles from the white paper and has pasted them in a line like a row of trees. No snowflakes for Samuel.

1.59. Four children at the 'snowflake' table. One child is yielding his place to another. There are four at the easel, all new faces. The children work quickly, painting over undesired results without hindrance. Mrs Martin holds an arrangement of cut, joined and painted cereal boxes so that one of the 'top' boys can take a measurement. With Mrs Martin overseeing his use of a sharp knife, he slices a cardboard coil to make a wheel. Mrs Martin is now standing by the easels; 'Um', nods her head indicating approval. To another child who has painted her paper completely dirt brown, 'You might want to use another color.'

2.05. Robert and Jeremy are packing up their maths game. Three children are completing an elaborate design with 'pattern blocks'.[6] Two boys have collaborated and produced a fantastic rococo ship of large and small Lego. Remarkably it holds together as they push it through the classroom drawing high approval from onlookers as they pass. A girl who sits just below me is fascinated, as am I, with a pair of scissors another has made from small Lego. She patiently attempts to copy it and I also try but with little success. Two boys cut photographs of mountains from magazines and mount them on construction paper. Two children at the sand table demolish sand cylinders they made with a plastic cup. I see three children sitting at table 1, the writing table, putting their names on new 'news' books and/or making themselves new 'dictionaries'.

Mrs Martin continues her circuits of the room, helping, guiding and making suggestions. 'Have a go at this'. She watches and listens from one location, then another, picks up a child who wanders and leads him to another activity. The observer follows her lead. Occasionally when our paths cross, we have a word. She tells me she keeps track of the Lego and the bricks and puts them away on occasion ('they can exhaust their value'). I see very little evidence of this yet. She reminds two children who earlier wanted a space in the hospital that there is a place now. They go eagerly. On occasion she will sit at her desk for a few minutes, examine the record books and make notations.

On this particular day Mrs Martin and I hang several recently completed paintings on the wall. We both admire them, agreeing that we would not mind having one or two of them in our front room. (Their quality to the observer's eyes contrast sharply with those in Mrs Eden's room.)

Mrs M: In the afternoons they choose themselves. They use their imaginations. Then if they want to make something specifically – well I help them. They do a lot of models and pictures, pasting and painting. Their paintings are really quite good and I'm not sure why.

Ann: I was wondering the same thing myself.

Mrs M: I don't know why – they've always been good.

Ann: In this particular year?

Mrs M: No, no they are always good. [pondering] I mix lots of colors. I make it nice and thick.

Ann: I think that's very important. The materials that they have – I was thinking that . . . . But there's also something else that's going on that gets their art going.

Mrs M: Well, of course. If you get one that's good and it's at the end of the lesson. You hold them all up and you say, 'What is it', you know, 'that's nice . . . I like that sort of busyness' or 'Isn't that nice' and they can see for themselves. Oh, and I tell them, I've told them always, when they first come they do a little type of squiggling. They make it in the bottom left-hand corners and I say, 'What about all this white, what is happening all around there', and they fill it all in with colors and they see for themselves how much nicer it looks.

2.25. Mrs Martin enters the hospital (this is at least her third visit). She notes the names of the 'patients' posted on the partition wall. Two children are busy with pots and pans preparing a 'good dinner' in the hospital kitchen. Two children are on beds. One is being admitted to maternity, a third being treated with salves by a 'doctor'. A few moments later one of the children is taken to 'X-ray'. She stands behind one of the silver corrugated boxes; the attendant works the two painted-black switches. A patient is helped to bed by one of the nurses. The doctors and nurses huddle conferring in hushed voices. Mrs Martin asks, 'And what's wrong with John today?' Her tone is appropriately somber. 'Indeed! A burn! And how did you burn yourself? . . . Well, John, what will you do with matches next time?' . . . 'Mary, are you going to have a baby girl?' A nurse intercedes, 'Mrs Martin, we don't know that yet. The baby's not been born.' Mrs Martin observes the X-ray scene. 'And why did you take your patient to X-ray?' 'To make him better.' Mrs Martin's inquisitive demeanor dissolves into a slight smile.

A few moments later I follow her into the hospital and engage another one of the children in a conversation. 'And what does this do?', I ask, pointing at the X-ray equipment. 'Helps see what's wrong.' 'How?' 'I forget . . .' (A few days earlier Mrs Martin had asked about X-rays and there had been silence. Two days ago she had held a discussion about X-rays during prayers with the help of two children who had suffered broken limbs. After the discussion the X-ray machine had drawn greater attention.)

2.35. 'Children, time to tidy up.' The painters finish up while others return materials to their places. The teacher pushes the hospital back a few feet and hangs up the nurses' and doctors' outfits.

3.05. The children refreshed by playtime and the teachers by afternoon tea are gathered for the final ritual. The children sit on the rug or in chairs and face Mrs Martin who sits on a child-sized chair near the piano. Tranquillity prevails. Mrs Martin comments, 'You did some nice work this afternoon. Steven and Jeremy made a lovely ship. Did any of you see the ship? [Oohs and ahhhs] Have a look at Joanne's painting. She covered the paper. And such clever shapes and nice colors. Lovely, Joanne.' Laying the painting aside, the teacher opens My Naughty Little Sister and begins to read to an eager audience . . . 3.25. The school day ends.

MR EDGAR: SECOND-YEAR JUNIORS

If one were to cast for a film the American stereotype of the English schoolmaster, Mr Edgar would be a candidate for the role. He is long, with a ruddy complexion, wears a starched white collar, tie, always a dark suit, slightly crumpled. His room could serve as the set for Tom Brown's School Days: thirty-eight wooden desks in rows virtually fill the entire floor space, facing Mr Edgar's desk which is at center front. There is barely room enough for an adult to walk the aisles. Windows along one side of the room, fixed blackboard running the length of the front and partly along the other side wall. There are some reminders of the twentieth century – the desks have formica tops, are not affixed to the floor, children's clothes show the benefits of mass production. A dozen excellent paintings are mounted on the wall and a large spirited mural, obviously a group effort, is mounted on one of the blackboards. Although this is not the only junior classroom at Port that looks relatively bare, where desks are in rows (in sharp contrast to the infant classrooms), Mr Edgar is the only one who engages almost entirely in what Mr Nigel calls 'class teaching' or 'chalk and talk' in all basic subjects. Nor is his the only junior classroom at Port where children follow a more or less strictly 'time-tabled' day. (Spelling sentences at 9.00; prayers at 9.30; maths at 10.00; English at 11.00.) Although the walls in Mrs Hendrik's fourth-year junior room next door are more barren, the children's desks are in banks of six or eight with children facing one another. Mrs Hendrik fits Mr Nigel's description of a 'group teacher', but she also engages in a fair amount of 'chalk and talk'.

Mr Edgar's is the only class where there are sufficiently long periods of whole class teaching that we are able to sit in one place and take transcripts of the one official, that is, teacher-led learning activity. (There are continuous unofficial transactions of course.) I sit in the middle row rear today. The children are keenly aware of my presence. I engage in conversation with them during off-times (between activities, while papers are passed or while children do their 'desk work'). I know from previous observation that I sit among the least enthusiastic participants in Mr Edgar's style of 'class teaching'. In general, his pattern is to ask a question, to which he has a more or less specific answer in mind, give a brief lecture, end with a question, followed by a series of five or six more questions. He has excellent command of the technique and excellent timing. (We see him another time in charge of junior prayers. Compared to Mr Nigel, who gets an indifferent response to his questions during prayers, Mr Edgar can have large numbers of children clamoring for the opportunity to make one-word contributions to his lectures.)

The class is virtually never completely silent. Although there is a level of continuous activity more easily observable from the rear, passing of notes, communal sharing of answers, there is no direct defiance of the teacher's requests and there are only rarely angry words. His tone is almost always kindly and a generally friendly air prevails that is not revealed by our transcripts. Tickles, pokes, verbal and written exchanges are continuous but the level of 'noise' permitted is within a range that the observers, after a few hours, can easily predict but cannot easily describe. Decibels and the differing qualities of noise set the limits, though there are always individuals who stumble or wander over the line — they are generally patiently reminded. He never shouts in our presence but we do hear several outbursts over the weeks of our stay through his closed door. There are occasional stern glances or a few curt words.

Sicily

I have come to watch a lesson using the school radio. The program, 'People from many lands', begins at 2.00. I arrive early. A child has completed reading to the class a story she has apparently written recently. It is based on a TV program on France they had seen the previous day.

Mr E: On the television . . . there were geese. What was it they were bred for? [no response] . . . They are bred for their liver.

C: A delicate food? . . .

Mr E: Can anyone tell me the name . . . [no response] . . . pâté . . . it is minced liver. [a few 'ughs']

C: I have a doll . . . from France [She holds up a doll in a national costume]

Mr E: Isn't that lovely! Where did you get her!

C: In France.

Mr. E: [Expressively as though it matters to him a great deal.] In France! . . . so geese are bred for their liver. Liver.

C: I don't like that at all. [widespread mutters, moral indignation over the injustice of it]

Mr E: Sh . . . Sh . . . Sh . . . Sh . . . [He nods knowingly; he anticipated the reaction and is tolerant of the sudden rush of conversation.] Sh . . . And what else would you get there? . . . [pause] . . . What is made there? [no response] . . . What kind of work were they . . . [several enthusiastic hands]

C: Farmers . . .

After several tries 'dairy products' is elicited. There follows a forty-five second lecture, 'French cream is not as famous as cream from Devon and Cornwall, . . . There are so many cheeses from France — more than from any other country. . . . Rene is from Cornwall, that's why she's such a big girl, eat's lots of cream.' He looks at Rene with a smile. She is delighted. Her eyes and face brighten. Mr Edgar smiles an acknowledgement.

At 1.50:

Mr E: 'People from many lands' is about the New World today. What's new in the New World?

C:	Mexico.
Mr E:	Yes. [childrens' arms are cradled in readiness]
C:	Canada.
Mr E:	Nods.
C:	[seated in front row peering at map] New York . . .
Mr E:	Nods.
C:	Australia.
Mr E:	Australia is new but it is not . . . [miss a few words] . . . The program is about Haiti.

He goes to the office and turns on the radio. Another program is finishing. He returns. 'Fetch your paper to write something down.' He passes out paper by placing it on front rows. Children pass the paper and the excess is returned to the front. He goes to the office and returns a few moments later with a coiled map.

Time: 1.58. He fits the map of the Caribbean on brackets on the front board. 2.00: 'This is Radio 4 for schools . . . today we will visit Sicily.' Mr Edgar looks at me (annoyed and resigned). 'The program guide said Haiti', he asides. The children listen. On the sheet of unlined paper I see many writing single words in columns as the program proceeds. The narrator raises moral and political issues about the future of Sicily. 'There is extreme poverty.' 'There are those who want change, but those who resist . . .' As the program continues I look around the class: one boy doodling on his paper, another bounces a rubber pencil, another boy without paper looks into space. Two boys who had been helping one another on their maths are carrying on a quiet conversation.

'The land is barren. It is difficult to scrape a living . . .' (The program continues.)

Mr E: 'ARE YOU LISTENING?' His voice is grave and loud. The boys who sit next to me terminate their conversation abruptly but only until it is clear to them that the admonishment, in the form of a query, was not directed at them. 2.15. The program ends. Mr Edgar goes to the office, turns off the radio and returns.

Mr E:	What's the name of the island?
C:	Sicily.
Mr E:	At the bottom of which sea?
C:	[Spoken as a child's rhyme.]
	Long leg'd Italy kicked Sicily
	Right to the middle
	of the Mediterranean Sea
	'long came France . . .
	[I miss the rest.]

Mr E: Was it easy to get a living?
In unison: No-o! [Hands are now being waved furiously.]

The familiar pattern is established. Some children never fully put
their arms down between questions. I see three or four who have
well-developed techniques for the reduction of arm fatigue – no
doubt a major problem of the heavy participant. Some alternate
arms used for hand-raising; some use their other hand to cradle their
arm to keep it in constant readiness. He continues:

Mr. E: Why?
C: Because they've not much money.
C: The woods were taken away.
C: They've no trees.
C: Moisture taken away from the land.
Mr E: [Provides a minute-long lecture on how trees help keep land from
        losing the moisture.] . . . What happened to the trees?
C: The people sold them.
Mr E: There it rains in what part of the year?
C: In the winter?
Mr E: So heavy rains come and wash the soil away. There were no trees to
        hold it in position . . . [continues for 35 seconds] the sun comes out,
        dries the soil and turns the soil into what?
C: Dust
Mr E: Along came the wind and . . .
C: Blew it away.
Mr E: The soil eroded. [Spells it out, e-r-o-d-e-d.] That's why in parts of
        the world there are deserts. . . . If you take it out what must you put
        in it?
C: Goodness.
Mr E: [Ignores the response] What you must do . . . [waits] what you
        must add is . . . [waits] fertilizer . . . manure. [Snickers from chil-
        dren. Mr Edgar pauses, looks stern just for a moment so as to put
        an end to excess joking. Gives a short explanation on how plants
        use up nitrogen.] What animal was mentioned at the beginning of
        the program?
C: Donkey
Mr E: What do they use for milk? [Now the non-official transactions are
        quite audible. About five or six girls and two or three boys attend
        the teacher consistently. Among them are several who scan their
        'notes' and sit with arms cocked to answer any question.] What can
        you make from goat's milk . . . ?
C: Cheese.
Mr E: [The questions continue.] . . . What was the name of the priest who
        tried to help? . . . What was the name of the English student?
C: [Gail who sits nearby to my great surprise recalls] 'Mr Jackson and

Brian.' [I peer over her shoulder and see a long list of words with Mr Jackson and Brian as entries. Gail is master of the art of successful pupiling in Mr Edgar's class.]

Mr E: [Continues explaining rotation of crops as he draws this diagram on the board]:

corn	grass
roots	X

Mr E: What do we call? . . . [points to 'X' box] . . . [no response] . . . We say it lies fallow. [The group of children near me and in the far left corner have been virtual non-participants for the last ten minutes. It is 2.30.] . . . 'Put your books away.'

JUNIORS: THE TEAM ROOM AT PORT

Three mornings a week at 9.00 a.m. all of the 'juniors' gather in what we will call the 'team' room, two fairly generous-sized classrooms that abut one another forming a 'T'. At the neck of the 'T' are wooden doors hinged as an accordion, probably the same age as the building. These may be used to divide the 'T' into two rooms. Previous to Mr Nigel's coming the doors were opened only for special occasions. Now Mrs Newhouse, Mrs Knowlton and Mr Vance together share responsibility for the seventy-eight third- and fourth-year juniors in the school. The doors are virtually never fully closed. Though intended as two rooms, the space has been divided into three distinguishable classrooms and a joint art area.

The three teachers in charge are the 'team' Mr Nigel created with the strong support and enthusiastic participation of Mrs Newhouse, and, as best we can tell, with the tolerance or forebearance of Mr Vance and Mrs Knowlton. Each teacher functions as leader for his/her group. Although we observed no evidence of cooperative planning (the three were always congenial with one another), all set out work requirements for the children in roughly similar ways – by the week. Also their timetables are so arranged that a portion of each afternoon is used jointly for activities. The children choose a craft (sewing, weaving, model-building), music, and 'library'. During this afternoon period identity by classroom disappears. The arrangement of time is coming closer to resembling Heathbrook's 'commitment', which is Mr Nigel's self-conscious model.

Junior prayers

The format (though not the style) for 'Prayers' at Port also bears some resemblance to 'Assembly' at Heathbrook. It is held in the 'team' room and two more classes, Mr Edgar's and Mrs Hendrik's, must be accommodated. The children from the first- and second-year juniors arrive in a more or less orderly line, find places on edges of tables and desks and sit facing in virtually all directions. Mr Nigel stands at a spot by the accordion doors that affords him the best possible view of the more than 150 children. At least a third cannot see him. The cramped look and feel of the room brings to mind the virtues of buildings that are suited to their use, and how the shape and arrangement of space in a building may make isolation more or less likely. It takes a person like Mr Nigel, intent upon change, to overcome the limitations of this architecture.

The proceedings begin with a psalm and a prayer, followed by a hymn from the *Church of England Hymnal*. Mr Nigel's tone is paternal, confident of the necessity for and his right to authority. Yet there is a quality of gentleness and respect for children.

In the midst of the hymn I hear Mrs Newhouse, say 'The museum man is here.' Mr Nigel leaves the assembly and is gone for almost fifteen minutes. Teachers and children sit, wait and chat. As far as we can tell no one seems to mind. The level of noise is high but its source is the density of people per square foot rather than any general unruliness. At 9.28 Mr Nigel returns and takes up the same position. Cheerfully, 'Let's see if the recorder people are ready.'

Three girls play the recorder. Mr Vance (who is also the school's music man) is seated unobtrusively nearby. The players' eyes occasionally fix in his direction. He nods and smiles at them giving both downbeat cues, and generous approval of their playing. The music sounds surprisingly competent to an ear reasonably familiar with the sounds of school orchestras.

The notes record 'attention like that in a church – not absolute but adequate'. Side whispering and comments are continuous and apparently accepted as within bounds.

At 9.31:

Mr N: I have a few things to say [voice is now more conversational as one

might talk to a peer]. Children's book orders must be returned
early next week. Because of the half-term break remember to bring
the right money for dinners – 48 pence – YOU! I'M SPEAKING TO
YOU MAN [to a child]. I'll have you out FAST. I'm talking . . . listen
to me.

He does not shout but the contrast with his previous tone startles.
My notes record, 'The effect is immediate, but I still hear whispering'. In a few moments the previous level of communication among
those present is restored. Mr Nigel turns to talking about the 'record
books' which is also a routine modeled on Heathbrook's. On each
Friday the children take twenty minutes to a half-hour to write down
their completed work in a record book. The children know that Mr
Nigel inspects them on a regular basis but there is not the same
intensity of concern that we were to find at Heathbrook.

Mr N: Record books are getting better. I am pleased at all the effort in
        mathematics . . . . It pleases me to see how well you are getting on.
        Some of you are covering 10 pages.
            How many of you enjoyed the Gilbert and Sullivan? [played at
        the previous Prayers; about a quarter of the group put up their
        hands.]

At 9.47 he plays 'Lord High Executioner'. A somewhat higher
level of whispering. I sit in a part of the room where children cannot
be seen by any of the teachers or the head. I see two girls having a
whisper and a laugh. They peer at me from the sides of their eyes to
gauge whether I will set any limits. I make a studied effort to appear
oblivious to their talking – it continues – the music ends.

Mr N: I think I enjoy that song best of all. [Talks about how we all have
        habits that irritate others.] Who knows some irritating habits?

The children respond half-heartedly. This has been an extraordinarily long 'Prayers'. Hands go up in the vicinity of where the Head
stands. The children appear to search for the correct response – or
correct type of response. I suspect Mr Nigel had something more
lighthearted in mind than the ensuing short list of what likely irri-
tates teachers of young children the world over. 'Fidgeting; breaking
windows; people who do not get on with their work; people who
steal; people who lie; people who suck their thumbs.' I miss the cue
to end. I hear Mr Edgar's voice, 'My class, lead on'.

As the children file out, Mrs Newhouse says to Mr Nigel, loudly
enough for the child to overhear, 'John has been here since January 4
and he is on page seventy-six' [in his maths book]. Mr Nigel is

earnestly pleased. He asks another child, 'Where are you? . . . Not too good'. To the whole group, 'How many of you are going to join the 50's club?' Four hands shoot up . . . then five . . . six . . . seven . . . (half up) . . . eight . . . nine . . . 'Splendid.' To a child, 'Page forty? . . . You can get to fifty by mid-term.' The children at a cue from Mrs Newhouse line up, then cross the hall to the library (and sometimes teacher tea room).

Mrs Newhouse's classroom

Her classroom is one leg of the 'T' of the team room she shares with Mr Vance and Mrs Knowlton. The following was taken from the chalk board one Monday morning.

5 pages maths
Own story (the cave)
5 sentences punctuated with speech marks
Nature observation
2 'Ladybird cards'
Topic; coffee

The expectation was that the children will complete this work by Friday, working mornings and that portion of their afternoons not given to 'choice' activities.

During these work periods children freely consult with one another leaving the teacher free to work with individuals or groups of individuals who wish and/or in her view require assistance.

This system, however, presents Mrs Newhouse with several problems. Though she is an experienced and skillful 'class' teacher, she is aware that she has not mastered the difficult art of keeping track of each child's work, particularly in mathematics. She finds herself clarifying the same mathematics concept (for example, prime number) several times as one child after another comes upon it in the mathematics book. Since she has twenty-seven children dispersed in three mathematics texts she says, 'I find myself spending all my time checking maths . . . with never enough time to teach any concept properly' or . . . 'to stimulate and encourage those who are sailing through their maths book . . . or are . . . falling far behind.' She has 'manipulatives' available but she cannot integrate them since she feels so pressed for time. An 'individual' teacher only since September, 'This way of teaching', she tells us, 'is harder'. But she is committed to a change, convinced, as she is, that the 'new way' develops children's capacities and keeps them more involved. 'I've

70

always wanted to teach informally and never did. I was interested in a post at this school because I found Mr Nigel's ideas close to mine. He encouraged and helped me.'

She is aware that she has traded off some techniques she values that she has refined over fifteen years, for example, 'talking as a class' – by which she means 'throwing an opinion to the class and say(ing). "Well Jane said that, what do you think about that?" ' We have an image of how she likely performed as a 'class' teacher by watching her as she gathers the children around her in a tight circle once or twice daily, usually for four or five minutes, or from the group lessons she teaches in the library. Though she, like Mr Edgar, poses questions and offers brief explanations, what she asks of the children differs. She stimulates their imaginations, presses them to think and encourages them to listen and respond to one another. 'What comes to mind with the word cave?' 'How would we find out why tea is so widely drunk in England?' 'Why is it, do you think, the train doesn't run to –?' Substance is more important than form. 'In doing your story . . . I expect proper capitalization and speech marks, but, above all, make your story interesting.' The agenda of these sessions varies but there is always a similar quality – a sense of intimacy. Though on occasion they may last twenty or thirty minutes it is rare for the children's attention to wander as is common in Mr Edgar's room. She rarely diverts in order to deal with side conversations that have got out of hand. The pattern of participation in these sessions, however, resembles Mr Edgar's in that those who are 'cleverest' by her standards are generally the biggest talkers; the 'bottom' rarely contributes. Mrs Newhouse does make an effort to draw them in and they almost always appear to be attentive. She, as does Mr Edgar, gives the one or two who are 'completely out of it' some private attention.

She attributes her easy transition to the 'new way' to the children, 'It is a village school'. She emphasizes in the recorded interview, 'The children have *manners*', which to her are essential for the new system to work. In her view, 'I didn't expect it but it was there. I don't know why.'

A session in the library

Once a day Mrs Newhouse takes her class across the way to the tiny library. There is a closeness, not easy to describe. Children sit wherever they can, Mrs Newhouse at the center. On this Friday it is 'record book' time; children spend twenty minutes recording their

71

accomplishments for the week. The book is collected by the teacher and regularly looked at by her and often by Mr Nigel. A page from a child's record book is reproduced below.

Record book
Mathematics
    Book 3, pp. 42, 43, 44, 45, 46, 47, 48, 49, 50, 51
Nature observation
    observation of mice
    observation of new dog
Activities
    TV – measuring
    orchestra
    recorder practice
    dancing
    P.E.
    slides of African animals
English
    'Ladybird card' No. 3
    Reading *Bambi* by Felix Salton
    Listened to 'Hunt Royal' by David Scott Daniel
Handwriting
    wrote poem called 'Cat'

(Note: Record of 'normal' reading progress is kept separately)

Mrs Newhouse sits on a chair. Though it is very difficult to move about, she does manage to circulate and look at virtually all record books as the children write. The children help one another recall the activities. She asks each child to repeat to her what pages they presently are on in their maths book and she notes the pages in her book.

Mrs N: Dale?
C: 43
Mrs N: Good, push yourself hard ... Steven what about you?
C: 22
Mrs N: That's four pages in three weeks, not enough. Peter?
C: 68
Mrs N: Colin?
C: 97
Mrs N: [to group] Colin has finished the book.
       ['I'm in book three', one child says to another, 'What page are
       you on?']
Mrs N: Dora?
C: 40

Mrs N: That's exactly as it should be . . . Andrea?
C: 19
Mrs N: Good, you are both good workers. Hands up for those who feel they need to do more. [A third of the hands are raised.]

Topics

One of the activities in virtually all the junior classrooms we visited was 'topic work'. With exceptions, 'topics' require the child, generally over the course of a week, sometimes longer, to write two or three pages of descriptive material based on a source book and to include an illustration or two. The label 'topic' was new to us but the ritual is a familiar one. We have often seen its counterpart in US classrooms but called 'projects' or 'reports'. Although Mrs Newhouse encourages children to select their own subject, she lists a subject on the board each week (for example, 'language', 'snakes', 'water', 'birds'). As Mrs Hendrik expressed it. 'It is supposed to come from their own interests but you steer them.' However, many children, in spite of the regular reminder that they may choose their own topic, virtually always take the teacher's suggestions. (Mr Scott from Heathbrook recognizes that this is the usual case, and to combat it, on some weeks he assigns children to choose their own topic. On these weeks he makes a special effort to help children find a topic which interests them . . . particularly those, he explains, 'who have a difficult time making choices'.)

In Mrs Newhouse's class the Ladybird books are the most often used reference. The encyclopedia is second. Several children tell us that one should not merely copy from these sources. (On one occasion Mrs Newhouse says to a child who wants to trace a sheep dog from a photograph; 'Draw it the best you can.' [To observer] 'I always prefer a child's own work.' For Mrs Newhouse topic work is a dispensable part of the curriculum. 'Some of them never get around to the topic work. They are coping with the bread and butter things anyway. If they don't show any interest, I don't think it is something you should necessarily push.'

Children also expressed to us ambivalence about the value of topic work. By far the most common remark by the children was they are 'boring', though several claimed to enjoy it. Daphne, who had in her folder several nicely written pages and diagrams on human biology, reported 'They are very valuable . . . because I want to be a biologist when I grow up.' Seven children chosen at random, when asked to describe 'work' in Mrs Newhouse's class, included 'maths, reading, composition [English], and nature' but omitted topic even though it is listed on the board with the others as work for the week. They have correctly interpreted Mrs Newhouse's priorities. The child who saw her future as a biologist summed up. 'Well, topic is what you do when you have finished your work.'

One boy described as 'dim' by Mrs Newhouse approaches me for some help on a topic he has chosen himself, electricity. We look in the library and in the classroom and I find nothing he is able to read, nor any apparatus to stimulate his interest. Whatever may have been his interest, it has disappeared by the next day – I notice him copying from the Ladybird book a paragraph on English birds, the topic for the week. I ask several children to read passages from the encyclopedia paragraphs they are 'summarizing' (more accurately copying and transposing a few words to make it 'my own'). They have a great deal of difficulty reading the dense prose. With several exceptions the task clearly has little meaning. It is a ritual to be completed. 'Topic', presumably one aspect of the curriculum intended to help children become informed about their social and physical world, is largely irrelevant to what counts for success at school.

Colin runs off

We have been observing and helping out at Port for three weeks when Colin Biggs, a boy in Mrs Newhouse's class, in a fit of anger runs off. During the three weeks of our stay there has been the usual run of expected violations – one day a war of clay between the third- and fourth-year juniors and on another, a brief skirmish with rulers while the teachers are at tea. Two boys are apprehended violating one of the school rules not to climb the wall to Mr Buxton's garden that abuts the school grounds and sentenced by Mr Nigel to two playtimes of hard labor (cleaning up the art area). Several children are caught and told off for tramping on the rain-sogged Common. Such events pass with hardly a notice, but Colin's breach is serious. Within fifteen minutes his absence is discovered and the news travels throughout the school.

Ann hears about it first while helping in Mr Edgar's room, Harold moments later from Mrs Martin. We converge in the library. (Mr Nigel, as fate would have it, is ill, and it falls to Mrs Carpenter, the deputy, to cope with the situation.) Mrs Carpenter, her face grim, has her coat on. Mrs Newhouse arrives a moment later with her coat in hand. Both leave the building to fetch Colin.

The precipitating event was benign. As Colin tells it, a girl sat on his desk. 'I asked her several times to get off so I could get on with my work.' When she did not, he opened the lid of his desk, converting it to an inclined plane, toppling her to the floor. Mrs Newhouse's view is 'he almost hurt her quite badly'. The girl, however, is unharmed. But Mrs Newhouse, who is not easily given to outrage or to raising her voice, reports that she 'shrieked harshly' at Colin. No one recalls the words she used, but there is little question that such a highly unusual event was not missed by the seventy-eight third- and fourth-year juniors in the 'team' room. Colin apparently left school unnoticed. As soon as Mrs Newhouse discovers his absence she goes directly to Mrs Carpenter who telephones Colin's home. Colin answers and hangs up immediately upon hearing her voice. Mrs Carpenter is ready to call the police, but Mrs Newhouse prevails upon her and they agree to go to his home. Mrs Newhouse tells us later that though she understands Mrs Carpenter's position, she was 'horrified' that Mrs Carpenter would consider calling the police. This is strong language for Mrs Newhouse.

Colin's father, we were told later by the two women, received them and Colin meekly returned to school. Mrs Carpenter, in her reports to all the teachers in the tea room during dinner hour, says with some amusement that Colin's father said to his son in their presence, 'I got into scrapes daily at school but I never ran home.' Mrs Newhouse later tells us that she told Colin that if he had been in 'senior school', the police would have come and it would be serious business . . . 'because you are the school's responsibility'. She tells us also that Mrs Carpenter told Colin to apologize to the girl and he protested angrily . . . 'I told her to get off'. Mrs Newhouse, to whom falls the responsibility of enforcing Mrs Carpenter's wish, lets it slide explaining, 'I wouldn't expect it if a child feels angry.'

V SCENES FROM THE OTHER SCHOOLS

HEATHBROOK JUNIOR

5 April. We are again visiting a school for the first time. We enter the front hall of Heathbrook Junior School, a building not more than five years old. The entire area and the school exude well being and prosperity. All is in order – the clean modern lines of the well-lit entrance hall, the obviously purposeful movement of the few children who pass, art and handicrafts carefully mounted on walls and in a glass case.

The head teacher, Mr Bolton, is out, we are told by the secretary but Mr Scott, the deputy headmaster, will be with us in a few minutes, and we are invited to walk about. We pass through the library and find ourselves in an area adjacent to Mr Scott's classroom. (There are no doors, and we hear his name spoken by a child.) A group of about 30 are responding to the teacher's queries: 'Why haven't more people written interesting stories? If you've lost interest you can't do your best work. Do you think your best stories are finished on the day you begin? . . . If so, you should finish on the day you begin . . . O.K.' At that signal, the children deploy themselves; some take out maths work from their trays, others begin to write, several boys chat in a corner. I draw closer to the set of chatting boys – football is the topic. Who will play at playtime? Several children approach Mr Scott with questions. He responds. They disperse as he comes forward to greet us. Without a word to the class, he leaves the room in order to give his American guests a tour of the school.

The fourth-year juniors are in a wing by themselves where Mr Carlson and Mrs Colton work as a 'team'. As we approach, Mr Scott gives us some background information on Mr Carlson. He was the 'most optimistic of all the teachers about the school-wide experiment last December'. At that time, the children were given 'total freedom'

76

:or two weeks, at the end of which all except Mr Carlson were ready to return to the *status quo ante*. Mr Carlson, we are told, insists it would have worked if they had tried for a longer time (Mr Carlson confirms this account in a subsequent conversation).

From the door of Mr Carlson's room, we see about 25 eleven-year-olds sitting at desks scattered about the room. On the board is a listing of work for the week: 'maths, one story'. Mr Carlson's desk is chaos; children's drawings carefully mounted adorn one wall. The teacher moves from one table to another, glares at four giggling, chatting girls, his voice deliberately caricaturing the authoritarian teacher, he booms, 'What's going on over there?' The girls smile. He speaks to a boy who is staring into space: 'You will do five problems, or else you won't be building any balloons this afternoon.' It is not said with the voice of an indulgent father, but in a this-time-I-really-mean-it tone. The child has a slight grin, his eyes meet the teacher's. The teacher's face is immobile. The child turns toward his desk and begins working. Three boys are looking closely at a card with a hand-lettered maths problem on it; two are copying from an encyclopedia. Several are painting. The girls continue to talk and giggle quietly. One tells the observer that she does her work at home so she will have time at school to be with her friends. (A few days later we ask Mr Carlson about this, and he tells us he considers 'social interaction' more important than maths.)

Mr Carlson walks over to the observer remarking, 'Some parents believe kids always have to be charging through books – they don't believe painting or just reading for fun is valuable. If a kid enjoys something, parents believe it's a waste of time.' One boy is recording something in a small book, using a ruler with extreme care to keep the lines straight. The observer asks him what he is doing so carefully and he explains that Mr Bolton checks these 'work diaries' each week – (later we discover he checks most classes about once a month and no one knows for sure the week their class will be checked). If these records of work aren't tidy enough, the consequences are (and the child points to a marginal note) 'See me'. Another child who has overheard the discussion reports that she does only one mathematics task a week 'because I don't like maths'. Three boys enter the classroom and slump in their seats. After a few minutes, Mr Carlson inquires 'where have you been?' 'Reading with Mr Bolton'. Their faces reflect in varying degrees distaste and resignation.

We are escorted back through the auditorium – the 'hall'. A dark-eyed boy stops Mr Scott to discuss the food he will need for his bird. We are told that Ian has found a bird and is caring for it in a cage in the courtyard of the school. Later, Mr Scott tells us that Ian, who spends a lot of class time caring for the bird, is a boy from 'St Agatha's', a nearby orphanage. 'St Agatha' is said in a hushed voice hinting there are special problems. Ian is an attractive child with a glint in his eyes; evidently he has not been squashed.

It is 10.00. Mr Scott invites us to join the children at the 'assembly', and we follow the orderly procession into the hall, not a queue – but close to one. Each child takes a place on the floor. The other classes are already seated. The teachers sit behind the children in chairs. We get our first view of the headmaster, Mr Bolton. He greets the children, 'Good morning, children' and in unison they reply, 'Good morning, Mr Bolton'. He then lectures for three minutes about the virtues of good music. There is not a sound. Who would dare? We also feel compelled to sit quietly. Mr Bolton appears awesome to us (how does he appear to the children?). He plays a recording – Beethoven. The music plays on as he reads the Lord's Prayer with ministerial timing and voice. He asks the meaning of 'trespass'; three children, the same ones we had seen practicing in the hall earlier, rise and perform a morality play – we miss most of the words but the message is unmistakable.

Mr Bolton then adds some closing remarks: 'I have one more thing to say to you. You'd better listen . . . Mrs A [the head of Heathbrook Infant School which is administratively separate but on the same site as the Junior School] has reported that the "fourth years" have been ruining the infants' ball games.' Heavy silence. Mr Bolton continues; each sentence is spoken deliberately, his eyes moving slowly across the assemblage. We feel the weight of authority in the air. His words awaken long-buried feelings from Harold's school days – guilt and . . . there's no question about it . . . fear. 'There will be no more junior ball games until further notice.' Each word hangs, bracketed by silence. 'And no war games. I will *not* have gangs in this school. You know what happens if I catch you' . . . silence . . . 'I won't let up on it.'

Following the assembly, Mr Scott shepherds us to the staff room for tea while the children have playtime. Mr Bolton pours our tea and tells us publicly that we have free reign of the school and may talk to any child at any time. Mr Scott introduces us to the teachers; they are congenial but do not interrupt their conversations to include us. We take seats and listen. There are several pieces of children's pottery that stand on a low table and the teachers are admiring some of the pieces. One says in mock hushed voice that some of the nicest pieces were made 'in the morning'. (We infer that pottery is customarily an afternoon activity.) Mr Bolton responds with what we later know as his characteristic wry humor, 'Someone must light a candle for repentance.'

At 1.30 all children at Heathbrook return to their classrooms and then disperse to 'commitment' until 3.10. We wander through the school. In the hall, twenty children are making a huge hot-air balloon from tissue paper – clearly several weeks of work here. In each classroom we find a different activity – inspection of fossils, body movement , singing, art, creative writing. One group of children is out on the school grounds at supervised games. Another group we are told is on a 'school trip' to the police station. Eight children are baking biscuits, supervised by a parent. There is also a group in the 'library' but what they are about is unclear. Mr Carlson tells us he doesn't think the children should decide what 'commitment' to attend since 'they often don't know what they are interested in', and we learn later that the children choose only within rather strict constraints: they must 'choose' a new activity each week, with the exception of Mr Edward's balloon group, which has been allowed to stay with that activity for several weeks, and they must choose each activity once a term. A quick calculation, number of weeks, activities, children, reveals that the amount of choice involved is not very great.

Mr Carlson is conducting the art 'commitment'. The children had gone on a field trip the day previous, and they must do an art project about the trip one day and write about it another. He lays out six choices of art media, and says a few words about the potential of each, nods, and the children begin to gather art supplies. Fifteen minutes later all are settled into an activity. Mr Carlson surveys the scene, walks over to three girls and tells them they are forbidden to do 'normal' paintings such as 'thatched cottages and Dutch girls'.

Meanwhile, in Mrs Colton's creative writing group children are writing stories about the balloon. As the observer enters, Ian is sulking, refusing to write. Mrs Colton is cross: 'I gave you the choice at the beginning of whether you want to come in and you chose to do it. Now you behave like everyone else.' Ian walks out, she follows and pulls him back bodily. Twenty minutes later, after Ian has written three lines, Mrs Colton, in a gentle voice, asks if he wants to go out to the fish pond in the courtyard. He nods and leaves.

Heathbrook: a morning in Mr Scott's classroom

The first half-hour and the final quarter-hour of each morning are the only regularly scheduled times when everyone in Mr Scott's classroom is engaged in the same activity. The first half-hour is devoted to 'reading', the last fifteen minutes to 'mechanical maths'. Between these two periods the children, Monday to Friday, like the juniors in the team room at Port, have a prescribed minimum of 'basic work' to complete.

'Reading' from 9.00 to 9.30 is a quiet time. The classroom appears as a reading room of a library, everyone sits quietly, whispering and low talking permitted. The children have each chosen their own books with the teacher exercising veto if he thinks a book is 'beyond the child's capacity to enjoy, or offers no interest or challenge'. 'I will permit a child to struggle with a book above his reading level if there is the interest.' We find nothing unusual of course for teachers to encourage children to find books they enjoy. But what is unusual is that there are no 'normal' readers, no reading groups or workbooks. Reading is reading real books, not 'readers'. Those children who, in his view, are the 'poorer' ones are called to his desk two or three times a week. He listens to them read, rarely interrupts, asking them to 'sound out' a word or to answer a question or two . . . ('What's going on here Geoffrey?' 'Why is it that Michael decided to leave?')

On some mornings at 9.30 or thereabouts Mr Scott seats himself on the cooker (cooking range) that affords him the best view of the room. He calls the names of those who are out of his line of sight to move, and proceeds to chair a discussion of ten minutes or so duration. He might ask a child to 'share' an interesting book — summarize the plot or relate an interesting incident.

This morning's discussion lasts almost twenty-five minutes. He begins in an uncharacteristic way:

Mr Scott: Some of you I noticed were not very attentive to your reading. Why?

S: It was boring . . . my book. I wasn't much interested in my book.

Mr Scott: [To Deborah whose attention I had noticed was rarely on her book during the reading period] I was disappointed that your book didn't hold your interest. . . . Books sometimes don't hold our interest and sometimes it may take a while to get into a book. Who has an *interesting* book; one they enjoy? [Nine hands out of twenty-seven are raised.]

S: I'm reading *Young Detectives*.

Mr Scott: Um. Tell us a part that caught your interest.

S: There are secret passages in a house . . .

The child goes on for about a minute. As he finishes others vie for an opportunity to be heard. Three children respond in a similar vein. Mr Thomas nods but only once does he ask for a clarification.

Mr Scott: [To Deborah] What is your book about? [She looks blank . . . and wounded.] . . . When you've read some, tell us about it.

He calls on Lois who avidly recounts an intricate plot. In spite of the growing disinterest, Mr Scott listens attentively and makes no move to shorten her monologue. Then:

Mr Scott: Richard, I know what you've been reading. [to class] He's read it *three* times. You can read a good book more than once. I have a favorite . . . I have read perhaps four times. I can put myself into each time . . . [Richard nods] Do *you* ever put yourself into it?

S: Yes, yes [in unison].

Mr Scott: How many of you put yourself into a book? . . . find yourself in the story? [A dozen hands go up.] Who can name a book you've read more than once? [Seven or eight asking for recognition.] What book is it? [Mr Scott nods and comments briefly on each. 'Yes', 'Ah, that's one, it held my interest' . . . 'Ah, yes', etc.] . . . If you begin a book and it doesn't catch your interest, it is time to find another. There are too many interesting books to stay with one you find boring. Perhaps some of you who haven't a book you like have heard about one that caught your interest. [9.50] Now think what you are going to do, then go to it.

Five or six children, who did not speak, remain in a circle around him and tell him about books they've enjoyed. At one point he suggests they should listen to one another. 'There are so many interesting books we may learn about from one another.'

The poorest readers (three or four children) have an additional half-hour of reading three times a week. We solve the mystery of the library group. It is remedial reading with Mr Bolton at 1.30 during the first half-hour of 'commitment time'. We are told repeatedly by the children that it is a fate to be avoided, if at all possible, for not only is there a stigma attached to being in Mr Bolton's 'library group', but there is no joy in the experience. Reading with Mr Bolton means using a 'normal' reader and a commercially-prepared workbook that resembles their American counterparts.

By 9.55 the children settle into a variety of tasks. Mr Scott consults his list of maths concepts on which is indicated those children who have asked for or he believes require assistance and calls three boys to his desk to show them how to work a probability problem, interrupting the explanation to reprimand Robert from throwing a 'unit block'; 'I had pleasure writing your report (card). Shall I fetch it and write that Robert throws unit cubes?' I ask one child why he is working on a particular task and he nods in the direction of the blackboard – 'I'm in group II.' We copy the following from the blackboard.

Group II[1]
Maths task
3 AEM
4 Rule cards
1 UFI
Reading work
Topic (A–Z: choose anything)

We ask another child who is writing a story about 'Red Indians' why he is doing that. 'That's my topic.' 'I'm in Group II', he says. 'Have you done 3 AEMs?' (We've understood the system.) 'No. If I don't want to, it's O.K. I'm working on my topic.' 'Will you do 3 AEMs this week?' 'Probably.' This boy's neighbor tells the observer he intends to spend the afternoon in the library in order to 'forge ahead in maths'.

During the morning I have kept a continuous record of the activities of a small, fair-haired boy for thirty minutes. During that period of time, he sharpens two pencils, talks with four friends, spills ink on Mr Scott's desk and wipes it up, and does five maths problems. A coincidentally fortunate choice of child, for at the end of half an hour, Mr Scott says to this child, 'You've spent all morning talking. Now finish up.' Ten minutes later, he has finished four more problems. Mr Scott checks them, correcting four of the nine, helping the child to see where he went wrong, saying, 'See how easy it is if you think a little.' His voice is gentle, supportive. Later he tells us Steven had been excluded by his peers last term and that he is glad to see the boys talking to him. 'I'm not concerned about his slow progress in maths.' He quickly adds, however, that he considers maths very important and is somewhat dismayed that the fourth years (Mr Carlson's and Mrs Colton's classes) are not doing quite as much in maths as he would like.

At 11.45 Mr Scott sits himself on the cooker once again. It is time for 'mechanical maths'. He passes out a mimeographed sheet with eighty simple subtraction problems (for example, $2 - 1 =$, $14 - 8 =$, $8 - 4 =$), directs, 'On the back write your name', holds a timer in his hand, 'Start now'. After two minutes he calls out 'Time: two minutes'. He puts the timer on a child's desk and asks him to be timekeeper. Mr Scott walks about watching the children work. 'Four minutes' the timekeeper calls . . . Susan is crying. Mr Scott walks over to her. She has completed fewer than ten problems. Mr Scott talks to her too low to be overheard but she is not easily consoled. 'Five minutes. All pencils down', papers are passed. Mr Scott announces that anyone who cannot complete 25 problems in three minutes is not doing well enough. Children line up on their own. 'Straight lines' but Mr Scott is not insistent. At the stroke of 12.00 most children pass to the assembly hall for dinner, several go home.

NEWTON PRIMARY – A SCHOOL FOR IMMIGRANTS

Standing at the intersection of two major streets in a relatively large city not far from the city center is Newton Primary, a grim, smoke-blackened nineteenth-century brick structure. We have been told that more than half the children are immigrants; mostly Asian, a few West Indians. We do not know quite what to expect. Most of the teachers and heads we have talked to have had little experience with 'immigrants' but they tell us that the city schools with immigrant populations are 'archaic' and 'troubled'. We have been told by a person in the local education authority, who suggested a visit to Newton, that Asian children are 'delightful', 'keen to learn', 'wanting an education' and that the 'West Indians are full of gaiety and laughter, but their parents are more concerned with Black power than with an education'.

Once inside the door we see the school has been 'purpose-built' for chalk and talk teachers and passive recipients of knowledge. Five hours spent within classrooms this day, however, reveals how ingenuity and commitment can thwart severe architectural limitations.

We cannot, on the basis of one day's stay, portray in detail the subtleties of schooling at Newton. In our notes are recorded the familiar signs of informal classrooms – Wendy houses, well-used easels and generously provisioned arts and crafts – wool, cotton, yarn, wallpaper. In one classroom (teacher to a child troubled by a maths problem), 'Go get the [unit] cubes, love'. A child tells the observer, children at his table 'do a story, number and reading everyday and then you can play'.

All this is familiar to us and unremarkable. Also familiar to us is the apparent concern many of the teachers show for their children whom they call immigrants. (We discover here within the first hour that even though the father, mother, or both, are born in England, the child is not necessarily called English if he is of Asian descent.) A high proportion of the children's parents were not born in Britain and many of the children know little or no English. Mrs Willis, the headmistress, tells us the teachers genuinely enjoy working with immigrants. The teachers are 'sympathetic, not sentimental'. One teacher tells us, 'They [the children] are able if one takes the time [to] find out what they can do.' She goes on to compare them to children from the 'council estates'. 'They [the indigenous English poor] are uniformly dull . . . many teachers leave the [council estate] schools . . . and those who stay are frustrated.' Here at Newton we find that teachers we talk to do not attribute children's educational deficiencies to their genetic endowment. However, there is far more certainty that the Asian children will make it ('they want to make it') than the West Indians who have the 'same lack of dedication to hard work as their parents'. One teacher tells us they (West Indian children) 'lie and cheat and are barely able to carry on an intelligent conversation'.

CASTLEGATE – AN INFANT SCHOOL FOR CHILDREN OF THE POOR

Our first day at Castlegate begins auspiciously; the sun is shining! We have chosen this school for a day's visit because the children who attend are poor. We have been told by several sources that it serves the 'roughest council estate' in the city. Though we will later visit a number of schools in this city that serve poor children, this school is the first.

On first impression the estate is completely unlike any of its American counterparts. The two- and three-story detached row houses are in good repair, most of the lawns tended. Later, we discover the school is situated on what we were told is the 'good' side of the housing estate and that visible signs of poverty and decay are in evidence not three blocks away. The two-story well-kept school building is completely surrounded by grass and there are well-groomed flower beds. We follow a path leading past three class-rooms. No one is in sight. Peering through the open doors into generous-sized rooms with plenty of windows, we see that the inhabitants have abruptly departed. In plain view there is evidence of a variety of school activities that have become familiar to us during visits to other primary classrooms: 'news' half-completed, crayons nearby; a half-worked number board, a bin of cardboard boxes and sundry junk, and several partially completed oatmeal-box lorries. We enter the central part of the building, observe a child, late to school, kissing his mum goodbye, and then quietly disappearing through double doors that lead into what appears to be combined assembly hall and gymnasium. As we stand in the corridor we notice a Wendy house in another form, a small café cheerfully decorated, complete with menus, food, price lists and cash box.

Without warning the double doors swing open and children stream forth. As they pass through the doors their sedate demeanor disappears and they talk in normal volume as they return to their classrooms. A teacher, obviously forewarned of our arrival, tells us that Mrs Hollins will be with us in a minute and nods in the direction of the hall. We realize that 'prayers', the morning assembly, has just been completed, that this day's prayers at least was attended by all classes. Through the doors we observe a woman whom we assume is Mrs Hollins at the piano, playing marching music as the children leave. When the hall is cleared, an ageless, imposing, well-tailored English woman approaches. Her mobile and smiling face suggests she is genuinely glad we have come.

Mrs Hollins's office is light, meticulously neat, decorated with children's work. It is the orderliness of the well-organized school mistress. On one table is a large assortment of shoes – certainly too many matching pairs to be 'lost and found'. We will ask her about those later.[2]

As is our custom we ask if she minds if we take notes and, being assured not, we wait ready for the expected orientation lecture in the head's office. On this day, however, it is brief, less than fifteen minutes. She tells us that half the children come from fatherless homes and do not have proper care; the teachers must *teach* (she underscores with a rise in pitch, not volume) reading, not merely listen to children read; that she herself hears each of the children read each week in the school term before they go to junior school; that the teachers work very hard with these children. There is an overriding concern for reading and a hint that she thinks of these children as different from others. She then tells us she will orient us by walking us through the classrooms. In each classroom Mrs Hollins introduces us to the teacher and the children, stops to chat with an individual child or a group about some work she has noticed and responds to children who solicit her attention. She seems to know each by name and dispenses praise liberally to one child's reading progress, another's story, a finger painting. Mrs Hollins also has something to say to us about each teacher's background – one's husband is very ill, another had expected a promotion to deputy-headship and was disappointed, a third is 'an excellent first-year teacher, but a novice nevertheless'. She is discreet and supportive of each. She has command of the details of the organization of each class. She tells us that in one class the children write at least twice a week, in another 'there is a lot of numbers but not a lot of written work'. In each room noteworthy children are pointed out. This one has an IQ of 75 and is 'low, not talented'; another 'is clever . . . it shows there is intelligence to be found' . . . 'John is too wild to work'. We are told that most of these children will go to a junior school where they will be told they can't read and will be humiliated, a junior school which 'is very formal; won't work with us at all'. Several weeks later, we visit Highrock Junior School for a day, find it to be among the most dreary and joyless schools we have seen anywhere, and share Mrs Hollins's despair.

In a classroom for second-year infants, two groups of six children are seated around a table; at one the children work at number tasks, with buttons and plastic cubes; at the other they write 'news'. The remainder are engaged throughout the room in 'choosing'. The teacher divides her time between the tables, spelling requested words, helping with a sum. Now she is seated at the writing table suggesting some 'write more'. One boy's news tells the story of his own death and burial. 'My mum and dad came to my cross.' She moves to the other table, watches a child work a maths problem, and poses a question.

As we follow Mrs Hollins through the classrooms we are treated to her ideas about good teaching. In two instances on that morning we are told no teacher can cope with more than two academic tasks simultaneously, and many teachers cannot work well with more than one. We are told that she expects each classroom to have a 'home corner', that children must not learn a phonetic approach until they can read some whole words 'so they don't split up every word'.

At 10.15 we are again at tea, but, in contrast to Port, Harold is the only male. Mrs Hollins, who has told us she joins the teachers for tea only once or twice a week – 'to let the teachers discuss things without me' – introduces us as American visitors; at this point neither we nor they know we will be settling in for several weeks.

After tea Mrs Hollins gives us some background on herself and the school.

I served during the war days on the land, my father being a farmer. After the war I started to teach in an unqualified manner – I taught in ten or eleven different schools. I was urged to 'train' and I did. I had three small children. I was fortunate enough to become 'student of the year'. . . . I went into a village school for three years . . . and then I came here. This is my fifth year now. When I found this school it was a very forbidding, grim and formal place, the children scurrying past, not looking you in the eye. . . . What they were doing was merely marking time. Every child wrote the same news — forty children copying off the board . . . We don't talk about the past. It's not diplomatic.

At 12.00 Mrs Hollins interrupts herself, telling us she must be in the hall to supervise the noon meal. We are each asked if we will help serve. We consent. In the hall we take places at the heads of tables of fifteen children. The children observe the formalities of mealtime procedure, prayer, then the measured passing of the bowls and plates of food. The children eat avidly and, in contrast to the other schools we had seen, there was little left for the garbage bin.

After visits to several other schools we decided to ask for permission to spend a month at Castlegate. As we worked in the school our fascination with it grew. Understanding it presented a special challenge, for it resembled, yet in profound ways differed from, the English infant schools for middle- and upper-middle-class children we had observed and from the schools we knew for children of the poor in the US. No school can, of course, be detached from the wider social context, but in this school we were daily reminded of the fact that these children were poor. We were reminded by the teachers' frequent unsolicited comments about children's impoverished backgrounds, by how avidly the children ate their school dinners, by the presence of the health visitor, a nurse, who came almost daily to inspect children for lice and to bathe some children.

We also observed more frequent expressions of anger and frustration from more of the children — aged six, seven or eight years old — than at schools for the more affluent — directed at each other, at teachers and at strangers. The notes taken the first day read: (small boy to Ann as we enter the school for the first time) 'I will spill hot sausage on you.' Another says, 'I'm going to cut you.' If there was any place where one could not escape daily the question of the complex relationship of economic and social stratification of society to the process of schooling it was here at Castlegate.

The patterns of schooling we observed, however, in many ways resembled those at Port and the other informal infant schools. The classrooms were enlivened by children's art work. Children moved about freely talking to one another, listened to tapes of stories they had chosen, engaged in sand table or water play. Some were constructing, others experimenting at the number board. In several classrooms children could be found sitting in cozy corners looking at books. In evidence in all classes were the familiar '3R' materials; the 'dictionaries' for writing words children needed for their 'news', maths apparatus – conkers, unit cubes, etc. – the familiar Wendy house, art easels, bricks, Lego, a variety of teacher and commercially-made games. In addition to the papier mâché animals, lorries and prams made of cereal boxes, in an area just outside many classrooms there were wood-working benches stocked with scraps of wood, a few well-worn but usable saws, hammers and wood files (nails were missing – we found out later that they had to be obtained from the head).

The use of time and the internal organization of each classroom appeared to be variations on what we had seen elsewhere. The distinction between morning and afternoon was less marked than at Port – the Wendy house and sand table were more likely to be used throughout the day and the 3R activities were not restricted to the mornings. Closer observation revealed that the organizational patterns of all the classrooms within Castlegate were similar. Each child in each classroom was assigned to a group with four or five others, each group designated by a color on the basis of estimates of reading ability. The teacher 'worked' two tables simultaneously; one of the tables was the 'writing table' and the activity at the other table varied generally according to the time of day. In the morning it would likely be language or a mathematics activity. In the afternoon one of the tables might be devoted to model building or perhaps a cooking project. The groups rotated through the tables at the teacher's direction. And while two groups were being overseen and helped by the teacher, the other was 'choosing'. Choosing included many of the same sorts of activities that were restricted to afternoons in Mrs Martin's room. However, choosing time was not as carefully monitored. Teachers who were busy at the two 'work' tables had little time to keep track of the choosing group, though teachers varied, and some planned these activities and monitored them more carefully than others. Some might allow the 'red' group to bang and hack around at woodwork to no apparent purpose, with no noticeable product. Others interrupted their time at the two managed tables to chat with 'choosing groups' and help them find a productive activity. One or two teachers were quite intent that the more able children use this choosing time to be 'stretched'.

The similarities among classrooms can be traced to Mrs Hollins's efforts during the five years of her tenure to shape her teachers to her scheme of rotating groups of children through the two teacher-monitored tables while allowing the remaining children to choose

from what she calls 'practical' activities. She gave us a detailed
account of how she went about shaping the teachers' patterns.

H: Can you talk a bit about the kind of changes you very clearly had in
          mind [when you took over the school]?
Mrs H: Well, I wanted the school to be run in a freer and more informal
          way. I wanted the children taught in groups; I wanted them off
          those chairs and I wanted to see the paint out; I wanted to see sand
          provided, and clay; I wanted to see home corners provided; I
          wanted to see the beds away in the nursery . . . abolished with just
          an odd bed for tired children. I wanted to see every kind of
          experience that I could for these children to have and everything
          that was beautiful and interesting. At the same time I wanted the
          academic achievement to improve too. In fact, I was asked if I
          could do something about the reading, which was important, by a
          member of the Authority. I was asked if I could do something
          about improving the reading in this school and that's what I set out
          to do – because it is one of my main interests, improving reading.
          But I wanted the children to have far more light, color and pleasure
          in their lives. And, at the same time, I want to arouse in them an
          interest in their work. I saw children in their so-called 'practical
          sessions' . . . I saw children merely dashing to and fro flinging
          paper airplanes about and it seemed to me that these activities were
          not very worthwhile. But I came with the idea that that's what
          you've got to get and that I was going to set about it forthwith and
          tried to make haste slowly, [I wanted] . . . no more copying sen-
          tences from the board.
H: So this was a common pattern, this copying a line . . .
Mrs H: A common pattern had been to copy a line from the board and . . .
          they might read it with the teacher. So I explained to one teacher,
          Mrs Paynter in fact, 'I would like you to have pin-boarding, rather
          than use the large blackboard, and here's a small blackboard for
          you to demonstrate. Maybe the children could do their work in
          their books individually.'
              I started out by approving of what they were doing. Something
          that I could approve that I found in each one . . . Mrs Paynter had
          quite a rousing first hour of the day with plenty of activities. After
          that it was all the way in the same pattern, down to sitting at the
          tables. Now I said, 'I like what you're doing, . . . there are some
          interesting things going on. I wonder if you could go on, you see.
          Keep your work out, keep your activities going.' She said, 'You
          mean keep all this work out? You mean all morning?' I said, 'Yes, if
          you like, keep it out all morning.' And she said, 'All right!'
              And . . . then when I looked again the swing had gone the other
          way. She'd . . . fallen in with only a part of my ideas. So I went in
          with that teacher (quietly since I'd done it, you know) – and

89

gradually . . . I said, 'Let the children have a book.' And I went in and sat down and worked with the group. I sat right there with them . . . I said to her [Mrs Paynter], 'I'll do it like this, everyone could do with a bit of help.' I tried to establish a friendship. I sat with the children. For instance, if they painted a picture I called them up into my room and showed them how to write underneath it instead of . . . copying . . . That was a beginning. And I sat with them and [talked] with them. And that's how we got this free writing established in one room . . . by sitting with the children myself and seeing that they all had a book . . . and had a pride in it . . . and didn't copy just a piece off the board.

   . . . And with another teacher I would go in and help take a reading session . . . 'Children', I'd say, 'Come sit around me . . . and have a little talk' . . . So I gradually got them all established a reading scheme. And that is uniform throughout the school.

H: You established it?

Mrs H: I established it.

After two years had elapsed and changes in the 3Rs were under-way, she turned her attention to the 'practical' activities. She clarifies:

Mrs H: Well, I refer to 3Rs as the skills of reading, writing, and number work . . . arithmetic. [Though] there's much practical work involved in those 3Rs, [I mean by practical activity] . . . the skill of cutting out, making train models, painting, sewing, making doll's clothes or embroidery . . . and there's the . . . the construction work, and ready-made practical work, such as building with the Lego, and the bricks, and all sorts of these things on the market today . . .

   And I feel that . . . you can just put constructional toys on the table. Fair enough. But I think you should only have one kind of those . . . The skill of sewing . . . and cutting . . . and clay-making needs to be taught . . . Now in the practical work . . . I always say to the young teachers in fact . . . you can only put out enough work with which you yourself can cope, singlehanded. It's no use think-ing to yourself . . . I'll have reading here, writing there, mathemati-cal equipment there, while they make doll's clothes there, cut pieces here, and paint a . . . wall frieze there, and do their colors there . . . each one of those is a difficult skill. And I think . . . I say to a teacher I don't think you can cope with more than one difficult skill at a time . . . activities need to be fairly simple, and I tell them . . . You must go and . . . show an interest in the practical activities.

In spite of the similarities between the infant classrooms at Port and Castlegate there are important differences in the ways teachers talk about the parents and children and in the way they teach. A most striking difference is the intensity of feeling in the teachers' descriptions of the children's parents. At Castlegate, though there was some variation, there was in general a strong disdain expressed for those parents who live on the 'rough' side of the estate . . . that portion of the council estate built most recently (where, we were told by several persons prior to our coming, the authorities collected together virtually all the social misfits and ne'er-do-wells of the city). It is from this area that the school draws 60 per cent of its children.

One teacher, whose husband is a clergyman and 'knows the people of the area', shares with us upon first meeting her view of the area – she tells us primarily about the 'rough' side. The following is a reconstruction of notes from informal conversation with her:

The 'older' side [of the estate] houses responsible, hard-working people who are concerned about their children. But life [after work hours] is 'club life' for parents who live on the other side. Their children often go to clubs with their parents at night and do not get enough sleep. Many women go out in the evening and leave the fathers as sitters. The women work in the factories which pay them well. But the mothers want to have a good time. They don't mend clothes for the children, they go to clubs instead. The majority of mothers are on some form of government assistance. They tell their children 'tell her [the teacher] you've got to have it'. They know their rights. The children won't hang up their coats because they are not taught at home. Care of materials is unknown. Their language is terrible, filled with bad [profane] words. The mums give food not [proper moral] training as love. The . . . [rough side of the estate] is a very dangerous area. They think you're the enemy if you go to take a sick child home. The children receive free lunches while the fathers bet away their money. Many fathers are not interested in working.

Her description is not useful so much for its factual content, which is at best problematical, as for the fact that she says at a single sitting what we hear in fragments from different sources over our five-week stay. Parents are seen as expecting to be taken care of by the government, ready to enjoy life, drinking and so forth, sacrificing their children to their own indulgences, suspicious and antagonistic to school, rarely appreciative of the dedication of the staff. However, we also heard on several occasions teachers talk about satisfactory discussions they have had with *particular* parents. In other words, though condemnations of *parents in general* are frequent, criticisms of *particular* parents are quite rare.

Castlegate teachers, though very often sympathetic to the children, view them as ill-mannered. When we ask Mrs Paynter if there are differences between the children whose parents live on different sides of the estate, she says 'fewer than one would expect'. But when asked about differences between children at Castlegate and at schools in the more affluent areas, she answers, 'Well I wouldn't know, I've never taught good ones . . . I've only had one or two good ones in my class.' And when she refers to 'good ones' she means those who are not only 'clever' (that is, capable of doing school work), but who 'get on with it' (that is, do their work without being pressed or continously monitored).

However, we are also told 'Castlegate children *can* learn'. Every one of the teachers (except one in the nursery) expresses this attitude and all but one attribute their optimism to Mrs Hollins and the positive staff relations she fosters. Mrs Hollins herself is conscious of her efforts to foster this view.

Although we do not hear the teachers speak of the children as a group as incapable of learning, it is also clear that they neither see great promise for them as students (not an unrealistic expectation), nor do they have great respect for the strength of their intellects, 'except for the odd one' as one of the teachers says. Mrs Hollins's comment, 'there is intelligence to be found', implies that, given the circumstances of these children's lives, one cannot expect as much from them as from those who live in more affluent areas. The word 'clever' is also used in this school but quite sparingly – applied to one, two or three children in each class – and the term 'thick' we hear frequently. In all the time we spent in the school we never heard the same degree of respect for children's potential as we heard from the teachers of immigrants at Newton.

Many of the teachers' views of the children were revealed by asides they made to us as we worked alongside them in the classroom. Mrs James's five-minute rundown of her students on our first visit to her class includes:

Charles is subnormal. I had him tested. . . . John is a problem child. His mother left his father – a lot of parents find it profitable not to work – the assistance [i.e., welfare]. He's wilder and wilder. I've tried kindness but he's beyond that. . . . He's too wild to work. . . . Sam hasn't a clue to phonics. David returned after Easter vacation behaving quite badly – he had too much contact with his older brother.

Although Castlegate teachers' patterns resembled Mrs Martin's the teachers also responded differently than she to the children. The sense of tranquillity and 'if not today then tomorrow' which was common at Port is missing. Here there is a sense of continuous

92

struggle against difficult odds – an idea that is expressed in one form or another by all the teachers in their actions as well as words. Our notes record (particularly in some classrooms) frequent controlling and chastising statements – what the children call 'being told off'. Anthony, the most frequent object of Mrs Lawton's chastisement, tells us in an interview that what constitutes 'being told off' is 'not what the teachers say but how they say it'. And in Mrs Lawton's room, as in the others, there is no doubt, in spite of pervasive tolerance of childish foibles and generally soft-spoken and patient manner, a far greater likelihood that tempers will flare. We see Mrs Hollins several time a week admonish a child during prayers for misbehavior. On a number of occasions teachers tell us they have decided not to confront a child who, for example, cursed aloud or refused to say 'no thank you' rather than 'no'.

There is also more frequent and intense conflict among the children to be dealt with. Teachers, unlike those at Port, are vigilant during tea time. They often glance at the playground from the window of the staff room – though the aide is supervising. Playfights among the boys (of the sort we see in all schools) do with more regularity degenerate into rows – someone is poked with a sharp stick or struck by a flung stone – that require teachers' or Mrs Hollins's attention.

Finally, there are some consistent deviations from the 'informal methods' that were familiar to us. The writing of the news is one example.

Castlegate, 17 April, Mrs Paynter, 9.45 – Five children take places at the writing table where their writing books have been placed by Mrs Paynter. 'David, writing table', she says and David joins them. 'Shall you write about puppets today?' [The children saw a puppet show staged by another class the previous Thursday.] Robert, who has a library book before him with a picture and a line written underneath – 'a big tree is near the house' – has begun to copy 'a big tree . . .' into his writing book for his 'news'.

Usually virtually everyone in Mrs Paynter's class writes 'news' about a picture chosen from a set of photographs cut from magazines and mounted on cards though writing one's own 'news' is not precluded. Mrs Paynter tell us:

A child who is very slow or a child who isn't capable of doing much . . . you do have to tell them what to do. . . . They just can't think for themselves . . . you have to organize . . . depending on what interests you're going to give them.

Except for a few children in the blue, 'top', group no one may leave the writing table until he/she is finished, and, except for those same few, 'choosing' activities may be engaged in *only* after a clear cue by the teacher.

9.00, Mrs Carter, 18 April – The red group will write today . . . get started on your pictures for your 'news'. Why don't you make a picture of your favorite story and then do a bit of writing about it?

9.40 – The children at the writing table have written very little. Teacher tells one child he may not copy from the book.

1.30 – A boy arrives late from dinner. He tells me, 'I ate a lot of dinner so I will be strong like daddy. My dad combs his hair lovely and goes out and gets drunk at night.'

[Mrs Carter tells us] – One or two will do anything but write . . . I try and find out if they've been anywhere or done anything, and if that doesn't work, I go on to stories or even to what they've seen on the television. Normally something comes up . . . if I stay with that child a little more than I probably would with the others . . . you've really got to coax them to do . . . lots of things.

In the class of Miss Gault, the deputy headmistress, who teaches the third-year infants, the news for the blue and green groups is to copy two or three lines from cards; for example:

Nip is a dog.
Nip can play with Dick.
Here is Dick.
Dick can play with the ball.

Each teacher – some more often than others – required the bottom groups – a third to half of the class – to copy sentences for their 'news' (the attempt to abolish their practice was one of Mrs Hollins's first acts as headmistress).

The reading program also differs from Mrs Martin's. First, approximately a third of the children work in a small group with the 'remedial reading teacher' twice a week for about twenty minutes. The reading teacher follows the same procedure for all. During the first ten minutes she holds up flash cards and the first child to call out the word receives the card. Since virtually all children want to get into the 'game', two or three call out the word in unison and, because they are competing, they call louder and louder until the teacher says shh . . . shh . . . shh and the cycle is repeated. Following this game each child reads a simplified reader that has been substituted for the regular one, and the teacher listens to one or two read at a time.

Second, Mrs Hollins reads weekly with all children who will be going to the junior school next term. It is a routine Mrs Hollins describes quite accurately as follows:

I usually have the children who are going to the Juniors this coming year . . . once a week . . . And the slow ones more. Well, depending, you see, if they're slow I might want two slow, four fast. I vary it. And if they're very quick as they are now, well . . . that's it. They'll come 'round this table as you see. . . . And the good ones, the very good ones, sit in the armchairs and read silently. . . . I encourage them to ask me big words and I praise them. . . . And then I hear a little bit of their reading. Or I ask them what the story is about and hear a little bit, just to show I'm interested. They don't really need me to coach them, but they shouldn't be deprived of the opportunity to come. . . . I don't only listen to them read you see. . . . I say stop a minute and all listen children. This is what this boy's doing. And show them how the word's made, how it's built up. Talk with them about the story. And they sometimes say to me in fact, this doesn't make sense. . . . I say well let's look at it. And then we talk about full stops, commas.

It takes a lot of time to hear them all read. Mrs Hollins comments on a trade-off which troubles her:

If I've got the time, then it's very gainful to go out to the corridor where there are music and dramatic play activities and listen to the play which develops the language. Or watch them serve at the café. They don't have any knowledge of cafés here. Or help them make a tune . . . if I did not have to be so with the reading. If there were not 90 children leaving this term, all of whom I want to hear once every week, I would go to the café and say, what are you buying, or have you tidied up, or how many packets of tea did you stack on the shelf? They are at least playing together, in the café, talking together, being grown up together. . . . They are doing well as far as it goes, but it would do more good if I had time to go out and be with them.

HIGHROCK JUNIOR

At our first meeting Mrs Hollins expressed her concern over what happens to many of the Castlegate children when they enter junior school. More than half attend Highrock. At Mrs Hollins's suggestion we spent a day there. After our visit she asked for a few of our impressions, then she volunteered her view:

Mrs H: The slowest children in [Castlegate] school were reading quite nicely because I had them every day . . . the teachers [at Highrock] say they can't read . . . They cannot read just because they cannot read the book [the teacher] has put in their hand. They put them in a reading scheme with *no books at all* [her emphasis]. They were so proud of their reading here. They love their reading and there they go to school where perhaps they may not even be given a book – they're told they *can't* read. One of these schools where our children go, they don't even want to receive a record on the child that we carefully keep throughout their school life here. They don't want to know what the reading schemes are [here] and they don't want to know anything about the school. They take the children and, after a week or two, give them a verbal reading test. I've seen it. You see the headmistress in the infant school cannot say anything about what the chaps shall do in the junior school. You just cannot. You do your best for the child. We say why are we bothering but we go on bothering. You've got to do your best for them. You send up their record and you hope for the best.

We were not quite prepared for what we saw at Highrock. As we enter the front hall of the nineteenth-century three-story structure, although the hallway and the stairs are filled with children, we are struck by the silence punctuated by adult voices. We climb the stairs to the head teacher's office and in those few minutes we hear a volley of angry commands: 'To the right'; 'Stand over here'; 'Wait at the door'; 'lead on'; 'quiet'; 'shsh'. We see a child approach a teacher standing cross-armed by a doorway. 'Please Miss . . .', she begins. It is a form of address we have heard before at Castlegate on occasion, and, though it is standard in UK schools, in the brief time we wait to be announced to the head by the secretary we hear it more than we have in weeks in other schools. Virtually every conversation between adult and child is preceded with 'Please Miss . . . (or Mrs)'.

The head, Mr Park, tells us he has been recently appointed to 'liberate the school'. There are three hundred children, seventy of whom are from the poorest council estate. He is earnestly concerned, beset by serious problems. One-third of the twelve teachers are first- or second-year teachers. Four years ago the school was 'middle class' but after a re-organization the middle-class children were moved to another school. 'Teachers were used to the middle class . . .' '[I] had to talk to the teachers about their attitudes to the children.' Mr Park tells us there are eleven classes and a 'special class'. This is the first time we hear the euphemism 'special class'. It is a class, he explains, for 'children who are far behind, who have other problems as well'. Mr Park's description of the children who attend the school is a catalogue of deficiencies – no redeeming virtues are noted. They don't play constructively, cannot concentrate, give up easily, physically are under par, socially retarded, fight all the time, have difficulty forming relationships with adults, they do not trust grown ups. They have learned 'grown ups let you down', he adds as an explanatory note. 'They do not carry out instructions. They test [teachers] by disobeying . . . cannot form relationships, are used to moving around, and they do not learn from books.' Mr Park's tone shows genuine concern and some bewilderment. 'We have four years for them to achieve basic literacy and we need a plan.'

At Mr Park's invitation we visit several classrooms and talk to several teachers. There are some variations in the classrooms, but the 'Yes, Miss', 'Please, Miss', 'Thank you, Miss' are omnipresent. The classrooms are barren. The atmosphere is cheerless for teachers as well as children. We see no hearty smiling face, adult or child's, the entire day. Teachers are continuously watchful as they talk to us, everyone alludes to serious intellectual and social deficiencies of these children.

11.40 – enter Mr Jerrid's second-year junior class. Children sit in rows. There are ten problems on the chalk board; for example, $(? \times ?) + 2 = 10$; $(? \times ?) + 12 = 26$.

Children are all seated at their desks with maths work. I sit in an empty seat. I see all maths books are open at page 12 and I see it is one of the books from the same series used at Port.

After five minutes: Mr Jerrid: 'Some of you are having difficulty.' There is virtual silence – some whispered communication among the children can be heard. It is furtive and, though I try, I cannot find a source. 'Shut up for a minute.' Complete silence now.

Mr Jerrid chooses one of the problems from those on the board. 'Something times something plus two equals eighteen. What times what equals sixteen?' (Waits, calls no name. Makes no motion.) Child answers: 'four times four'.

He writes $4 \times 4 + 2 = 18$ on the blackboard. He continues with several other problems. All answers emanate from the left front of room. Some children appear to be asleep. 'Put your desk lid down', he calls out. Several minutes pass. He begins again to ask a series of questions that are answered in barely audible voices. No names are called and all answers, once again, from the left front. 'How many tens in 55?; How many twos in twelve? How many twos in twenty?' 'I've told you once Billy! Perhaps you would tell us your two tables.' During the question and answer sequence, an undercurrent of whispers becomes more distinct.

11.59 – 'All sit up' . . . A noticeable change. All children now are quiet, seated head high in their seats. They are dismissed by rows, in the order of the row that falls silent first. They line up by the doorway. 'Stand up straight, Jessica.' 'I can hear your voice.' The door is opened. 'Lead on.'

MR SPRINTER – OUTSIDE THE RANGE

It was in one classroom in one school in the center of a massive, treeless new housing estate less than three miles from our English home that we found Mr Sprinter, the teacher who most approximated informal teaching as it has been romanticized in the books and pamphlets that first caught our interest several years earlier. A brief glimpse at his classroom illuminates a form of informal practice that appears qualitatively different from all but perhaps one or two classrooms we visited.

Perhaps not coincidently, Mrs Calthorpe, headmistress of the school, had just two years prior been headmistress of a village school of forty-three pupils and two teachers (including Mrs Calthorpe) which had been portrayed, in a film and a booklet published by a US Research and Development Center 'as an example of primary education of the sort . . . highlighted in the 'Plowden Report' – freedom, self-motivation, self-discipline and the 'integrated day' '.

Mrs Calthorpe and Mr Sprinter reiterate and confirm what we have seen and been told by others, teachers, heads and LEA officials, that the style Mr Sprinter's teaching practice exemplified was far from typical even of informal teachers. Mrs Calthorpe acknowledged that many Americans came to think that 99 per cent of primary teachers work like Mr Sprinter, but that very few actually do. Mr Sprinter told us 'of the people I know perhaps two are working in a similar manner'.

On first look Mr Sprinter's classroom appears little different from many others we have seen: a variety of activities, the buzz of apparently self-motivated study, the relaxed teacher moving from one child or small group to another. Using our techniques acquired over the past months to uncover the underlying structures that explain the apparent self-direction (for example, the accordion cards, list of work for the week), as we usually do, we ask a child about requirements. Queries of a series of individuals and pairs turn up the same answer. A certain amount of maths is required *during the year*. Otherwise, we are told repeatedly 'nothing is required, not for the morning, day, week or month . . . nothing'.

Another difference becomes apparent, the greater *variety* of activities – one boy sawing a wooden 'ornament'; another beginning a picture of 'an explorer'; Mr Sprinter sitting down with a child building a terrarium to help him understand the directions given in a book; a girl adjusting a microscope, 'bringing fish eggs into focus' she tells us. One child is working on an old printing press; two play chess, while two onlookers follow the game; four are thinking up limericks to say to skipping (jumping rope). Mr Sprinter suggests that after they record them on paper they 'go outside to try them out'. Two boys are drawing tanks and trucks, a girl is making paper pompoms, another apparently daydreaming in the midst of drawing a hand. Two boys are deeply engrossed in Lego construction – the likes of which have not been seen in any classrooms we visited – a motorized cable station. A book on transportation lies open nearby as reference. Mr Sprinter returns to help the girl adjust the microscope again, then assists the boys to tighten the cable, asks them if they heard about the power station outrage on the news. Two girls who have been watching a snail for forty-five minutes ask him a few questions as he walks by. He helps them record their observations, then, in an aside, tells us they have reached some unwarranted conclusions, yet 'have done some thinking on their own', and that 'their record is very primitive'. Mr Sprinter stops at the workbench, shows the boy the wood is warm from the saw, tells him it will make a lovely pattern. 'It's hard wood. . . . I told you it would be hard work.' 'Just two playing chess, please. . . . James and Penny you do something else.' He returns to the Lego project at the request of the boys to help them with the pulley. The displays of seashells, bones, hamsters, a variety of books attract sporadic interest. One boy is reading *Charlotte's Web*, two are doing maths.

At 2.15 the same day, the teacher and three boys are playing the recorder; a microscope area has been set up, evidently by those who were earlier looking at the eggs; one girl is still drawing a hand. The Lego pair are taking down a Lego castle and transporting it across the papier mâché mountains with the cable and pulley. The boy who has completed a complex picture of an explorer shows it to Mr Sprinter. One of the 'snail' girls calls the other excitedly – the snail has 'come out'.

What is the structure in this classroom that appears so unlike the others? Are the children learning the 'basics'? Here is Mr Sprinter's view:

Ann: I'd like you to say a little bit about how a student's day is structured in your classroom – what would go on with a couple of students, typically?

Mr S: Well, that's rather difficult because they're at times doing very different things. Probably, if we just took two as an example, say two girls and give the names Karen and Debra, it's easier. They come in in the morning and they've been doing a lot of work on snails and small insects and that kind of thing, and collecting them, and then say on this hypothetical morning, they just come in and they say, well we've done snails now and we want to do earwigs, and so they want to go out and collect these on the mound outside the school. So they ask me can we go out and collect those. They go out and they spend more time out there looking for them and then they'll bring them in and set up a little tank with grass and that kind of stuff for them to live in, and then they'll probably watch them and I'll talk to them about it if I have time to. You know, and that will probably be the starting point for some writing at some point. It may not be that day – oh, I've jumped a stage there. Probably the next thing I would suggest they do is find some books on them because we have some nice books on insects and small animals you find just all around, very common small animals, so we'd look for books. That would probably be the first thing. After they have set up the tank and a place to live, I should encourage them to read the books and see what they could find out about them, and then go on to doing some writing about it. You know, I missed a stage – I said that they would do some writing and that was, you know, in some ways a slip – it was the sort of slip that all teachers make, they miss out about half a dozen stages really, and the biggest one we miss out is sitting and looking. The greatest strength that kids have that we don't have any more really, that we have to recreate in ourselves as adults, is that way of looking. [This approach] is not very common because you know I take a stand on the 'work and play' thing. The way most people work it here is that they have assignments and they say you do your work and then you can play – and that seems to me morally a very, very different system. I think that is in fact a very traditional school system in a different guise. It maybe sounds very arrogant, but I think a lot of people don't do it because they don't understand the difference . . . they see school as a place where you work a system . . . you may not like maths at all but you know you've got to do maths before you can build with the bricks . . . it means that the whole idea of learning is that somebody decides for you what is important . . . it seems a very serious thing to do with education you know to say that reading is more important than music . . .

Ann: Well, I might as well be direct about it. I was beginning to wonder as I'm sitting here – so what – so the child knows that there are 100 species? What are the goals of spending some time with children on this kind of nature . . . what are the values that you see in it?

Mr S: Certainly involvement, you know . . . I know from experience . . . the children become very, very involved in that and that was very, very much the prime concern.

Ann: More important than the 3Rs for example, or at least of equal importance?

Mr S: Well, I think it's impossible to grade those. I think, yes, some children will have the 3Rs anyway. I think basically most kids, you just put them in a room surrounded by books and you know a good half of them are going to be interested in the books and most of them are going to make it anyway in academic terms. I don't have very high standards. I think that they should all be able to read. They should be able to read poetry fluently by the time they're eleven and they should be able to write reasonably well and write legibly and that they should have reasonable and not very advanced maths concepts – so those standards are not very high and without a lot of pressure it's possible for them to reach those standards. So, you know you don't need the pressure there. The pressures I would put on most of those kids would be on involvement ...

I think you should have kind of a magic cupboard. Which to some extent I have. That's a matter of building stuff up and you have a lot of stuff you keep in there. And on a wet Friday morning there may be three or four kids slouching about looking fed up. Then you produce something from your magic cupboard. ... I think that's pretty important and you know you need to have as much stuff as you can in it ...

Ann: Can you think of a kid you have to lean on quite a lot?

Mr S: Yes. David. He's an unusual character, this one, but he's eight, he reads very well (you may have met him). Little David, he reads very well and writes not at all – simply not at all.

Ann: And so what do you do?

Mr S: Well, what happened, I'd left this for a long time and ... kept on trying to encourage him – he's very interested you know. He reads a lot and very wisely ... it just didn't work and it didn't work and kept on not working and so in the end I just sat him down and said he had to do some practice with me. I just sat down for a whole morning and he did writing for a whole morning and every morning for a week and now he's got hold of some of it – he still doesn't write very much but he does write more now.

Mr Sprinter's classroom is an island sheltered by Mrs Calthorpe who says it is rare to find someone who can 'do it right'. Presiding over a school where most teachers are variations on Mrs Martin, Mrs Eden and Mrs Newhouse, the headmistress labels a new teacher (who teaches in a classroom adjacent to Mr Sprinter's and thinks of himself as a Mr Sprinter) as 'dangerous' – he is 'the ultimate in non-structure; there is no feeding ... no teacher expectancy. Chaos. The kids are crying out for feeding'.

Mr Sprinter is aware that his way of teaching contradicts the expectations of numbers of parents and describes his efforts to deal with their concerns:

Mr S: Well they [parents] complain about roughly the same things. Discipline is one thing they complain about. The children are moving about and talking and sometimes making a row. The fact is I can control them; that is a fairly easy one to deal with.

If they come in – you've got to be sure of yourself, you know. You can say, 'Well just look around – this space is about as big as your main room at home . . . You know you normally don't have 32 children in your main room for 5 hours. Just have a look at how much equipment there is in here. Can you see any damage to the equipment? Can you see any signs of the children running riot in here? Can you imagine what your room would look like with 32 children after they've been in for 5 hours with just you as the one adult?' I go on to say that there is control but a very different kind of control. So if you don't win on that one, at least they accept your point and they realize that you're not an idiot which they're coming to tell you you are.

Their other complaint is the curriculum one and that is more difficult because you can't convince them about anything. They disagree with you you are.

Ann: What is it they want?

Mr S: Well, they basically want I suppose what most parents want, that their children should be better than they are. And if the parents didn't succeed in school, they may push even more for their children to succeed in school. It's a kind of vicarious success for them.

Ann: What do they define success as that you are not giving them? Good spelling?

Mr S: They should be good at maths – good at reading and good at writing . . . handwriting as well.

You know if they're a genius at the clarinet, they couldn't care less. There are at least two parents that have children in my class who would take that line. It doesn't matter a damn what else they can do – they must be able to do the basics.

Ann: They probably wouldn't complain in a traditional school.

Mr S: No, because there is every sign in a traditional school that they are working.

NOTES TO PART TWO

Introduction

1 The description of the entire day, morning and afternoon are composites drawn from notes taken on separate occasions. The descriptions of particular lessons and schooling events are based on notes from a single setting. We have taken some liberties with some of the descriptions in order to protect anonymity.

Chapter IV

1 Though policies vary from school to school, children generally enter infant school when they are 'rising fives', that is, the school term in which they will celebrate

102

their fifth birthday. Junior schools are for children 7 to 11 years old, roughly equivalent to second to sixth graders in the US.

2 Observations were made and recorded by both writers. Sometimes, for reasons of style or clarity, we write in the first person singular.

3 For our North American readers, these are 'buck eyes', used in a number of classrooms for counting and working out math problems.

4 A rubber is a pencil eraser.

5 Some cards represent a class of tasks, others portray particular tasks. We inferred the imperative implicit in each card from what we saw and what Mrs Martin and the children told us. Our information is not complete.

X set	Task
1 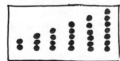	Write name in 'copy' or writing book.
2 	Do 'news'; that is, draw a picture and trace, copy or write a sentence underneath.
3 	Do a jigsaw puzzle.
4 	Choose any non 'normal' reader and look through it.
5 	Choose one of the various counting apparatus and perform the tasks. This card represents a sequence of mathematics activities. The child is expected to choose the same or roughly equivalent apparatus he/she worked with the previous day. A child chooses a different type of card after Mrs Martin instructs him/her in its use.
6 	Choose a *blue* card if you are not yet in a 'normal reader'. Draw and color the object portrayed. (Each object is shown in simple line drawings or in stick figures; e.g., a pram, a man walking.) Or, choose one of the *pale blue* or *white* cards if you have advanced to one of the readers. (On these cards are pictures of characters in the reader and the directions: 'draw Janet; color Janet's dress blue; draw a dog, write "Janet and the dog".')

7  Choose and copy one from a set of 'writing readiness' cards intended to provide the child practice in learning to control a pencil. (All cards are variations of the illustration.)

8  These are the 'copying cards'. The children duplicate the word into their writing book. There are two types: single-word cards (a picture of the object and the word basket, kitten, dog, Janet, etc.) and sentence cards (a picture and underneath 'This little dog is here.' 'Here are three dogs.'). The persons, objects portrayed and the words – though not the sentence itself – are taken from the readers.

9  Cards nine and ten represent a set of mathematics activities that are the same as those described below in the Y set. Only the 'cleverest' children at tables 4 and

10 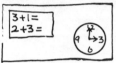 5 are expected to progress to these activities.

The Y cards are located at Y (see floor plan). These are intended for the 'top tables', 1 and 2. One should, however, note the overlap. The two sets, in spite of first appearance, are, in fact, a single continuous set.

Y set   *Task*

1   Write name on 'news'. (Same as X set.)

2  Write 'news' (same as X set), except that children using the Y cards use their 'dictionary' as soon as they know the alphabet – names of letters, vowel and consonant sounds; they write their own 'news'.

3 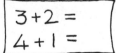 Do 'sums'. These are not literally addition problems but represent the most complex sets of cards. The progression of activities indicates what Mrs Martin defines as quantitative literacy. (No effort will be made to describe the cards in their entirety.) The more advanced cards require use of apparatus and recording in the 'number book'.

4  Do 'shopping cards' which are a sequence of cards intended to teach recognition of English coins and currency and once these are known, to learn how to make change. There is more than one series of cards. The more advanced maths problems require making change and recording answers in the 'number book'.

5

Do 'clocks'. This includes a set of cards and 'ditto' sheets. Corresponding 'apparatus' is a cardboard clock face with movable hands. These are also sequenced in terms of difficulty; first the child matches word and number symbols (six o'clock, 6 o'clock) to representations of clock faces. Then the process is repeated with quarter, half hour and 'quarter to' in that sequence. And then there is a reversal; matching clock representations are shown for times given in numerals alone (3.25, 4.45, etc.). There are practice cards and, finally, simple time problems. (Jim left at 6.00. He stayed for 20 minutes. What time did he return?)

6

These the teacher calls 'writing' cards. Our information is sketchy here but apparently it is expected that the child should make up several original sentences (or brief stories) using the words on the cards. (We would liken these activities to what American teachers often call vocabulary development.)

7

These are called 'missing word' cards. They record phrases or brief sentences with blanks to indicate words are missing.

Maths

The 'sums' cards, the clock and 'shopping' or 'money cards,' and the maths games that children may choose during their unscheduled time constitute the official 'maths' program. There is also the 'informal' maths program – a set of activities that teach a number of basic things that are traditionally and sometimes explicitly maths in many US classrooms. During the afternoon 'activity time', children, as they go about a variety of constructing activities that are set out by Mrs Martin on the 'arts and crafts' table, learn the elements of topography and geometry – angles, shapes, two- and three-dimensional relationships – and linear and two- and three-dimensional measurement. Formal introduction of units of measurement occurs in second-year infants. Finally, the sand and water tables are aspects of the maths program. We have very sketchy notes on the details of these activities. Moreover, it is clear that, compared to other informal reception classrooms we observed for a day or two, relatively little use was made of the sand and water activities at Port. We may have missed significant details since we were not highly attuned to mathematics curricula and we also never thought to ask Mrs Martin about it in much detail.

There were three general categories of 'sums' cards: those that help children develop basic concepts of numbers – e.g., the ordering of the numerical symbols, the correspondence of the symbols to objects (1–1 correspondence); those that teach the understanding of basic operations of addition, subtraction, multiplication and division; and a third set that, for want of a better label, we call 'number practice'. These give children practice in doing simple calculations to the point that they can call out from memory the answers to one-digit and simple two-digit problems. American teachers call them 'number facts'. 'Mechanical maths' is the term we heard most frequently in the schools we studied. Corresponding to these three types are 'apparatus'; for example, manipulative objects that can be used for counting and matching, such as conkers or buttons; for teaching the concept of 'addition', 'subtraction', 'multiplication' and 'division' there also are 'unit cubes', bits of plastic of differing colors that snap together and disassemble easily as children work through problems. For learning place value and basic operations there are the 'unit cubes' and white containers (that once served as containers for yogurt or cottage cheese) and colored plastic chips. Some of the maths materials (cards and apparatus), where sequence is crucial, are kept in gray trays in one of the new pieces of furniture. The early cards in the sequence do not require writing by the child. The child merely displays his matchings or countings on the card itself using the appropriate 'apparatus'. As soon as the children have advanced to writing numerals and have a satisfactory concept of number, they are expected to work out the problems presented on the cards using the appropriate 'apparatus' and to record the problems and the answers in their 'number book'.

The reading scheme

In addition to the task governed by the accordion cards, there is a 'reading scheme' which must be understood as an overlay on the entire card system. Within a month of entering school, as soon as the child can master approximately a dozen flash cards, he/she receives a first 'normal' reader (approximately 36 pages). Three of eight children who entered four weeks earlier had not yet mastered the set. Two non 'first termers' also have not. One of these children, David, has been shifted to a set of pink cards and a special book made by hand by Mrs Martin. In the first several weeks the children begin the 'normal reader'. The teacher listens to them read virtually every day. The top readers she usually hears every other day. In addition there is often a 5–7 minute group lesson, generally for those who have not yet mastered the letter names and sounds or the 'sight' vocabulary.

'Hearing a child read' normally means listening to him/her read 3, 4 or 5 pages. (There is not much reading matter on each page, particularly in the earlier books of the reading series.) The teacher overlooks minor omissions and even a mistake (substituting 'a' or 'an') as long as it appears to the teacher that the child reads it meaningfully. If a child falters, Mrs Martin does not allow him/her to struggle for long. She encourages the child to try the initial sound but says the word if he/she fails or pauses too long (so, Mrs Martin says, as not 'to lose the thread of the story'). If a child repeats a mistake, the troublesome word or sound (e.g., th, sh) is recorded on the back of the white marker where she also writes the pages the child has read to her. Mrs Martin also keeps at her desk a notation of the books the child has read and for each makes an entry on a 'list of skills' indicating 'mastery' or 'need for further attention'.

6 A form of apparatus used for teaching basic geometry and exploring spatial relations.

Chapter V

1 The maths book is divided into segments or 'tasks'. Each includes directions for how to complete the segment. There is a *de facto* work rate per week of approximately 2–3 tasks. AEM are a set of commercially-produced maths cards, which augment the maths book and regular reading and maths 'apparatus'. Rule cards are practice cards for mechanical maths: +, −, ×, ÷. UFI are reading and comprehension tasks.

2 We found out subsequently that she collects shoes and other clothing and distributes them to children who are in need.

PART THREE
TOWARDS A THEORY
AND LANGUAGE OF SCHOOLING

INTRODUCTION

The schooling process we have portrayed in Part Two reveals the regularities and uncertainties, constancies and apparent contradictions of everyday social behavior of teachers and children in schools. Our problem became how to find language that simplified the complexity without over-generalizing or distorting the nuances and problems of school life. After only a few days of observing at Port Primary, the first of the schools we studied, it was apparent that descriptions of teachers' schooling patterns in terms of the familiar 'informal v. formal', 'progressive v. traditional', 'teacher centered v. student directed' and the like, whether used as dichotomies (either–or) or continua (more – less), even with qualifications added, distorted the realities. And whatever accounted for the variations in schooling patterns, teachers' 'commitments' or 'beliefs' had at most a tenuous connection to their schooling behaviors. For example, what might be said of 'freedom' in classrooms? Mrs Martin prescribed the range of activities each child was to do every morning, yet children, some regularly, others on occasion, were exempted from the requirement. In Mr Scott's room, Jeffrey, who chose to study 'Red Indians' was not expected to do the 'required' work for the week. Mr Carlson walked by a group of giggling girls but chastised a boy for not doing his maths. Yet this same teacher, among the staunchest advocates of informal methods, who at a staff meeting argued for giving the 'experiment in freedom of choice' at Heathbrook a longer try, refused to allow children to paint pictures of costumed Dutch girls or Second World War fighter planes, so beloved by eleven-year-old girls and boys respectively. And what might we say of motivation? Those teachers who were reputedly the most 'informal' did not rely consistently on 'intrinsic' motivation which is claimed by advocates of informal methods as a guiding principle. Children in Mrs Martin's class did choose to paint and play in the hospital, but they were required to do a host of tasks whether or not they had the least inclination and were infrequently, but on regular occasions, given 'sweeties' for teacher-approved behavior. And Mr Sprinter, who encouraged children to write and do a variety of art projects by evoking their interests, insisted that David write every day against his will. Mr Scott, who was among the best organized for providing for children's interests and most often encouraged and honored a child's chosen interest in 'topic', or fiction, fully supported Mr Bolton, the Head's record-book checking routines, and insisted upon documentation that all work had been done properly and diligently. Could we say that informal methods were more 'individualized'? In Mrs Martin's classroom everyone was expected to complete one of two sets of prescribed activities, but children could alter the order and work at their own rhythm within limits. In Mr Scott's room, no child arranged his time the same as any other and more often than not worked individually, yet the work minimums were not unique to each child and all children had to work through the same maths and handwriting sequences, though always with a significant number of exceptions recognized.

We found that the terms of the dilemmas provided a way of describing these variations, regularities and apparent contradictions. By speaking of *dominant and exceptional patterns of resolution* to one or more dilemmas we were able to represent the variations characteristic of individual teachers, and the similarities and differences among the English teachers, and within and between English and US schools.

Once we settled upon describing schooling in terms of dilemma resolutions, the troublesome question of what was the relationship of teachers' commitments or beliefs to their schooling behavior could be recast in terms of what were the antecedents *or origins* of teachers' patterns of resolution. Put in this way, the over-simplifications of the effort in the Plowden Report, and by Roland Barth and others to explain behavior in terms of 'beliefs', 'values', or 'ideals' became more clearly evident. Sometimes teachers' patterns of resolution appeared to be consciously chosen, deliberate efforts to put social and educational values into practice, though these choices were always qualified by situational constraints, some of which teachers recognized and discussed openly; at other times teachers' patterns seemed almost totally mindless, sheer habit, or formed by cultural and social experiences and forces, or by internal needs of which they were but dimly or not at all aware.

Similarly, we found that we could recast many of the evaluative questions we were asked and were asking ourselves (for example, What were the effects upon children of this form of schooling? Do children learn as well as in more formal schools? Will they be better 'adjusted'? What are the differential effects on poor v. middle-class children? Will differences in schooling patterns have any significant effects on the society at large?). We reformulated such questions in terms of what were meanings, social and cultural, that children take from teachers' patterns. The effects of schooling could be studied in terms of how these meanings taken from patterns of resolution influence persons' social, political, economic and cultural activity in the immediate and long-range future.[1]

These three general concerns, describing schooling, understanding its origins, and its consequences were inextricably linked, and efforts to articulate their inter-relationships and clarify our background assumptions about rationality, and societal and individual change led us to George Herbert Mead's social behaviorism and later to an exploration of its connection to several Critical social theorists.[2] In Chapter VI, we state the social theoretical underpinnings of the dilemma orientation, drawing upon the works of these theorists. In Chapter VII we set out the terms of the dilemma language using examples from the narrative, and from our own experiences in schools in the US.

VI TOWARDS A DIALECTICAL ACCOUNT OF TEACHER ACTION

Language sharpens perception and understanding of experience, but it simultaneously distorts and obscures. Most of our everyday and scientific languages fragment social activity, including schooling, into the separate and distinct categories of consciousness (for example, values, beliefs, attitudes, motives, personality traits, etc.), observable behavior, and social context (for example, socio-economic status, classroom climate). These separations in our languages make it extraordinarily difficult to talk and think about schooling as a continuing social process wherein context and consciousness are joined in the acting moment.

Persons' activities cannot be understood apart from their biographies and the histories of the groups with whom they identify, which live on in consciousness; or apart from the time and place in which they act (a particular school, local education authority, nation or state at a particular juncture of human history). The dilemma language of schooling is an effort to represent the thought and action of teachers as an ongoing dynamic of behavior and consciousness within particular institutional contexts of schools for the young. The dilemmas are not to be conceived as entities that may be physically located either in persons' heads or in society. Rather they are linguistic constructions that, like lenses, may be used to focus upon the continuous process of persons acting in the social world.

Our effort to clarify the problem of the relationships of thought, action and social context in the schooling process led us to the writings of George Herbert Mead,[1] and to Marxist thought as interpreted by the humanistic Marxists, Georg Lukács, Raymond Williams, Antonio Gramsci, C. Wright Mills and others.[2] In this chapter we briefly outline Mead's social psychological perspective, focusing on the concept of the 'act' which is central to the dilemma language and orientation, and introduce some Marxist concepts that helped us relate Mead's social theory to the part material forces, individual action and the schooling process may play in social change. In the second half of the chapter, we use a classroom situation to illustrate how the Meadian concept of the 'act' and the concept of 'dilemma' enable us to portray the flux of schooling life and overcome at least some of the distortion of common and social scientific languages that construe human social relations in terms of the mutually exclusive – though perhaps 'interacting' – categories of behaviour, thought and social context.[3]

MEADIAN NATURALISM

Mead's work was a response to what he saw as a fundamental problem in western philosophical and social scientific thought – how to portray the relationship of man to society and to the physical and biological world.[4] Does a proper understanding of man and society require going outside of nature and hence lie beyond scientific explanation? Is the ambiguous concept of mind, like the study of morals, to be ignored or consigned, if one has interest in such matters, to poets, novelists, metaphysicians, moral philosophers, theologians and moral visionaries, those outside the traditions of science? Or is 'mind' or 'consciousness' a phenomenon that can be studied and understood as one would other natural phenomena – migrations of birds, the growth of plants, the tides, the movements of the galaxies?

Though Mead's conception of man in society is naturalistic or 'non metaphysical', he explicitly rejects the model of man as object, as machine, taken by the then newly emerging and increasingly influential science of psychology and by the Social Darwinists.[5] He, like other American pragmatists,[6] sought to provide an alternative to the philosophical traditions that preserved the dualism of mind—body; thought–action; and to avoid the deterministic assumptions of behaviorism and Social Darwinism. He rescued the concept of mind from its historical, philosophical and linguistic confusions, and pointed the way for the development of a science of society that provides a satisfactory account of the relationship of individual human behavior to the basic question of continuity and change in society. Although he never published a systematic exposition of his thought during his lifetime, the reconstructions of his lectures, largely through the efforts of his students, together with his relatively few published pieces, provide us with a remarkably consistent emerging theory, which includes a naturalistic account of morals, aesthetics, philosophy of history and knowledge.

Reflective action

Mead's position has been labeled a 'biosocial account of man and society'.[7] In the following passage he places human thinking in the realm of natural phenomena – both the more rudimentary form of 'thinking' observed in animals as well as in humans and its more elaborated and articulated form that he (and Dewey) takes to be among the highest forms of human activity – scientific inquiry.

The animal, even the plant, has to seek out what is essential to its life. It has to avoid that which is dangerous for it in its life. . . . A plant shows its intelligence by driving down its roots, in its adjustment to the climate . . . [while in the] animal kingdom, you get much more adjustment in an environment . . . [where] the getting of food, the avoiding of enemies, the carrying-on of the process of reproduction, take on the form of an adventure. Intelligence consists in the stimulation of those elements which are of importance to the form itself, the selection of both positive and negative elements, getting what is desirable, avoiding what is dangerous . . .
What the animal needs is food [and] freedom from its enemy. If it responds to the right stimuli, it reaches that food, that safety. The animal has no other test . . . [of] whether it has made such a proper selection except . . . [as it presents itself by] the result. . . . You can test your stimulus only by the result of your conduct which is in answer to it. You see, that takes the research method over into life. The animal, for example, faces a problem. It has to adjust itself to a new situation. The way in which it is going brings danger or offers some unexpected possibility of getting food. It acts upon this and thus gets a new object; and if its response to that object is successful, it may be said to be the *true* object for that stimulus. It is *true* in the sense that it brings about a result which the conduct of the animal calls for. If we look upon the conduct of the animal as a continual meeting and solving of problems, we can find in this intelligence, even in its lowest expression, an instance of what we call 'scientific method' . . . [This] basic outline has been developed by man into the techniques of . . . science. The animal is doing the same things the scientist is doing. It is facing a problem, selecting some element in the situation which may enable it to carry its act through to completion. There is inhibition. . . . It tends to go in one direction, then another direction; it tends to seek this thing and avoid that. These different tendencies are in conflict; and until they can be reconstructed, the action cannot go on. The only test the animal can bring to such a reconstruction of its habits in the ongoing of its activity. [The] experimental test is, can it continue in action? And that is exactly the situation found also in science.[8]

In this passage Mead emphasizes the continuity between responses of plants and animals, human and non-human, to problematic situations – those situations where there is a 'lack of adjustment between the individual and his world'.[9] Intelligence for all living things consists of some sort of adjustment to new situations. The adjustments by humans that are most similar to animals' are habituated actions.[10] Habituated responses are evoked by a stimulus or set of stimuli in the present situation of which we are only dimly or not at all aware. These habituated responses are the 'tail ends' of dispositions to act or attitudes that are accompanied by feelings and 'imagery, taken from past experience, about the likely result of a person's response to the situation'. For example, my fear of and disposition to punish a disruptive child may have had their origins in my early schooling experience, the way I was treated and saw others treated. These images and feelings may have been evoked again during my student teaching by a supervisor's criticism of how I handled a disruptive class. Such feelings and dispositions to act (and these may be contradictory), whatever their sources, remain in a person's consciousness and are likely to be evoked in a future situation often without our awareness. Alfred Schutz, a noted European phenomenologist, uses the concept of 'recipe knowledge' – trustworthy, accepted ways 'of interpreting the world and for handling things and men' [11] to capture those tendencies to act that underlie habituated behaviors.

Though persons may more often respond with recipes when confronted with problematic situations, they also have the capacity to respond reflectively – to examine critically their own recipe knowledge, or to become *'self-conscious'*. As Mead uses the term, *self-consciousness* means awareness of one's own and others' perspectives on our inclinations and actions. Development of this awareness advances our understanding of the possible consequences of alternative courses of action and is therefore requisite to an intelligent choice from alternatives. The systematic, critical search for alternatives, employing logic and evidence, is, in Mead's language, 'minded' or 'reflective' activity. Reflective or scientific thinking is from Mead's perspective an elaborated process of persons adapting, adjusting, attempting to alter the social and physical environment. In his account Mead has extended the Darwinian concept of 'adaptation' to include 'mind' – the capacity of the thinking individual to examine a problem self-consciously from different perspectives and to create novel – heretofore unknown to the individual – solutions. The persons are not merely passive objects in this 'adaptation' but subjects, active changers, creators of their world.

The I, the me and the generalized other

Critical to understanding Mead's view of mind or consciousness are three metaphors: the *I*, the *me* and the *generalized other*. The *I* is a biologic *I*, an acting organism, the initiator of solutions to environmental circumstances and problems. The *me* may be construed as the process of viewing oneself as an *object* in the environment. To view oneself as 'object' is to see oneself from the point of view of another. The root idea of the *me* may be exemplified by the teacher in a classroom who stops in mid-sentence and thinks to herself, 'No, that's not what I meant to say', indicating that she hears herself as others hear her, or, in other words, sees and hears herself as an object. She (as subject or acting *I*) may reformulate what she has said based on what she heard herself say (or was about to say). One's overt behavior – that which may be seen or heard by another – from a Meadian perspective is only a portion of an act. The entire act includes a *continuous* reflexivity or dialectic 'within' the individual, between the *I* and the *me* or the many *mes* – the various alternative perspectives on one's action one has incorporated knowingly or unwittingly from one's experience.[12] This thinking or 'minding' process may precede, proceed reflexively with, or follow overt action.

The *me* metaphor represents persons' ability to see themselves from the point of view of another. However, the perspectives of other persons may become *generalized*: thus, one's own and others' behavior may be seen not only from the point of view of *particular* others, but in terms of *generalized* and *abstracted* norms, values, beliefs, etc. of groups of others. These generalized perspectives may include sex-role norms, political values, implicit and explicit norms of doing scholarly work in a specialized area, generally accepted standards of beauty, worthwhile knowledge and justice. The *generalized other* then represents the constraints and possibilities of our own culture and the cultures of past and contemporary others that, through social experience, direct and vicarious (reading, for example) become part of each of us. Individuals, though bound by their *generalized others*, may seek to enlarge their accepted perspectives on themselves and their society.

Social continuity

How is it that the basic form and structure of a society and the attitudes, norms and values of persons living in it come to resemble those of prior generations? These questions are formulations of the problem that the social, political and historical sciences are, in the final analysis, designed to solve – the mystery of social and cultural transmission and change. In the following passage Mead shows how the *generalized other* explains social continuity – the shaping of individual behavior by society.

Only insofar as he takes the attitudes of the organized social group to which he belongs towards the organized co-operative social activity or set of activities in which that group . . . is engaged does he develop a complete self . . . and on the other hand, the complex co-operative processes and activities and institutional functionings of organized human society are also possible only insofar as every individual involved in them or belonging to that society can take the general attitudes of all other individuals with reference to . . . the organized social whole . . . and can direct his own behavior accordingly. It is in the form of the generalized other that the social process influences the behavior of the individuals involved in it and carrying it on, i.e., that the community exercises control over the conduct of its individual members; for it is in this form that the social process or community enters as a determining factor in the individual's thinking.[13]

The act

The concept of the act is the central epistemological concept in Mead's social behaviorism and in our dilemma language. The concept is a deceptively simple one. In order fully to comprehend its implications, we had to struggle with the separation in our own thought, and in western society generally, of theory from practice; thought from feeling; ideas from action. Mead's efforts to overcome such dualism is represented in his concept of 'act'.

The unit of existence is the act, not the moment, the organism adapting and interacting in the environment. (W)ithin [the act] there is nothing [but] successive phases. There are no static elements. There are things that do not change although they pass. These are but two sides of the same situation, at least in the world that is there. There is no thing that does not change except insofar as it passes, and there is no passage, except over against that which does not change. Motion, or change of position, is a change of that which in certain respects remains without change, while change of quality involves that whose substantial character remains unchanged – but neither takes place except in passage. Abstractive thought isolates phases of the world that is there.[14]

The opacity of this passage disappears if one reorients one's view from a world of objects to a world of continuous transformations. From the Meadian standpoint, to say an act has a history and consequences is distorting. *The act is a process* that includes its history and is continuous with its future. The act includes what in our common language we call the *psychical* or *subjective*, as well as what we call *objective* or *real* forces that are, have been, and persons anticipate will be, in the situation. Overt behavior for Mead represents the observable 'phase' of the entire activity.[15] The entire act includes all our attitudes or dispositions to behave that may be evoked by our present experience in the situation. Feelings and images from the past about the likely consequences of alternative actions are also part of the act. These images and feelings are not always, indeed, they may be rarely, within a person's awareness.[16] From the perspective of Mead's social behaviorism the observable – the recordable conversations and events – are wed to the subjective (or to our consciousness) and to the context or situation, all of which are in a state of continuous change.

To summarize, the concept of the act rests upon Mead's conception of person as a conscious being who is simultaneously an object, acted upon, and a subject, an initiator of action. The act itself is a continuous dialectical process of homo sapiens adapting. The objective reality (the head teacher's (principal's) real or implied threats or promises, the size of the classroom, number of disruptive and hostile children) is 'in' the act, as are the history of the actor, the history of his culture, and images of possible futures that are in one's consciousness. Thus, past, present, future intersect in the moment – as persons act in situations. The concept of act as used by Mead represents these intersections. The objective forces and other persons we encounter in the world are real; for Mead the social world does not reduce to subjective states of mind. (The fact that we may be deluded, may have delusions, is significant but not our concern here.) The realities – the objective circumstances that are forming or have formed and been informed by our encounters with the world – be they known, unknown or partly known to us are 'within' the act. These realities, past and present constraints and opportunities, shape – though they do not determine – the future.

Social activity and the development of the generalized other

Meaning

The capacity of individuals to see themselves as objects, as others see them – to stand outside of self – is necessary for the process of reflective or critical – as opposed to an habituated – adjustment of persons to their social and physical environment. How does this critical capacity develop? 'The central factor', Mead argues, 'in

117

adjustment of individuals to environment is "meaning". *Meaning arises and lies within the field of the relation between the gesture of a given organism and the subsequent behavior of this organism as indicated to another human organism by that gesture.'* [17] In other words, if a gesture suggests to an observer (any observer, not necessarily the one to whom the gesture is addressed; a social scientist, for example, sitting in a classroom), what another organism, human or sub-human, may be going to do or say, then the gesture has meaning.[18] The growl of a dog prior to attack *means* imminent attack, the expression *au secours* prior to drowning *means* 'I am in trouble', even if the person or animal to whom the gesture is directed does not hear or comprehend the words. An observer of dogs or drowning Frenchmen may infer the meaning of the verbal or non-verbal gesture from observing the relationship of the organism's gesture to its subsequent behavior.[19] These examples indicate that the capacity for taking meaning is shared by humans and animals and need not involve use of language.

It is not necessary for the acting animal, human or not, to have an idea in order to say the gesture has meaning. The meaning 'of a human or animal gesture is *not* a process going on in the mind . . . *it is an external, overt, physical or physiological process going on in the actual field of social experience'* [20] that may be inferred by partici pants or observers in a social situation.

Significant, non-significant gestures and self-consciousness

I thumb my nose at my friend; she laughs; the meaning of that gesture *to my friend* is manifest by her response, her laughter. The nose thumbing and dog growling clarify the distinction Mead makes between significant and non-significant gestures. When I thumb my nose, it can be said I have an idea 'in mind', and I assume that others to whom it is directed and any observers will take meaning from my gesture (though it may or may not be the meaning I intended). What is crucial to the concept of *significant* gesture is that I, the actor, had an idea in mind when I gestured, and that the gesture had the capacity to arouse the same idea in my friend as I had in mind when I made it (though it may not succeed). The growling dog likely had no 'idea' in mind when he growled, nor necessarily any 'idea' the other dog would respond to the growl. Thus, the growl is a non-significant gesture.[21] When I say to myself, 'If I use the word 'Negro' many of my Black listeners will likely discount what I say, or if I wear a swastika on my arm I will provoke trouble', I am self-conscious of my own (significant) gestures; that is, I am able to see or hear them as would others, though I may be mistaken, of course. To become increasingly self-conscious is to become increasingly aware of the meanings that others in the society or in other cultures and historical epochs, take or would take from one's gestures; to enlarge one's understanding of how one's own experience is seen from the perspective of others. To Mead, developing self-consciousness[22] makes possible the adjustment of individual and group to one another, that is the development of cooperative activity or social life.[23]

Language is a form of significant gesture[24] that enables persons to evoke in themselves and others meanings that non-verbal gestures cannot transmit.[25] Though animals other than humans may conceivably make significant gestures, the elaborated language of humans changes qualitatively the order of complexity in such communication.

Its importance, then, is that language is capable of facilitating cooperative activity. 'It [a language gesture] calls out [or increases the possibility of calling out] in the individual making [it] the same attitude towards [a social act]... that it calls out in the other individuals participating with him. This makes the speaker conscious of their [others'] attitude towards it... and enables him to adjust his subsequent behavior to theirs in the light of that attitude.' [26] For Mead, thinking is an 'internal conversation of gestures' which is greatly extended through the use of language. Thus, it is language or communication that enables persons to *shape the conditions of their own adaptations to the environment.*

Only in terms of gestures as significant symbols is the existence of mind or intelligence possible; for only in terms of gestures which are significant symbols can thinking – which is internalized or implicit conversation of the individual with himself by means of such gestures – take place. The internalization... of the external conversations of gestures which we carry on with other individuals in the social process is the essence of thinking. This capacity gives humans the power of adapting to and also altering the social and physical environment. Man is constrained, as are other creatures, by the existing social and physical arrangements but in homo sapiens there exists not only the capacity for alteration of the existing constraints of his physical environment – wild animals do that – but of imagining a future and attempting to avoid or achieve that image.[27]

Language and other significant gestures make it possible for individuals to view themselves as do others, specific and generalized others – in and out of the individual's immediate social community – and to 'adjust' their responses. By 'adjust', however, Mead clearly does not mean uncritical acceptance of others' perspectives.

119

Marxist and Meadian dialectics

Mead's 'social behaviorism' lays the groundwork for a dialectical social psychology that links patterns of individual human behavior, human consciousness and society. Geoffrey Esland summarizes the Meadian conception of dialectic as follows:

> Meadian epistemology incorporates a dialectic view of man as world producer as well as a social product. Moreover, not only does this represent the dialectic between self and others, but, also, the inner dialectic which occurs when the individual reflects on his actions.[28]

Although he explored a great many questions, Mead did not provide a critique of society and history, nor show how prevailing forms of social, political and cultural life are the product of historical developments. Thus, although he set out a basis for linking individual consciousness and social structure, he could not provide an account of how consciousness is related to particular forms of social life and culture, and the place individual and collective action may play in changing society's history.

Marx, like Mead, was a naturalist who contended that there is nothing supernatural about persons, what they experience, the societies and cultures in which they live. Both sought to provide an account of man in society that overcomes philosophical idealism and the dualism of mind/body, subject/object, ideal/real, theoretical/practical. Marx, however, did not develop the conceptual links between individual consciousness and society. Mead's social behaviorism, as extended, modified and clarified by scholars within the Critical Marxist tradition,[29] provides the connections between historical forces, social and cultural structures and forms, and the alternatives persons perceive, act upon (or might create) in given situations.[30]

Dialectical materialism

Central to an understanding of Marxist dialectics is the recognition of the crucial role that particular forms of economic production play in human history.[31] For Marx, the central feature of the productive process prevailing in capitalist societies is that labor has become a commodity that is sold for someone else's use and profit. Norms, laws, social forms, morals, all cultural and social relations have a complex and problematic, but undeniably strong relationship to this motor force of capitalism.[32] Persons are not, however, mere objects shaped by economic forces and structures. Like Mead, Marx portrays human beings as both autonomous actors who have the potential to shape history, and as objects whose thought and action are shaped by forces they are often unable to control or even understand.[33] Marx's version of the 'I' is *hoo faber*, man as producer and creator of the circumstances of his own existence. The capacity of persons to become self-conscious – to see themselves and the existing institutions from the perspectives of other epochs and social arrangements – enables them to transcend rather than to be merely driven by history. Conscious creative activity is limited by prevailing social arrangements, but human actions and institutional forms are not mere reflections of them. Thus, the familiar aphorism from Marx: 'Men make their own history, but they do not make it just as they please; they [do so] . . . under circumstances directly found, given and transmitted from the past.'[34] The process of society transforming itself is, then, conceived as a dialectic wherein the individual (*homo faber*), possessing a creative self (or an 'I' in Mead's language), though 'conditioned and limited . . . like plants and animals',[35] is also an '*active* natural being' who has the power to rearrange social conditions. As Georg Lukács puts it, ' [in the Marxist notion of dialectic] the most essential interaction [is] *the dialectical relation of subject and object in the process of history*.'[36] 'Fatalism [determinism] and volunteerism [free will] are only contradictory in a non dialectic, non historic perspective.'[37]

Shaping of consciousness: ideology and hegemony

Though the experience of living in a society may not *determine* what people believe (and do) it affects their images of what is true, desirable and possible. The prevailing cultural forces push in the direction of justifying and legitimating the privileges of those who presently control the means of production. The term 'ideology' is used by Marxists to refer to the 'relatively formal and articulate system of meanings, values, beliefs'[38] that legitimate and justify culture and society as it is. Ideologies from this perspective portray existing social arrangements as given, as inevitable, that is, the result of forces or factors beyond human control, and as benefiting everyone by casting the interests of dominant groups as congruent with the public interest (for example, what's good for General Motors is good for the country).[39] Ideologies present particular forms of work and human preoccupations as more valuable and deserving of greater status and economic reward than others; persons who engage in these socially and economically rewarded occupations as generally, if not always, meriting their superior place and the political power that accompanies it because of their greater skill, intellect or drive; work as unable to be satisfying and meaningful for all persons.[40]

Such beliefs, cast by ideologies as plausible, true or as self-evident, are in part mere illusions that maintain the existing structures of political, economic, social and cultural life and the accompanying inequalities of regard and power among persons.[41] Moreover, ' [w]hile ideologies serve the interests of dominant groups, they also have some grounding in reality. . . . This helps explain why they can become taken for granted.'[42]

The concept *hegemony* as commonly used in Marxist analyses refers to the *lived* system of social relations rationalized by the relatively formal system of beliefs and meanings represented in the ideology of a society. Hegemony refers to the 'whole body of practices and expectations . . . a *lived system of meanings and values . . .* which has also to be seen as *the lived dominance and subordination of particular classes'*.[43] 'It is lived to such a depth . . . saturates the society to such an extent [that it] . . . even constitutes the limit of common sense for most people under its sway.' [44] Hegemony is then not only the articulated beliefs represented by the 'ideology',[45] but the lived relations, taken as legitimate and given, which are justified by and serve to maintain the ideology.

Social and cultural change – counter and alternative hegemonies

If the 'hegemony' of a given social order is so powerful, how then can social change occur? Answering this question has been a major preoccupation of the several contending Marxist schools. The basic premise of Marxism of the nineteenth century was that the contradiction between wage labor and capital would lead inexorably to a proletarian revolution.[46] Though Marx laid out the idea that social transformations have their origins in the transformation of consciousness, he never systematically developed what today we would call a social psychology, that is, an account of how social experience shapes human consciousness and of the relationship of human consciousness to human agency – the willingness and capacity of persons to control the circumstances of their own lives – which includes of course engaging in the intentional process of social transformation. Several Marxist Critical social theorists address this question of the relationship between consciousness, including human agency, and social and cultural transformation (for example, Georg Lukacs, Antonio Gramsci, members of the Frankfurt School of Critical

Marxism, most notably Max Horkheimer, Theodor Adorno, Herbert Marcuse, and Jürgen Habermas). We weave in the next several pages a loose argument drawn from these sources, linking consciousness to social change using the concept of hegemony which, in our view, clarifies and elaborates Mead's most significant but problematic concept of the 'generalized other'.

Hegemony is 'continually resisted, limited, altered. . . . It is never either total or exclusive, (and) counter-hegemony and alternative hegemony . . . are real and persistent.'[47] In other words, ideas and social structures and relations are not merely reflections of productive forces and economic structures – there is no simple correspondence between the two.[48] Nor do the various institutions – schools, communications, the courts – directly correspond in form or function to one another. Though related to structures of power, each of these institutions has a relative autonomy from the others.[49]

The possibility of overcoming 'false consciousness', or demystifying the social process, that is, coming to question the inevitability and beneficence of prevailing institutions, which is necessary if people are to gain control over their lives,[50] is explained in part by these contradictions between hegemonies, between ideology and reality and between various institutions. 'Since complex totalities are comprised of a number of elements and tendencies, these processes may change at different speeds or in incompatible ways, leading to contradictions within the system and ultimately, perhaps, to the transformation of the system.'[51] For example, the capitalist ideology that hard work, individual enterprise and initiative are rewarded independent of social or economic status is contradicted by the reality of limited opportunities to advance, even for those who are, from the point of view of the present social structure, meritorious. As individuals become aware of these sorts of contradictions they may 'penetrate behind the historic conditioning of the facts . . . (no longer) accept them as given . . . [and come to] understand the difference between their immediate appearance and inner core'.[52] In short, though, we all are under the sway of the dominant hegemony, consensus is never complete. Some members of society will respond to the contradictions of society by becoming aware of alternative interpretations of reality. This awareness is requisite to and makes possible minded action and intentional change.[53]

The role intellectuals (teachers, writers, scholars) play in this process is unresolved in Marxist writings.[54] On the one hand, some point out that it is difficult for *non-intellectuals* who are immersed in daily activity to escape their social immediacy, to grasp the dynamics underlying surface appearances. Other theorists see *intellectuals* as hopelessly blinded by their privileged status in capitalist society. One response to this dilemma is 'to construct a dialectical bridge between the extremes',[55] of depending upon the intelligentsia for the raising of consciousness or denying it a role altogether. From this perspective intellectuals play a critical role, thus have some 'directive' function in the raising of consciousness, but in a close organic relationship with non-intellectuals. Professional intellectuals must not separate themselves from the world but guide their efforts in such a way as to erase the distinction between intellectuals and non-intellectuals, thus dispersing widely the intellectual function.[56] Organization and association among non-intellectuals can, however, contribute directly to the raising of consciousness (without the intervention of professional intellectuals). As people come into contact with one another they become aware that their fate is not subjective, particular and contingent, but is shared by others,[57] and flows not from individual situations but from a larger dynamic.

The dilemmas and Meadian and Marxist dialectics

The dilemma language and each of its terms – each dilemma – captures contradictions that are simultaneously in consciousness and in society. The dilemmas may be seen as a way to represent the generalized other, or dominant, alternative and counter-hegemonies that are in the lived situation of teachers as they school children. Mead has been criticized over the years for viewing the *generalized other* as representing consensual or shared attitudes, values and norms, rather than attitudes, values and norms that may conflict with one another.[58] It is not, however, inconsistent with Mead to view the *generalized other* as the internalization of contradictions and conflicts within the culture and the political and social system, as representing not only consensual but alternative possibilities for acting and/or evaluating potential or completed action. The individual, confronting problematic situations that arise within the social and physical environment, is capable of choosing from among the alternatives represented 'in' the generalized other (or more correctly, generalized others), and in so doing be a creator not only a creature of culture.

Each dilemma captures not only the dialectic between alternative views, values, beliefs in persons and in society, but also the dialectic of subject (the acting true 'I') and object (the society and culture that are in us and upon us). It does so by formulating in each *act* both the

124

forces which shape teachers' actions (those forces that press toward particular resolutions to a dilemma) and the capacity of teachers not only to select from alternatives, but to act to create alternatives. Each of the dilemmas thus represents contradictions in the society that reside also in the situation, in the individual, and in the larger society – as they are played out in one form of institutional life, schooling. The dilemma language and approach lays a groundwork for engaging in 'critical inquiries' by providing a means for conducting systematic empirical studies that relate alternative courses of action in particular situations to social and cultural contradictions and the process of social and cultural change. As we shall show in Part Five, the dilemmas can be used by both practitioners and researchers to illuminate the often hidden connections between everyday social experience and broader social and cultural questions. In the next several pages we illustrate the theoretical account of teacher action that we have outlined in the previous pages.

A LANGUAGE OF ACTS: AN ILLUSTRATION

We call the language we developed to represent the schooling process a 'language of schooling acts'. As with any language, the dilemma language brings into focus qualities of experience hidden by our familiar languages. In contrast to many research and everyday languages, the dilemmas focus on the contradictions, the flux and the reflexivity of the social process that are encapsulated in daily encounters of teachers with children in the social setting of the schools.

In the remainder of the chapter we offer an illustration to clarify what we mean by a language of acts. We attempt to show how the terms of the language – the sixteen dilemmas – may be used to represent schooling processes that are in constant flux, and to illuminate the relationship of past, present and future.

We begin with a summary of observations recorded one day in March at Heathbrook and add some quotations selected from conversations and interviews that occurred during the several weeks of our stay.

'We ought to chain it to your desk so you don't lose it again', Mr Scott says to Susan as he hands her a lined composition book to replace the one she lost. Susan's head droops; tears look imminent. Another child, whose eyes catch Susan's, responds with a grin. Susan twists her half-brooding mouth into a half smile and she returns to her chair, new composition book in hand. Several children's heads turn toward the doorway. The Head enters carrying 'work diaries', lined composition books wherein [each child every Friday morning lists the learning tasks completed during the week]. He says a few quiet words to Mr Scott as he hands him the stack of books, looks quickly about the classroom which has become noticeably more silent upon his arrival, and departs. Mr Scott from his vantage point in the middle of the room scans the room, his eyes passing over individuals, pairs and trios, some of whom appear to be working diligently while others every now and again become engaged in intense conversation. His eyes fall on Steven and Bruce moments longer than the rest. These boys, who yesterday had been seated on opposite sides of the room, are today seated together, intently examining one of their football cards, engrossed in what appears from a distance to be a particularly vigorous and extended exchange of ideas, their mathematics work as presented on a set of cards cast aside, temporarily forgotten. Mr Scott leaves his place at the center of the room, approaches Mary, and responding to her request, reads a portion of the story she is writing.

Over the course of the next several weeks Mr Scott tells us a number of things that can be related to the events of the morning. A week before:

Steven, for instance, is a very creative boy and he can't settle down to work; he's got to be left alone before he produces his really best work.

Later:

I separated the football fanatics and they became miserable, so I let them sit together again. I didn't want them to be miserable.

Later:

If I can't interest them in what they're doing, then it becomes a case of them having to do it . . . I don't say that in forty-five minutes a child should spend the first half-hour slugging his guts out and then have a break for fifteen minutes. I just expect at the end of the three-quarters of an hour he will be able to have done what I expect.

Later:

Children realize it [their record book] is going to be looked at either by me or by Ralph [the head]. . . . Ralph is interested in seeing what they've done for the week.

Later:

I have yet to come to terms with myself about what a child should do in, for instance, mathematics. Certainly I feel that children should as far as possible follow their own interests and not be dictated to all the time, but then again . . . I feel pressure from . . . I don't really know how to explain it, but there's something inside you that you've developed over the years which says the children should do this. . . . For example since I've been here I've been annoyed that some children in the fourth year haven't progressed as much as say some less able children in the second year in their maths, because they've obviously been encouraged to get on with their own interests. But I still feel that I've somehow got to press them on with their mathematics.

Mr Bolton, the head, in the course of a long recorded conversation says:

The way I see it is to make sure the teachers know that you've got to have certain standards in the school, that the children get up to those standards that you want them to reach before they go up to [the local comprehensive school]. But at the same time, that must not be all they know of it. Because I think that in addition to sending out children who are good at reading and competent at maths, they've also got to be well-adjusted. But you don't get well-adjusted children unless you get children who are competent at mathematics and reading. . . . Hang-ups come from the fact that they can't read. I think we've also got to provide a place which is pleasant; almost as a refuge from some homes. You almost have to get between some parents and the children.

Later (summarized from field notes):

In the teacher's room Mr Bolton, Mr Scott and the two of us wait for tea water to boil. Mr Bolton tells us of a [radio or television] program discussion of the decline of mathematics standards in the schools and its effects on students' qualifications for university entrance. Mr Scott nods assent and says, 'Yes, there is probably something to that.'

Mr Scott this morning walks past Steven rather than telling him to get back to work. One could view this as a null-event since Mr Scott did not do anything to Steven. However, this 'non-event' stands out for several reasons – because he treats Steven somewhat differently than the others and differently than he did yesterday. It also stands out because Steven isn't doing his maths, and Mr Scott, in word and deed, considers maths an especially important part of the work of school. How can we make sense of this non-event? Had we not spent time in his class nor had some access to Mr Scott's and Mr Bolton's views, we might not have noted that Mr Scott looked at Steven but said nothing, or we may have passed it off as something of which he was not aware. We had no way of knowing by observation alone whether, for example, his non-behavior was studied indifference or benign or even malign neglect. But as Mr Scott tells us about Steven's 'creativity', about the misery of the football fanatics when they were separated from one another, about the press he feels to get the 'fourth years' to progress, as he tells us what in his view lies behind what he did, we discern his response to Steven as part of a pattern. This pattern includes both his bypassing of Steven and his later confrontation of him, and only becomes apparent if we take as hypothesis that Mr Scott has consciousness.

The act, what Mead calls a 'unit of existence', is the fundamental conception on which the dilemma language rests. It includes the observable instances of Mr Scott's behavior, his visions of the future, images from the past, and the circumstances of the present situation (some of which he is aware). To view Mr Scott's schooling behavior in terms of the dilemma language is to see it not as a set of disconnected, contradictory, discrete, situational behaviors, but as a complex pattern of behaviors that are joined together through his consciousness. We have some limited access to his consciousness as he talks to us about what we see him do in his classroom and through our observations of the context in which his behaviors are embedded. The act portrays Mr Scott not only as a mindless reactor to inside or outside forces, social, physical and psychological, but as a person who is and may become critical, in Dewey's and Mead's terms *increasingly* able to engage in reflective action. It appears to us, and apparently to Mr Scott as well, that he at times makes choices, more or less consciously, more or less throughtfully, from among the alternatives as he sees them. This sense of choice is suggested by 'I have yet to come to terms with myself', and as he shares a few of his continuing internal conversations about whether Steven and children generally should be pushed to do mathematics.

As Mr Scott talks to us and as we watch him teach, it becomes apparent that he is responding with some degree of awareness to a wide range of contradictory social experiences and social forces, past and contemporary, both in his classroom, his school and beyond him in the wider community. He has internalized these contradictions and they are now 'within' him, a part of his *generalized other*. We infer these contradictions by observing his behavior and listening to what he says about it — 'something inside you that you've developed over the years which says children should do this' and 'I didn't want them to be miserable' — and from his frequent admissions to us in conversation that he accepts of his own accord the Head's views on standards in mathematics, and also agrees with him that 'children need a haven'.

We represent these contradictions as dilemmas that are 'in' Mr Scott, in his personal and social history, and 'in' the present circumstances (and, as we shall later show, are also fundamental contradictions in the culture and society). These contradictions and the 'internal' or 'mental' weighing of these forces that sometimes occurs are joined in the moment he looks at Steven, then by him, and focuses his attention on Mary.

The act, then, includes Mr Scott on this day looking past Steven pursuing his 'fanatical' interest in football and the internal conversation which precedes it. It also includes a great complex of human behavior, both his own and the behavior of others, past and contemporary, that lives on in his present activity. Implicit in Mr Scott's responses over the course of any period of time are alternatives he perceives that have arisen from previous social experience with others, encounters with his wife, children, friends, former teachers, parents, his present colleagues and superiors, children in his classes now and over the years, and indirect encounters – watching and/or listening to people via the media, or reading fiction, biography and the daily press. The past that is in the present situation includes Mr Bolton returning the record books to Mr Scott on the morning we took observation notes and Mr Scott's reconsideration of Steven's talents and weaknesses only yesterday when he for a moment recalled one of his own painful school experiences during our conversation. The dilemma language captures Mr Scott's activity as social, that is, as connecting past and future – Mr Scott's non-encounter with Steven forever may remain part of Mr Scott's and Steven's social experience to be recalled by one or both in some future present. It also connects individuals to one another – Mr Scott's non-encounter is reflexive – it both affects and is affected by Steven's acts.

The concept of the act is difficult because it ignores a set of distinctions that are taken for granted in both practical and technical language. In addition to unifying thought/action/context, it treats as a dialectical unity what we generally call 'values' (that is, images, vague or explicit, about what are desirable or preferred set of relations among persons and between person and environment), and 'beliefs' (what persons take to be empirically true of the world and what will be the likely consequence of acting in this way or that). It also intentionally bypasses dualisms implicit in our common and scientific languages when we speak of rational v. intuitive, practical v. idealistic, freely chosen v. determined.

As Mr Scott directs Steven back to his mathematics work, what we observe may be the manifestation of a continuous tension within him that includes both 'beliefs' and values; for example he may believe that if Steven (and boys like him) do not 'buckle down' they are destined for second-class citizenship, or that if Mr Bolton, the Head, sees the boys messing about with trading cards during maths, he will lower his estimation of Mr Scott's professional competence – hence influence the recommendation he receives when he applies for a headship to which he has told us he aspires. The dialectic may be said to include what are commonly termed 'values' – his unexamined and frequently expressed commitment to the 'work ethic', the importance of making it in a society which he believes rewards mathematics competence. His may be a carefully or carelessly deliberated 'compromise' between the 'values' of success in a dog-eat-dog world and of the importance of experiencing some pleasure in learning, particularly for children. Both 'beliefs' and 'values' are inextricably interwoven in this act.

The dialectic cannot be said to be a process that is either engaged in freely or shaped entirely by outside circumstances; it is both. Both Mr Scott's 'beliefs' and 'values' have been shaped by social, political and economic circumstances (in Meadian language, taken in as meanings through experiencing the significant gestures of segments of the generalized other with whom over his lifetime he has come into contact). The external realities over which he may have exercised and now can exercise minimal control are 'in' his behavior – the fears of parents of his students about hard times ahead transmitted to him via the Head in the form of increased pressure to improve children's maths performance, the images portrayed on television of what it means to make it in today's society, his own fear that he may not advance, etc. – all may be potent factors in his predictions about the consequences of his acts, and in what he takes to be good or true, whether or not he is conscious of such connections.

Although Mr Scott's perspective on 'getting ahead' may have been profoundly shaped by his history, it may also have been influenced by his *reflections upon* his history, by his self-conscious observations that the competitive and individualistic culture has shaped his teaching but in ways he does not presently approve and will attempt to alter. When we say that persons' behaviors are manifestations of conflicting dispositions or attitudes it is as mistaken to take this to mean that they are the outcome of a deliberate choice between conflicting subjective states of mind, as it is to say the behaviors are determined with or without their awareness, by external economic and social forces or by 'pragmatic' considerations.

The language of acts takes schooling behavior to be determined neither by the 'structure of society' nor by internal states of human consciousness; rather, following Mead and Marx, the relationship between the 'internal' and 'external' dialectical. The dialectic is

130

'within' persons who are simultaneously pawns and originators of action, and between persons and an outside world that at every moment is in them and upon them. The concept *act* brings into focus Mr Scott as a potentially active agent, a person who is capable of processing external experience but is also limited by that experience. The act thus conceptualizes those occasions when Mr Scott, perhaps for the first time, consciously asks himself whether, *in this particular set of circumstances*, he values getting ahead over allowing this child to share his excitement with another child over having located a card of his favorite football player, and for the first time resolves his competing tendencies to act in a way that appears discontinuous with his past behavior.

Patterns of resolutions as patterns of acts

Mr Scott responded to the problem of whether or not to allow Steven to play with his cards on this day by turning a blind eye to Steven's use of morning work time to pursue his football interest rather than his mathematics. However, on the following day, Mr Scott announced to Steven that he must solve correctly a minimum number of maths problems or some future privilege (sports during playtime) that he, the teacher, bestows will be withdrawn. We view this observed alternation as the tail end or the manifest parts of a dialectic, an 'internal' processing (which may proceed 'intuitively', mindlessly or rationally) of diverse and conflicting 'values' and 'beliefs', 'ideals' and 'practical realities', past and present. In terms of our language, the apparently inconsistent behaviors we observe are viewed as alternating modes in a pattern of resolution, to a single (or to multiple) dilemma(s) of schooling. As he goes about teaching at any given moment, Mr Scott is pulled and pushed towards numbers of alternative and apparently contradictory behaviors. One set of alternatives is whether to allow Steven to discuss the football cards – or to chastise the child, or in one way or another remind him that he must complete his maths – but at a given moment Mr Scott cannot both remind and overlook.

In this instance, one pair of conflicting tendencies underlying the observable behavior is, on the one hand, towards allowing Steven to enjoy the present, and on the other, insisting he forgo the pleasures of the present in order to be prepared for the future. Our knowledge of these competing tendencies is taken from what Mr Scott tells us about the variations in patterns of behaviors we observed. We represent this apparent contradiction *in behavior and thought* as a dilemma we label *childhood unique v. childhood continuous*. In abbreviated form, the dilemma captures the pull, on the one hand, towards viewing the early years as a special period in a person's lifetime, qualitatively different from adult periods, and, on the other hand, towards viewing children as people-becoming-adults who must be prepared for that time when they will assume adult responsibilities.

Our research indicated that many of the teachers were self-conscious to some extent of this dilemma and resolved it in ways that could be construed as somewhat unique and creative responses to their past and present social experiences, and with some degree of reflection upon their experiences. This is not, of course, to say that teachers are in every moment conscious of these pulls and reflect upon them at each turn. Some resolutions may be the outcome of conscious reflection that took place immediately prior to the teacher's act, or simultaneously with the act, or at some time earlier in the individual's teaching career and are now habituated behavior.

However, we need not assume that a teacher has ever been aware (self-conscious) of any particular dilemma. A dilemma exists even if nowhere in the individual's past the claim or pull of one horn of the dilemma has 'entered' his or her *generalized other* or consciousness. Although it is likely that teachers will have internalized to some degree the contradictions of the culture represented by the dilemmas, it is possible that some individuals may not have become aware of some of them. In Mead's terms, they have not incorporated these 'others' perspectives into their *generalized other*. In Marxist terms, their consciousness (or some aspect of their consciousness) has not been raised, that is, they do not see that the resolutions they take as given are not given, but are the product of historical forces and represent only one of the possible ways to complete an act. This is what we mean when we say that dilemmas 'exist' whether or not persons are aware of them. Implicit in this position is a modification of Mead in that we see the generalized other as incorporating the contradictions of society and culture.

In our language, a teacher is viewed as an individual who, although he/she may resolve the dilemma passively, mindlessly and habitually, is also capable of reflecting on and evaluating the alternatives and sometimes does so.

If we take a *pattern of resolution* as a unit of analysis, apparently inconsistent or exceptional behaviors are not ignored, but are seen as a part of a dynamic, reflexive *combination of opposites*. A pattern of resolution then, will include behaviors which, though apparently inconsistent with each other, are consistent with one or the other horns of the dilemma. Thus, one may identify the less frequent 'minority' or *exceptional* modes of resolutions as well as the *dominant* or more frequent modes. By characterizing schooling activity in terms of patterns of dominant and exceptional modes of resolutions rather than only in terms of dominant modes, the language can be used to describe some of the complexity and diversity of teachers' schooling activities.

The pattern of alternating opposites does not, however, exhaust the possibilities. Mr Scott need not either bypass Steven or turn him to working his maths cards, although these may be the only alternatives he perceives in that moment. It is possible to conceive of a solution wherein Steven's intense interest in football is joined to Mr Scott's concern that Steven do maths to the teacher's standards, although on this occasion Mr Scott does not construct such a solution. (Nor did we find any teacher who was able to direct junior-aged boys' interest in football-card trading toward maths, though many of them certainly tried.) Such a resolution where the pulls of both poles are joined, we call *transformational* to designate those (rare) instances when the contending presses of the culture at least for the moment are synthesized and thus overcome.

CONCLUSION

The dilemmas are a *language of acts*, a means of representing in language the diverse and apparently contradictory patterns of schooling. Dilemmas do not represent static ideas waiting at bay in the mind, but an unceasing interaction of internal and external forces, a world of continuous transformations. Because they are capable of becoming aware of these internal and external forces that bear on their own *de facto* solutions, persons are capable of altering their own behavioral patterns and/or acting with others in efforts to alter the circumstances in which they act.

Mr Scott's past and present experiences are 'in' his patterns of resolution; he is not only a pawn to these experiences but also an originator of action. Since Steven, like Mr Scott, takes meaning from experiences and may reflect upon them, then Mr Scott's patterns of resolutions may be seen *as both* transmitting and transforming the society. The problem of the relationship between Mr Scott's past and present experience, his patterns of resolution, and the meanings Steven takes from them, is a representation of the problem of the relationship of past to present to future in the social process and is, thus, one way to formulate the question of the role schooling plays in social transmission and transformation. By recognizing *patterns* of resolution, including dominant and more exceptional modes, and viewing teachers' behavior as both determined and free, the dilemma language enables one to consider the relationship of school to society while avoiding the oversimplified, but surely not wholly incorrect, position that schooling merely reproduces the ideas, values and beliefs of those who are most powerful and influential in society. Just as it is a mistake to identify the *I* with social change and the *me* with reproduction, similarly, it is an over-simplification to identify common patterns of resolution with social reproducton and exceptional patterns with social change. The consequences of social activity are often paradoxical – oppressive national or classroom regimes have in their own perverse way contributed to personal liberation and social revolution. Focus on the paradoxical consequences to students of dominant and exceptional patterns of schooling complicates one's analysis considerably, but it is this complexity that is likely crucial to gaining an understanding of how ongoing social life within institutional settings is related to political, economic and social change.

The place of schooling in social change continues to be problematical. We can neither decide in advance that teachers are willing or oblivious henchmen of the social system or creators of social change, nor how important are their activities relative to activities of those within other social institutions. The dilemma language only provides a way of formulating and inquiring into these issues while acknowledging the continuous reflexivity of person and environment as these may be related to change and stability in the social process.

VII THE DILEMMA LANGUAGE

The sixteen dilemmas are intended to serve as a language of inquiry for describing schooling and exploring systematically the origins and consequences of the schooling process upon children, and its contribution to social and cultural reproduction and change. The purpose of such inquiries is practical – to clarify alternative courses of action. This chapter is an exposition of the dilemma language, and Parts Four and Five explore and illustrate its uses.

Though the main business of the schools is shaping students' lives, the form and substance of this control continues to be disputed. Disagreements over how much and what kinds of control reflect the contradiction that, on the one hand, schools are expected to pass on to the younger generation the generally accepted knowledge and ways of knowing of a society – thus insuring continuity of future with past; and, on the other hand, are expected to develop in the younger generations the inclination and ability to deal with changing circumstances – to seek out solutions to problems with knowledge of the generally accepted answers of past generations but not to be limited by them. The dilemmas are intended to formulate the range of tensions 'in' teachers, 'in' the situation and 'in' society, over the nature of control teachers exert over children in school.

We divide the dilemmas into three sets – 'control', 'curriculum' and 'societal'. The four control dilemmas are intended to capture the tensions over *locus* and *extent* of control over students. The contradictions in teachers and situations that underlie the patterns of control (revealed by teachers' resolutions to the control dilemmas) are represented by the twelve remaining dilemmas, which we divide into two sets. The curriculum set is an effort to capture contradictions and controversies over transmission of knowledge, and ways of knowing and learning. The societal dilemmas focus on contradictions in schooling patterns related to equality, justice and social relations between ages, sexes, and ethnic and racial groups. There is no distinct line between the curriculum and societal dilemmas. *Both sets together in some sense explain the tensions in persons and society over the form and content of the patterns of control, and behavioral patterns of a teacher may be viewed through one, several or all the dilemmas simultaneously.*

THE CONTROL DILEMMAS[1]

The four control dilemmas as a set may be used to describe and analyse differences in the locus and extent of classroom control. Patterns of control may be described in terms of teachers' dominant and exceptional patterns of resolution to each of the four control dilemmas, and in terms of their inter-relationships. For all except the first (whole child v. child as student), teachers' behavioral patterns may be compared in terms of the relative predominance of teachers' v. children's control. Because teachers may resolve each of the dilemmas differently for different children, at different times of the day or year, and for different subjects or domains of children's development, there are virtually an infinite number of analyses possible using the control dilemmas as a set or individually. A pattern of resolution at times may not be represented as more or less teacher or child control but as 'transformational' – in the sense that neither the teacher nor the child can be said to be controlling the situation. Control becomes transformed into a qualitatively different form whereby both simultaneously may be said to be exercising control.

Whole child v. child as student – (realms)

Mrs Martin coaxes Mary into the hospital; Mrs Paynter at Castlegate permits children to play at café if they ask; Mrs Carpenter is ready to call the police to fetch Colin; Mrs Newhouse believes Colin's behavior is the school's responsibility; Mr Scott, pleased that Steven has made some friends, allows him to chat about football during '3R' time; Mr Edgar arranges chairs in rows to focus children on their schoolwork rather than upon one another. Mrs Hollins sets aside time during the day to talk to a child who has come to school struggling to repress his tears, but she considers exploration of the sources as beyond her range of responsibility. Mr Carlson requires more maths of the boys than the girls, but pays far more attention to the emotional development of the latter. These variations represent different modes of resolution to the dilemma, whole child–child as student.

This dilemma focuses on the pull, on the one hand, towards taking control over or responsibility for a wide range of *realms* of the child's development, represented as *whole child*; and, on the other hand, towards defining the range of control more narrowly, *child as student*.[2] The whole child emphasis is towards assuming greater responsibility for children's aesthetic, intellectual, physical, social-emotional and moral development. The child as student pull is towards taking responsibility for children's learning of a narrow range of school subjects – focusing primarily on intellectual and cognitive development. Whole child resolutions are often associated with a 'progressive', 'child-centered view', while the child as student emphasis is on a 'subject-centered', more 'traditional' view of the

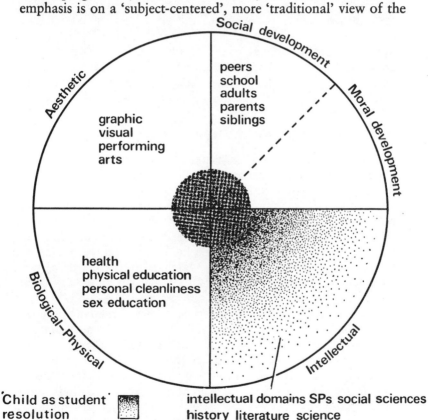

Figure 2 Realms of a student's development

137

teacher's range of responsibility. Advocates of each often portray the alternative view perjoratively; the child as student view has been characterized by its critics as failing to recognize the interrelations of emotional, social and intellectual life of persons, while the whole child emphasis has been characterized by its detractors as overstepping into the private lives of children and/or theirparents.

Figure 2 presents the differing realms of a student's development that distinguish a whole child from a child as student emphasis.[3] The shaded area represents a dominant child as student resolution.

We can compare teachers' patterns of resolution to the whole child –child as student dilemma by analyzing how much time teachers require individuals or groups of children to spend in the various realms, or the quality and quantity of time teachers devote to preparing lessons in, or materials related to, each of the realms.[4] Whether or not and how teachers evaluate children's development in a particular realm, and differences in teachers'/students' control over time and operations in the various realms will reveal teachers' dominant and exceptional pattern of resolutions to this dilemma. How such patterns of resolution may be analyzed will become clearer in the discussion of the remaining control dilemmas.

Teacher v. child control – (time)

Mr Scott assigns roughly ten hours of work per week, and allows children, with exceptions, to schedule their own time during morning work periods – several children who are able to finish their work by Wednesday or Thursday may (within limits) choose what they will do the remaining mornings. Mr Edgar schedules exactly when and for how long children will engage in each curriculum activity, according to a timetable in which he allows children one or two hours of choice each week. Mrs Martin permits children to write their news when and, within limits, to work on it for as long as they wish; Mrs Paynter at Castlegate sets *begin* and *end* times for each child at the writing table. These represent differing modes of resolution to the *time control* dilemma.[5] The dilemma captures the pull, on the one hand, toward teachers controlling when children will begin activities and the duration of the activity and, on the other, towards allowing children to control their own time. An analysis of control over *begin* time for a particular child or group of children, across different subjects, can reveal *if*, *when* and *how frequently* children or particular sets of children have the opportunity to write a story, not according to a timetable, but when they have an idea or thought to communicate, or to do mathematics when they feel their minds are keenest rather than when the clock requires. Control of *begin* time is exerted not only by expecting students to initiate an activity at a particular time (for example, maths, at 10.00; spelling at 10.45, etc.), but also, by a teacher's control of sequence ('do "basics" first, then you may paint', or 'follow the order of activities on the board until you have completed them all'). A teacher may vary her control over *begin* time according to school subject, realm of development, or type of child: Mrs Martin tells Samuel and a few others when to do their news, although she allows most children to arrange the sequence of their own morning activities. The Castlegate teachers specify when each group of children will begin work in the basic subjects as well as activities such as physical education and singing (though exceptions are allowed) – but permit children *begin* control over dramatic play and woodwork. Neither at Port nor Castlegate do teachers schedule time to deal with peer relationships.

Control over duration may be exercised by specifying how long children must work on a particular activity, for example, 'read for forty-five minutes', or requiring they work until the task is completed, for example, 'read until you finish'. Castlegate teachers specify duration in each 'basic' area, but for the most part allow children to exercise control over duration in many of the graphic arts. Mrs Colton specifies *begin* time for all but controls *duration* only for Ian and a few others. Time control may be represented on a matrix using as a unit of analysis a given time frame (day, week, month, year), subject area, or groups of children (see Figure 3).

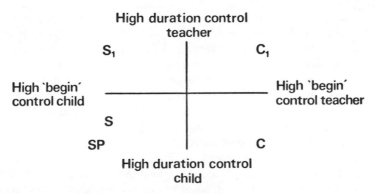

Figure 3 Matrix representing time control

139

In Figure 3, S represents Mr Scott's general pattern of time control in the basics *on any given day* for all children. S_1 represents Mr Scott's control over time in the basics *over the course of a week*. SP represents the dominant pattern of Mr Sprinter by day or week, the one teacher in forty who left many *begin* and *duration* decisions on even the basic subjects to the children. C represents Mrs Colton's general pattern of controlling begin time in the 3Rs but leaving duration to children, while C_1 represents her exceptional pattern for Ian.

Teacher v. child control – (operations)

Mr Carlson permits the children to choose from a wide range of art media for projects on the topic 'water'; Mrs Paynter specifies how the children are to fashion Easter bunny cards, using teacher-made cut-out forms and a limited set of colors in a given sequence. Mrs Martin shows each child how to cut out snowflakes but allows Samuel to cut as he wishes. Mr Sprinter allows children to spend time browsing through books or comic books of their choice, Mr Scott requires some – Mr Edgar virtually all – reading time to be spent answering questions on 'SRA' or 'Ladybird' cards *in prescribed order*. Teachers at Highrock rigorously enforce particular forms of 'good manners' (children are chastised publicly if they forget 'Please, Miss', 'Yes, Miss') – while Castlegate teachers set and enforce a few very general rules for how children should address adults, and even then permit exceptions. These differences in degrees of specification are conceptualized by the *operations control* dilemma.

This dilemma captures the pull, on the one hand, towards the teacher exerting detailed and specific control over how children are to behave in the various curricular domains (that is, within particular realms of development) and, on the other hand, towards allowing children to exercise control over their behavior. 'Programmed learning', and most forms of 'behavioral management', in theory at least, represent the most extreme forms of control over operations, with students granted virtually no control over what is to be learned, how it is to be learned, or how much one must do. 'Complete as many as you like' and 'I don't care how you do it, as long as you get the right answer' represent the other extreme.

Teachers' control of time and operations *taken together* determine students' work rate. One could describe relative differences in control of work rate – in all subjects or in one subject relative to others, for one child or group of children as compared to others – by

140

analyzing and comparing their patterns of resolution to the *time* and *operations* dilemmas.

Teacher v. child control – (standards)

Mrs Newhouse monitors weekly the number of pages of mathematics each child has completed. Mr Sprinter sets no requirements for how much maths a child should do. Mr Scott gives speed tests of multiplication tables, but for a while allowed Steven to avoid maths. Mrs Martin gives Cheryl her first 'normal' reader only after she has mastered the requisite sight vocabulary, but encourages every child to use the easels and paints. She tells David he could do better on his news, but ignores another's obviously erroneous understanding of X-ray. These behaviors are manifestations of teachers' responses to cross-pulls in themselves and in society toward teachers controlling standards and towards allowing children to control standards themselves. A distinction may be made between who *sets* and who *maintains* or monitors standards. Mrs Martin has set as one of the standards for a good painting 'filling in the paper', but she very rarely monitors whether the child has successfully met the standard.

The setting of standards and monitoring of students' performance in terms of these standards is one of the most powerful means of control in school settings. In attempting to represent a teacher's pattern of control over *time, operations* and *realms* of development, one must therefore also look at the locus of standards' control. Use of the standard dilemma brings into relief an often subtle but powerful way that teachers or other school authorities exert control over time, operations and some realms of children's development. A teacher may control how a child does a task not by specifying operations or directly controlling time but by the monitoring of standards of performance. We see this in Mr Scott's classroom. Children would appear to have greater control over time and operation than they actually do if one failed to take into account the Headmaster's inspections of the record books.

By examining the locus of control over standards, one can also identify contradictions in control patterns within classrooms. For example, a teacher may tell children they may write any sort of story they please, but grade them according to her implicit standards of a 'good' story. A teacher may apparently exert little *begin* and *duration* control, but students' time may be tightly controlled by virtue of the schedule of examinations.

141

USING THE CONTROL DILEMMAS AS A SET

The four control dilemmas can focus narrowly or broadly depending upon the practical or research question one is asking. For example, a broad or general representation of the relative amounts of control over children is achieved by charting teachers' operation control against their resolutions to the realm dilemma as in Figure 4.

Point T represents the teacher who assumes responsibility for a limited range of realms – perhaps only the academic – and controls the operations in these realms quite tightly – the American 'school marm' and English schoolmaster stereotypes. Point P is the stereotypical progressive-informal classroom teacher – concerned with virtually all realms of the child's development, but with very loose prescription of tasks. (As our portrayal of the schools in Part Two reveals, none of the more formal or informal teachers fits these stereotypes.) Point M represents an informal teacher like Mrs Martin, who exerted relatively greater control over several realms beyond the intellectual (greater whole child emphasis), greater control over operations in the 3Rs, and over standards of performance than did the more formal teachers, who, like Mr Edgar are rep-

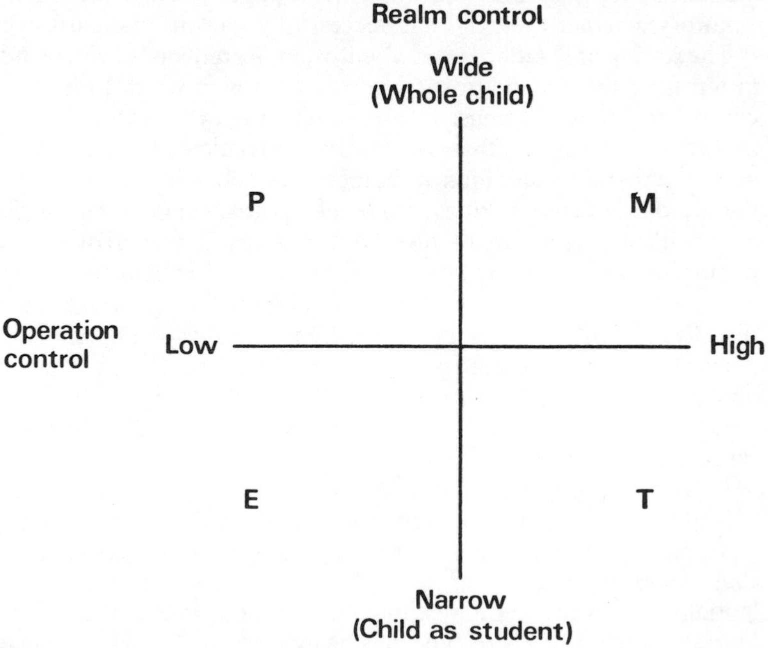

Realm control

**Wide
(Whole child)**

P   M

**Operation
control**   Low ——————————————— High

E   T

**Narrow
(Child as student)**

Figure 4 Degrees of control over realms/operations

142

resented by point E. Although he maintained tighter control over time and duration, he exerted relatively little operation control, and took more limited responsibility for realms of development beyond the narrowly intellectual.

The four control dilemmas may be used to make more limited comparisons among individual teachers or sets of teachers. For example, Figure 5 represents a comparison of two teachers' patterns of control in two subject areas.

Here E represents a teacher like Mrs Eden whose dominant resolutions in the language curriculum area focus rather widely on several aspects of children's language development (oral reading, writing, comprehension, vocabulary development) with relatively close attention to operations in each. E_1 represents Mrs Eden's patterns in the art curriculum where she focuses almost entirely on graphic art with relatively little attention to operation controls. B represents a teacher (in the classroom adjacent to Mr Sprinter's) whose attempts to deal with aspects of children's language development is as broad as Mrs Eden's but who is entirely *laissez-faire* in terms of operation control. B_1 represents this same teacher's resolution in art – a relatively broad conception of artistic development, but relatively little control of operations. These comparisons are merely suggestive.

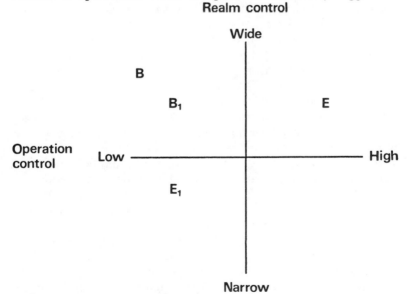

Figure 5 Representation of two teachers' realm and operational control in language and art curriculum

They point to the ways teachers' control patterns may be compared using combinations of several control dilemmas.

THE CURRICULUM DILEMMAS

All social groups pass on to the younger generations ways of looking and thinking that assure some continuity with the forms of cultural life of the group. The curriculum dilemmas together provide a way of inquiring into how teachers through their schooling acts transmit knowledge and ways of knowing and learning.

Personal knowledge v. public knowledge

Mrs Hollins devotes a significant proportion of her time to encouraging children to read for pleasure; remedial reading at Castlegate is, however, primarily a process of memorizing words. A boy in Mrs Martin's class grasps the meaning of measurement as he and the teacher together fit a wheel to his cardboard lorry. Children do 'topic work' by copying, with minor changes, sentences from an encyclopedia. A teacher at Highrock accepts successful completion of maths workbook pages as demonstration of a child's ability to count with coins and make change. Miss Gault asks the child to make change with play money. A teacher spends a week setting up a 'simulated' government as part of a unit on politics, while another spends several weeks 'covering' the political theories of Plato and Hobbes. A teacher overlooks questions a child asks about the discrepancy between her own experience in her family and the definition of 'nuclear' family she has been asked to commit to memory from a school text.[6] A teacher expects children to memorize the dates of the Crusades, although the children have no understanding of the meaning of these events, the persons involved, nor of the relationship of these events to their own lives. In one teacher-education program, knowledge of Dewey's social and educational philosophy is deemed essential. In another program knowledge of any particular philosopher is seen as expendable. These reveal differing emphases in resolutions to the *personal–public knowledge* dilemma.[7]

This dilemma represents, in its most general form, a cleavage in the western tradition over what is worthwhile and adequate knowledge. On the one hand, teachers are drawn towards the position that worthwhile knowledge consists of the accumulated traditions of the ages, traditions which have a value external to and independent of the knower. On the other hand, teachers are drawn towards the position that the value of knowledge is established through its relationship to the knower. For some teachers in the United States in the 1960s the 'romantic' educational writers and reformers (Carl Rogers, George Dennison, John Holt, A.S. Neill) provided a rationale for the press toward *personal knowledge*.[8] The present call for 'back to the basics' represents a movement toward a particular conception of *public knowledge*.

From the *public knowledge* perspective a body of information, skills, perspectives, facts, ways of knowing is valued because it is accepted within the traditions of knowledge, that is, it has received some degree of acceptance using 'public principles that stand as impersonal standards to which both teacher and learner must give their allegiance'. Public knowledge may be seen as composed of traditions of knowledge which have stood the test of time.[9] An educated person, from this perspective, is one who has been schooled and certified by persons who have themselves demonstrated mastery of such knowledge and who hold credentials as educated persons in that particular tradition.[10] Thus, the value one places on public knowledge would in theory at least be related to how much control one believes students should be accorded over what is learned.[11]

The emphasis on public knowledge is perhaps best exemplified by the humanist who holds that understanding the cultural heritage – the classical traditions and bodies of knowledge in the arts, sciences and humanities – is essential to the process of individual learning and growth. At its worst this position is seen as a 'sabre tooth' curriculum – learning of outmoded and irrelevant content and methods.[12] In both its ideal and corrupted versions, however, there are assumed to be bodies of knowledge and ways of knowing to be mastered by students whether or not at any given moment they perceive the relevance to their present concerns. Implicit in the more extreme public knowledge emphasis is a view of learning as a process of reception.

Implicit in the *personal knowledge* emphasis is a view that worthwhileness of knowledge cannot be judged apart from its relationship to the knower. Knowledge is useful and significant only in so far as it enables persons to make sense of experience. Personal knowledge is gained from the 'inside'. To know in this sense has the connotation of *Verstehen* or holistic understanding. 'Street sense', a familiar way of talking about personal knowledge, has all these connotations.

As with the other dilemmas, teachers are drawn in both directions simultaneously. Public knowledge modes of resolution are common in the schools. Occasionally one finds shifts to personal knowledge modes unaccompanied by any attempt to relate that knowledge to public knowledge, as when Mr Edgar stops briefly in the midst of his lesson on France and notes a child's interest in her French costume doll, then as quickly shifts back to a public knowledge mode.

When a child struggles to represent his own experience in his news, when the boys in Mr Sprinter's class utilize a book on transportation to help them build their cable-car system, they are fusing or joining personal with public knowledge, and the teacher may be said to have set the conditions for resolutions to this dilemma that are transformational. Dewey's argument to reject 'knowledge of the past as the *end* of education and . . . emphasize its importance as a means . . . (as) a potent agent in appreciation of the living present' [13] is an argument for the transformational mode – a wedding of personal and public knowledge.

If children experience public knowledge resolutions that are divorced from personal knowledge do they learn to respect public knowledge and its purveyors? Or do such patterns of resolution lead students to simultaneously revere and ridicule teachers? Do patterns of resolution that emphasize public knowledge promote social stratification based on educational credentials? [14] Is the personal knowledge of minority children more likely to be ignored in schooling situations than the personal knowledge of 'mainstream' children? (For example, is the personal knowledge of black children in the US, who have spent vacations in rural areas of the South, discounted by teachers who claim 'these children never go anywhere'?) Do teachers in particular classrooms or educational institutions reserve or emphasize certain sorts of public knowledge for boys over girls, children of particular social backgrounds, race, or presumed intellectual abilities? We return to such questions in Part Four.

Knowledge as content v. knowledge as process

Mr Edgar asks specific factual questions about France; Mrs Newhouse asks questions of the sort: 'How do you know that? How could we find out?' Children doing 'topic' copy with minor changes sentences from the encyclopedia; in Mr Sprinter's class several boys figure out how to use a pulley to transport weights. One teacher's astronomy unit focuses on children learning significant names, facts, generalizations, concepts (for example, names of planets, Kepler's law, parallax); another teacher's unit focuses on how astronomers gain their knowledge. These are examples of distinctions represented in the *knowledge as content v. knowledge as process* dilemma.[15] This dilemma formulates the pulls toward viewing public knowledge as organized bodies of information, codified facts, theories, generalizations, on the one hand, or as a process of thinking, reasoning and testing used to establish the truth or adequacy of a body of content or set of propositions, on the other. There are in the culture and within and among teachers deep divisions over whether content or substance should take priority over 'skills' or 'critical thinking'.

Within the *knowledge as process* perspective there are alternative definitions of what this process is. A teacher may treat scientific or critical thinking as a process roughly comparable in all disciplines and in practical problem-solving, or may teach modes of inquiry as though they were distinctive to particular domains. Those who emphasize knowledge as content will also have alternative definitions of what sort of content is of most worth. (These alternatives might also be formulated as dilemmas.)[16]

Do teachers reserve some patterns for particular types of children (mechanical maths for 'dull' children, conceptual for the bright ones)? What meanings do children take from patterns of resolution where process is emphasized over content? We suppose that teachers who resolve this dilemma more frequently in knowledge as process modes will not necessarily transmit a critical stance towards the processes themselves, nor towards the knowledge gained through them. Patterns of teaching that may be more closely related to the development of social critics are conceptualized by the dilemma, knowledge as given v. knowledge as problematical to which we now turn.

Knowledge as given v. knowledge as problematical

Mr Edgar asks children to name countries of the 'New World', and he rejects Australia as a correct answer without comment or reason. Mr Bolton accepts 'disobeying your mother' and 'getting cross' as examples of immoral acts but he does not open to question his implicit view of morality. Mr Scott teaches the idea that there are number systems other than the familiar base 10, while Mrs Newhouse takes base 10 for granted in her maths curricula. One teacher presents a definition of social class, a second presents three definitions and asks the students to find the implicit ideas of a good society. One teacher teaches the concept of nation – while another shows that the concept of nation-state as we know it has evolved historically, and ask the children to examine their own ideas of 'Great Britain'.

This dilemma focuses our attention on the pull toward treating knowledge as truth 'out there', and the alternative pull towards treating knowledge as constructed, provisional, tentative, subject to political, cultural and social influences. Geoffrey Esland, writing from the knowledge as problematical perspective, says of 'knowledge as given' that it 'disguises as given a world that has to be continually reinterpreted'. From the knowledge as problematical perspective what is most important is looking critically at what has been taken as given. An emphasis on *problematic* in one's resolutions is reflected in activities and experiences that develop children's creative and critical powers. Implicit in this emphasis is an assumption that persons are capable of creative and critical examination of the world that they take for granted.

There is only a limited emphasis on learning how to criticize culturally accepted truths in *any* society. Jules Henry suggests as reason: 'Man is yet afraid that unchaining the young intellect will cause overthrow and chaos. . . . The function of education has never been to free the mind and the spirit of man but to bind them . . . were young people truly creative the culture would fall apart, for originality by definition is different from what is given and what is given is culture itself.'[18] Patterns that are predominantly *given* would, we suppose, convey unquestioning reverence and respect for the public knowledge transmitted by society through its agents, and ultimately for the society and its institutions as well, while heavily *problematic* patterns would convey a disposition towards criticism and analysis, of culture and society, and encourage creativity. If this is so, how this dilemma is resolved differently for different children and different subjects is of crucial interest to those concerned with how resources of society are differentially allocated by schools. Using this lens one might ask whether the teacher communicates *knowledge as given* to particular racial or socio-economic groups and reveals its problematical nature to only a chosen few as Basil Bernstein, Pierre Bourdieu and others suggest,[19] or whether knowledge in some subjects (economics, sociology, history, geography, for example) is treated as given but in other realms (physical science and art) is treated as more problematical?

Intrinsic v. extrinsic motivation

Mr Scott asks the children to share with each other good books they have read; Mrs Newhouse and Mr Nigel comment on the number of pages each child has completed in maths; Mr Sprinter allows the girls to wander outside among the earwigs for an entire morning, but requires that David sit beside him for several weeks and write. Teachers the world over use praise, rewards, corporal punishment, expulsion from school to motivate students. These are indications of patterns of resolution to the motivation dilemma. The pulls of this dilemma are, on the one hand, toward the position that the impetus for learning comes – and should come – primarily from within and, on the other hand, to the notion that action by the teacher is required for learning to be initiated and sustained by the learner. Positions on the dilemma often take on an ideological cast – the enthusiasts of *extrinsic motivation* (behavior modification, or programmed instruction, for example), being accused of moral opacity as well as failure to understand children, while the critics, the defenders of *intrinsic motivation*, are themselves accused of denying the realities of human nature, the importance of reward and the fact that there are parallels between human and animal learning.

As with the other dilemmas, teachers' resolutions to this dilemma may be examined in terms of resolution to others of the dilemmas. For example, do teachers determine that some realms and forms of knowledge are less interesting (motivating) to children than others (parsing sentences is a bore, experimenting with chemicals is not; solving problems is intrinsically more interesting than memorizing spelling rules)? Do teachers treat particular children or groups of children, as more or less intrinsically motivated ('these kids have no interest')? Do teachers feel it is important that a particular child or group of children be intrinsically motivated in a particular realm of knowledge (it is not important that the girls be intrinsically motivated in sports)? Each resolution to this dilemma, then, involves a value judgment (it is more or less important that children be intrinsically motivated); and an empirical judgment about where the 'flashpoint' is for a given child in a given subject. 'Flashpoint' is a metaphor for the teacher's subjective estimate at any given point in time of how much is required to get children or a given child to want to learn in a given domain. (Little push seen as necessary in a given child assumes a low flashpoint.)

These two sets of judgments – one empirical and the other valuational – are represented on the two-dimensional space in Figure 6. The horizontal axis represents the value (high or low) a teacher places on a particular set of children being intrinsically motivated in a particular subject and the vertical axis represents the teacher's estimate of the flashpoint for those children in that subject. The points in the space refer to a teacher's patterns of motivation that are continuous with the intersection of these judgments. Point A represents a teacher's behavioral pattern of richly 'provisioning' the classroom, that is, arranging the environment with stimulating materials and planning activities in order to make it as likely as possible that the child's interest will become ignited without external push. This is a transformational resolution. B represents the absence of reinforcements or rewards (for example, sweeties, threats) and the absence of provisions for igniting children's interests, since these are seen as unnecessary. Point C represents a popular image of the traditional teacher where there is, like pattern B, little effort expended by the teacher to spark interest, although, in contrast to B, there is much use of extrinsic motivation.

Using this lens we can ask whether teachers are more committed to intrinsic motivation in art than in maths, or for clever children than for 'dull' ones. We can then consider how such differences affect children's interest in maths and art differentially, and differentially stimulate children to control their learning internally, or to become dependent upon external reward.

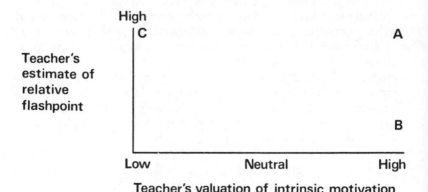

Figure 6 Relative importance of intrinsic/extrinsic learning

Learning is holistic v. learning is molecular

In Mr Scott's' class children read books each day for half an hour; remedial reading with Mr Bolton is reading short paragraphs and answering questions. In Mrs Martin's class children are expected to know letter sounds, and recognize a set of whole words before they are given their normal readers. At Castlegate children learn to make change at the play shop; in Mrs Martin's room by working through a sequenced set of 'shopping cards'. One teaches children to dance by encouraging them to try a movement of several steps and turns without regard for the technical nuance in each movement; another segments the movements, teaches each one and insists upon some mastery before the next is introduced.

The dilemma *molecular v. holistic learning* is a way of analyzing differences in teachers' responses to tensions within them (and in the culture) over how people learn and retain what they have learned. From the *molecular* perspective learning is the taking in and accumulation of discrete parts or pieces; when one has mastered the pieces one knows the whole. Retention of knowledge from this perspective depends on introduction of parts properly divided, sequenced and reinforced. From the *holistic* perspective learning is the active construction of meaning by persons, the understanding of a whole, a process that is in some essential way different from learning a series of parts or elements. People remember better what has been learned because it has 'meaning'.[21]

The root idea of the holistic position is that for learning to occur the student must think, mentally act upon the material, and 'make sense' of the piece (idea, skill) by seeing it in relationship to something already known. Thus, aspects of knowledge are introduced when students are ready to integrate them – in other words, when the students are able to place them in some context. George Dennison in *Lives of Children* describes the necessary fit between what the learner already knows and what is to become known as follows:

They [the students] had known all along in some unstructured way, that devices and illusions [in a film] were passing before their eyes. It needed only a touch to bring this subliminal knowledge to the surface and give it a meaningful form.[22]

Since learning and retention from this perspectice require a 'fit' between what is already known and what is to be learned, teaching may entail a variety of modes depending upon the situation. Concrete experience and play will be important ways of setting up this fit for particular children. Abstraction and verbal communication will promote learning in other instances.

From the molecular perspective a person learns if the teacher breaks down what is to be learned into parts that, if properly sequenced, 'add up' to the entire skill or knowledge. There is no concern that material to be learned be seen as 'meaningful', that is its parts understood in relationship to a whole either before, during or after the learning experience. The fit between what the learner already knows and what is to be learned is not salient. Prior public knowledge is likely to be regarded as more important to learning than personal knowledge, the relevance of which is largely discounted. Finally, motivation is viewed as depending heavily upon extrinsic reinforcement properly regulated.

A strongly molecular pattern of resolution is implicit in virtually all 'basal' programs widely used in US schools.[23] Basal programs, in the form of a graded series of readers and associated workbooks, divide the reading process into a set of component skills (for example, word attack, vocabulary mastery, understanding sequence, making inferences etc.) that presumably add up to reading competence. Through a combination of group and individual instructional activities wherein each of the components is mastered, the child learns to read. Standardized and criterion referenced tests are also based on the same epistemic logic. Thus a *particular* pattern of resolution underlies the presumably morally neutral process of evaluating student achievement.[24] What has come to be called in the UK and North America as the 'language experience' approach to teaching reading, if done according to Hoyle, is, in our terms, a transformational resolution to this dilemma: it insists that taking of meaning (*Verstehen*) virtually always must accompany mastery of molecular skills.

The holistic–molecular dilemma may be used to analyze how teachers or groups of teachers treat children differentially and what are the consequences of such differential treatment. For example, what is the effect of using with poor children programs that have a heavy skill mastery, that is, molecular emphasis.[25]

Each child unique v. children have shared characteristics

All children in Mrs Martin's class follow accordion card set X or Y each day, but they do each task in any sequence, at their own pace; Mrs Paynter's children read individually, but do maths and writing as members of one of three groups and at specified times; Mr Scott's children usually work individually in the basic subjects, though on occasion he will call a few together in groups of shifting membership. In all of the above cases, however, nearly all children go through the same maths and reading sequences though at different speeds. These modes of classroom organization are indications of differing patterns of resolution to the *each child unique v. children have shared characteristics* dilemma.

This dilemma focuses on two contrasting conceptions of how significant are differences among children for selecting knowledge and organizing for teaching and learning. On the one hand, teachers are drawn towards dealing with children in ways that focus upon how they resemble one another. An extreme *shared characteristics* resolution is to take children as sufficiently similar so that everyone in the classroom can be taught the same material in the same way at the same time. A somewhat less extreme resolution is viewing children as sufficiently similar that teachers can prescribe the same curriculum for all children – varying only the pace and standards of performance – as in a Skinnerian type learning program. On the other hand, teachers are drawn towards seeing each child as a unique mix of an infinite number of dimensions, an idiosyncratic configuration of social, intellectual and physical skills, interests, histories, emotions, learning rates and learning styles.

The pull towards *each child unique* can be taken in two ways; first, as a tendency to see each child as a unique 'whole' person who defies categorization, no matter how complex and differentiated the categories. This sense of uniqueness is conceptualized by the *child as person v. child as client* dilemma. The second way is the meaning of uniqueness encapsulated in this dilemma – the learner is seen as a unique combination of a complex and highly differentiated set of attributes. From this perspective teachers see children's uniqueness in terms of their membership in multiple categories.

Two questions may be asked to clarify teachers' patterns of resolution: how many categories does the teacher use to draw distinctions among children, and how many gradations or variations does she use within a category? For example, a teacher who tends toward *shared characteristics* may see reading ability as a unitary trait and see three categories of reading ability: good, fair, poor. An extreme *shared characteristics* perspective may be implicit in treating children stereotypically: grouping children on the basis of assumptions such as 'girls aren't interested in cars', 'blacks are poorly motivated', 'the troublemakers are not very sharp', 'five-year-olds don't know how to read', etc. Teachers with a strong *each child unique* emphasis will make almost as many distinctions in skill or interest on a given dimension as there are children. They will also view 'reading ability' itself, as an array of capacities (for example, not only in terms of a child's ability to respond correctly to comprehension questions, but also in terms of the capacity to discover subtleties of meaning in poetry or fiction, to identify the value judgements implicit in a newspaper story, to read expository material critically, etc.).

An inquiry into how teachers' patterns of resolutions to the each child unique–shared characteristics dilemma relate to resolutions of other dilemmas will clarify how their resolutions to the other dilemmas are patterned. Both the characteristics of children that teachers treat as shared and those that they use to differentiate children in the resolutions to all schooling dilemmas will have consequences for the meanings children take from classroom experience. For example, if teachers resolve the *standards* dilemma by treating black children as more or less alike, but differentiate the whites in terms of a much larger number of categories, this will likely have consequences for the ways children of both races view racial characteristics, and how they regard educational standards as well. If teachers recognize a variety of levels of accomplishment in reading, but treat all (or sub-groups of children) as more or less alike in art, or recognize different learning styles in reading but not in maths, children's views about these activities as well as about themselves and each other are also likely to be affected. Using this dilemma in conjunction with the *distributive* or *corrective* justice dilemmas can reveal how the teachers' patterns of dispensing justice are related to the number and kinds of distinctions they make between children.

Learning is social v. learning is individual

Mr Scott gathers a group of seven together to encourage them to help one another with their maths. Mr Edgar – officially at least – expects children to work alone on 3R work. Mrs Newhouse gathers children around her to share their views of a verse of poetry. Mr Edgar and virtually all the teachers at Highrock arrange the desks so the children all face front. Mrs Martin encourages everyone to become involved in the play hospital. Each child in Castlegate's remedial reading class competes with the others in order to collect the maximum number of vocabulary cards. Groups of boys work together in Mr Sprinter's class to create a motorized cable station.

In one classroom a teacher conducts a group discussion about whether grandparents should live in the house with their children and grandchildren (as they may have recently learned this is a common pattern among many peoples and cultures). In another classroom the teacher pursues the same general subject with a recitation lesson after children have read about the advantages and disadvantages of nuclear and extended families. These behavioral patterns represent differing emphases in resolutions to the *social v. individual learning* dilemma.

The dilemma captures alternative orientations toward how learning proceeds best. From the *individual* perspective learning is a private encounter between child and material or between child and teacher. The ideal ratio of student to teacher, though hardly possible in the real world, is one to one. From the *social* perspective learning proceeds best – most efficiently and effectively – if there is interaction among the persons learning. Involved in the social perspective is often a view of knowledge as socially constructed. Thus the pull toward *learning as social* may be related to whether the teacher views knowledge in the area as *problematical* or *given*.

The *learning as individual* perspective often receives tacit support from administrators and parents concerned with quiet classrooms and with individual rather than team performance in sports and games. The individual learning perspective may also be supported by the ideology of independence, individual initiative and self-reliance. In schools this implies that students 'own' responsibility for their own progress. The press toward the social learning perspective may be buttressed by the value society places on cooperation among peers, a value that may, however, be more often rewarded or at least less often punished in the workplace than at school.[26]

In some socialist societies patterns of resolution in primary schools are apparently heavily learning as social. Rudolf Steiner schools located throughout the western world are also organized to emphasize learning as social resolutions. In both cases the press seems to be the desire to transmit values of cooperation and group responsibility. One would expect teachers' resolutions to this dilemma to affect children's present and future willingness and ability to work together on political, familial or work tasks.

Child as person v. child as client

Mrs Paynter allows children who 'can't think for themselves' to copy 'news' from a storybook; Mrs Martin and Mrs Eden celebrate Julia's birthday with great fanfare; Mr Nigel acknowledges boyish delight at pushing over cans in a supermarket; Highrock teachers bark orders at obedient children; Mrs Martin arranges the afternoon room for her children's pleasure and well being. These behaviors are indications of patterns of resolution to the *child as person–child as client* dilemma. This dilemma captures conflicting orientations within professionals toward those they have contracted to assist. The child as person pull is towards relating to the child as a fellow human being, acknowledging the common bond of humanity between teacher and child. The alternative pull is towards treating the child as a client, as a receiver of professional services – time, energy, knowledge, skills – that fulfill the child's needs. The dilemma speaks to generalized attitudes, dispositions and qualities of interactions that are manifest in how teachers respond to children and arrange the learning environment. The *client* position emphasizes what divides the child from professionals, focusing on the child's 'problems' which require expert diagnosis and treatment. It is this general view that in the social work profession is pejoratively labeled 'clinicalism'. [27] However, it is important to recognize the positive aspect of the client perspective: professionals committed to a dispassionate serving of others without prejudice or favoritism.

Although most of the patterns of teachers we studied and know from firsthand experience are complex combinations of these alternate pulls, it is not uncommon, particularly in schools that serve the poor, for children to be treated as objects,[28] though even here there may be more significant variations than are often acknowledged.[29]

THE SOCIETAL DILEMMAS

The societal dilemmas as a set formulate contradictions that are implicit in the ways children are dealt with in all forms of institutional life including, but not restricted to, schools. The societal set serves to describe differences in resolution with respect to conceptions of childhood, the allocation of resources, the definition and control of deviants, and the relations of 'sub'-groups to the more dominant groups in society.

Childhood continuous v. childhood unique

Mrs Martin provides the play hospital with salves and bandages; Mr Sprinter shares skipping (jump-rope) rhymes with his eleven-year-olds; Mrs Eden checks to make certain the infants have eaten some vegetables before they are allowed to leave; Mrs Hollins sees to it that children have access to a play corner and dressing up clothes in every classroom. Mr Jerrid at Highrock conducts a maths lesson without any concrete objects or apparatus to help children understand the equations. Mr Scott, in spite of a direct question by a child, avoids discussion of a controversial month-long coal miners' strike, though its consequences are clearly evident – the classroom is dark and cold. Mrs Newhouse, in a discussion with a child doing a project on 'Red Indians', raises questions about problems Native Americans experienced a century ago. (In an aside afterwards, she indicates an awareness of the alcoholism and unemployment problems among Native Americans today, but tells us she considers these grim realities an unsuitable subject for third-year juniors.) Mrs Eden, without anger or admonition, asks a five-year-old to clean up the paint he accidentally overturned; another teacher in a similar situation admonishes a child for spilling paint, tells him to 'grow up', that paint is costly. Mrs Eden, in contrast to Mrs Carpenter and Mrs Martin, requires that children complete their maths before spending time at the art easel, water or sand tables. These patterns represent differing emphases in patterns of resolution to the *childhood* dilemma.

The dilemma focuses on two contrasting conceptions of childhood. On the one hand, teachers are drawn to a view of childhood as a special period in a person's life that should be prized and nourished, and a view of children as qualitatively different from adults in the ways they perceive the world, communicate and learn. On the other hand, teachers are drawn towards treating children as persons who differ, not in kind, but only in degree, from adults. Childhood is seen from this perspective as a time of preparation for adult life, for learning what one will need as an adult to cope successfully with the workaday world. As with the other dilemmas, teachers' resolutions are, of course, neither totally in one direction nor the other but a combination of opposites, and are in rare moments transformational.[30]

The distinction between the two poles is perhaps clearer if we recall that 'childhood' is not a state of nature, but an historically-evolved, socially-constructed conception. While there has always been a time in a person's life when physical, mental and social capacities have not equalled their adult forms, views about the length of time required for 'growing up', and the qualities that distinguish the mature from the developing person have varied within and among societies. Whatever may now be considered unique qualities of children, they were not considered sufficiently important in the US and Britain a hundred years ago, to prevent the young from doing 12 or more hours of physical labor every day.[31]

Implicit in the childhood continuous–unique dilemma are conflicting views of how children learn. From the *continuous* perspective, children learn in ways that differ only in degree from those of adults – while from the *unique* perspective children learn in ways

157

that are qualitatively different; for example, they are incapable of learning abstract social concepts (freedom, social class, power) in the absence of direct experience, must have extended and continuous opportunities to manipulate objects in order to understand the meaning of $+$, $-$, $\times$, $\div$, and have a unique capacity to represent thought and feeling in painting and/ or in writing.

Differing conceptions of childhood are also revealed by what teachers select as appropriate for children to learn in school. Teachers are drawn toward selecting knowledge, skills and work attitudes necessary for adulthood; and, on the other hand, towards selecting knowledge that nurtures the creative, intellectual, aesthetic, social, physical development of children whether or not they are instrumental to success in the world of adults.

Differing conceptions of how one should define and treat deviants (see the *Equal justice under law v.* ad hoc *application of the rules* dilemma) are implicit in these two views of childhood. The differences are parallel to these suggested by the previous discussion: from the *continuous* view, obligations and responsibilities resemble those of adults and those who do not fulfill these are considered deviant. From the *unique* perspective, children have responsibilities and obligations that are qualitatively different from those of adults and deviations from adult behavior norms are not treated as grievously.

If respect for the uniqueness of children, their ways of thinking, their interests, is necessary in order to teach them, successfully,[32] and if a disregard for the uniqueness of children, including the capacity to 'play', allows these qualities to atrophy, then differences in teachers' patterns of resolution to this dilemma, and how a single teacher resolves it differently for different children, are important questions. We might inquire, for example, into the differential effects of resolutions that require children to complete their 3R work before they may 'play', what are the consequences upon children who work more slowly of experiencing significantly fewer *childhood unique* resolutions? What are the consequences of very striking differences in resolutions to the *childhood continuous–unique* dilemma we find between American and British teachers or of the abrupt shift in patterns of resolution that apparently occurs between kindergarten and first grade in American schools?

Equal allocation of resources v. differential allocation

Mrs Martin hears every child read every day; Mrs Hollins hears all the second-year infants read once a week and, like Mr Bolton, provides additional 'remedial' tuition for the poorest readers. Mrs Martin allows Elaine to wander on occasion for extended periods of time but keeps close watch over Samuel and the 'newer ones'. A teacher may spend several hours a week organizing mathematics materials for four particularly good mathematics students but does not take similar pains for four potential artists or poets; she may give more time to counseling emotionally troubled children than to those who are behind in maths (or the converse); spend more or less of some discretionary funds on art supplies than on reference books, stimulate 'middle class' or 'clever' children but rarely find time 'to stretch' those who are 'socially backward' or 'dim', suggest to boys more often than girls that they undertake a scientific or engineering project.

These represent variations in patterns of resolution to the *allocation* dilemma. It brings to the fore the continuous problem of the bases for just allocations of school and teacher resources – materials and quantitative and qualitative differences in attention and time. The dilemma represents two contrasting conceptions of *distributive* justice. On the one hand, teachers are pulled towards the view that all children deserve equal shares and, on the other, towards the idea that some students merit more than others. Throughout history the criteria for deciding who deserves more or less of these resources and how much more or less one deserves have been a source of strife. Should the allocation of valued resources be based on individual merit or on the public good? If the criterion is individual merit, should this be defined in terms of native ability, individual effort, history of oppression of a group, or cultural 'disadvantage'? If the criterion is social benefit, should this be defined in quantitative, material terms, or in more 'subjective' terms such as the degree of alienation or satisfaction in one's work?

The pull of the dilemma towards equal allocation is towards the principle that a literally equal allocation is by its very nature fair, in the sense that a child might hold that everyone deserves equal-sized pieces of cake. However, because some persons may begin the 'race of life' with discrepancies in socially and/or financially valued talents (skills and knowledge), the outcome of adherence to the principle of literally equal shares will likely be to preserve existing inequalities. Thus, both *equal* and *differential* allocation may conceivably increase or decrease equality of results in the classroom or in the society.

In order to describe relative differences in patterns of resolution within or among classrooms on this dilemma, we must analyze variations in terms of individuals, and groups of children. Do some groups or individuals experience some types of resolutions to the control, curriculum and the other societal dilemmas more than others? These variations, qualitative and quantitative, in patterns of resolution reveal the *de facto* emphasis in teachers' resolutions to the basic societal conflict over equality. Who receives more? The individuals who are viewed as 'deprived' because of inequities in the treatment they or their parents have received (for example, they are 'poor' or 'immigrants'), or individuals who display certain traits (shy, withdrawn, unusually creative or intelligent children)? Or those who have demonstrated that they will work hard and will take advantage of opportunities (the hard-working, dedicated ones)? Giving more to each of these groups is not only contradictory to the idea of equal share; the giving of 'more' to children in any of these categories conflicts with giving more to those in another. (Teachers, of course, differ on the criteria they use to categorize children as deserving of a greater share of resources. Such differences are conceptualized in the *each child unique v. children have shared characteristics* dilemma.)

The significance of patterns of resolution to this dilemma also lies in *what* resources are being differentially allocated. The resources which teachers control and allocate are many and varied – attention or time, both qualitative and quantitative, and materials are perhaps the most obvious. However, the most significant resources teachers allocate are knowledge, and the quality of the learning experience by which the teacher transmits the knowledge. A teacher may transmit analytic skills and critical literacy (that knowledge is permeable, provisional or *problematical*) differentially – perhaps, as is widely believed, giving more of this valuable resource to the higher social classes, or to a particular sub-set of children from these classes (and in this way controlling the content and distribution of educational and societal opportunities). A teacher may provide more *social learning* experiences to the well-behaved than to the troublemaker, more holistic maths experiences to the boys than to the girls, and may in meting out dispensations take extenuating circumstances into account more often for white children than for black or the reverse.

Finally, an understanding of patterns of resolution to this dilemma requires an analysis of how much extra is given – is it to the point (a) where all individuals or groups at least reach a minimum level of competency (parallel to the minimum-wage idea); (b) until the growth of each keeps pace with that of the others; (c) until all reach approximately equal competency; or (d) to the point where the special skill and talents of the most talented are nurtured (the child who has great potential as a musician realizes his/her potential).[33]

Self-reliance of the economically disadvantaged v. special consideration is a particular case of the allocation dilemma, mentioned separately because of the special place this issue apparently plays in economically developed, western, liberal capitalist economies that presume to operate within the tradition of equality of opportunity. It focuses on the question of how those who are socially or economically disadvantaged relative to others are to be treated. It could be called the 'affirmative action' dilemma and it raises the same questions that have been raised in Britain over the desirability of the policy of establishing Educational Priority Areas, a policy of 'positive or 'reverse' discrimination.[34] The dilemma formulates the cross-pulls on teachers towards having all students, regardless of social position of parents, race, gender, national origin, take personal responsibility for reaching the intellectual and social standards of the culture, and giving special consideration to those who are regarded as victims of social and economic circumstances and previous policies, in order to help them escape the effects of these conditions.

In a society where there is an assumption of equality of opportunity based on merit, teachers are drawn towards the position that extra allocation of resources may be necessary to make equal opportunity a reality for those students whose ability to succeed in school is limited by a history of economic disadvantage or prejudice.

Teachers (or administrators or other policy-makers) allocating more resources to some children rather than others – spending more money on 'remedial' books for poor children, offering more encouragement for girls to engage in sports, choosing the 'best citizens' for a limited number of spaces at a concert, rather than those who have never attended – represent differing emphases in resolution to the *self-reliance v. special consideration* dilemma.

Equal justice under law v. ad hoc application of rules

Mrs Newhouse prevails upon Mrs Carpenter to fetch Colin rather than calling the police; Mr Edgar directs his anger more often at the regular non-participants, although the eager participants are often equally noisy; a teacher may 'keep after school' anyone who arrives late from playtime (or recess) or she may make an exception to the rule for Mary, who has been having trouble at home, or for John, who has been working especially hard at being punctual. Mrs Eden

161

allows one child to go to the Wendy house with work unfinished, yet applies the well-established rule of 'work before you play' to the others.

The dilemma captures a tension implicit in the acts of teachers and others who confront the problems of dealing with transgressions upon the rules and norms of groups – judges as they sentence, foremen as they report or overlook breaches of work rules, parents as they consider whether to exempt a child from a sanction applied to a sibling. On the one hand, there is a pull toward applying equal and uniform sanctions for the same transgressions, no person to be above the law and all exemptions based on public and clearly defined principles. The opposing pull is toward exempting or punishing individuals for idiosyncratic or individual reasons.

The development of the 'equal justice under law' position is often characterized historically as a great advance over the more personalistic means of dispensing justice that frequently made exemptions for the rich and the powerful.[35] This principle of equal justice includes exemptions, but only for publically declared categories, for example the 'temporarily insane', the young, etc. The equal justice emphasis focuses upon enforcing the rules, without regard for what makes an act different for each individual; maintaining common and public standards of justice, with categorical exemptions and predictable sanctions, is seen as the cornerstone of a just moral order. Punishments applied equitably are deemed essential to establish and maintain this order, both for those who are the onlookers and those who have broken the rules (for example, 'the children will get on you if they think you play favorites'). Implicit in the equal justice pull in schools is an assumption that children are just about as capable of following the rules as are adults.

The equal justice position is not, however, an absolute principle of justice in western societies. The pull towards *ad hoc* is similar to the conception of equity in western law. Equity tempers a strictly equal distribution. The pull towards the *ad hoc* position is not towards capricious or unpredictable exemptions. A teacher may be pulled towards *ad hoc* resolutions by her view that her primary role as teacher is to be responsible for the growth and development of each individual. She may also be pulled by a concern for community responsibility and equity, as against an abstract 'legalism' (as when a teacher punishes a child for potentially destructive gossip even though there is no publicly articulated prohibition against it, nor any known consequences).

Teachers' general patterns of resolution to this dilemma and how

162

their patterns differ for some children or groups are of interest because of their potential effects on children's notions of justice. One might consider whether particular sets of children are regularly treated as exceptions or under what circumstances are particular forms of rule-breaking tolerated and sanctioned on an *ad hoc* basis? If *all* children are expected to finish maths work before playtime, does the teacher in fact exempt 'dim' children for failure to do so, but punish them more severely when they speak uncivilly to adults? When girls engage in horseplay are they more frequently than boys treated individualistically? [36]

Common culture v. sub-group consciousness

Mrs Martin allows Samuel, a Jehovah's Witness, to leave her classroom during prayers; another teacher might ask such children if they would like to inform the class about their religious ideals. At Newton, with over 60 per cent immigrant population, no notion of the uniqueness of the several cultures represented is evident in the curriculum, neither in the songs, art projects, fables or literature. In several schools we hear teachers at tea talk about 'English', 'West Indian' and 'Pakistani' children, although virtually all the children to whom they refer were born in England. A teacher tells a Black child that her statement 'her my friend' is improper as written English, while another might read, and encourage children to write stories in Black vernacular English. One teacher omits discussion of the system of Black slavery from a unit on 'Labor in nineteenth- and twentieth-century America' while another includes Black history, buts omits mention of Chicanos (Americans of Mexican descent). A teacher periodically entices boys into the home corner (Wendy house) but when helping boys find books to read, promotes the usual male fare of guns, motorcycles, airplanes, hot rods and rockets. A girl strikes back at another child who has been taunting her and the teacher admonishes, 'girls don't do that sort of thing'. Every year there is the Christmas pageant and public Easter egg hunt, but although Jewish children are exempt, no corresponding celebration of Jewish history and folkways is held. The foregoing represent patterns of resolution to the *common culture v. 'sub'-group consciousness* dilemma.

The dilemma is an effort to capture the tension, on the one hand, towards developing in children a common set of social definitions, symbols, values, views of qualities that 'good' men and women in that culture and/or 'good' citizens of that nation should possess and, on the other, towards developing in children consciousness of themselves as members of a 'sub'-group, distinguished from others, perhaps by distinctive customs, language, dress, history, values and appearance. The movements for teaching Black history and Black culture and instructing Spanish-speaking children in Spanish as well as English represent what appears to be a growing *sub-group consciousness* pull in the United States. Lee and Groper[37] suggests two 'models of cultural' – the cultural difference model, which focuses on the differences between cultures, and the bicultural model, which focuses on the compatibility and overlap between two cultures as well as the differences. The former may be seen as a pattern of resolution that emphasizes sub-group differences. The latter is what we label a transformational pattern.

The centripetal forces – those that press toward a common definition of, for example, a proper English or all-American child – may be parochial (that is, may represent a highly restrictive and highly prescribed view of characteristics and behaviors that members of the group should possess) with deviations seen as heresies, that is, a proper Englishman speaks BBC English; an all-American boy is a 'jock', but never a dancer; the all-Americal girl is 'popular', but never aggressive. However, the common culture may be defined in terms of a more tolerant and universalistic set of ideals.[38] Thus, a common culture perspective in its most parochial forms may ignore and demean a minority and/or oppressed group, a pattern of behavior we might label (and rightly) as racist, sexist, anti-Semitic, xenophobic, etc. However, the more universalistic definition of common culture in a classroom may represent a press toward some common commitments to tolerance, freedom and equality, etc.

CONCLUSION: PUTTING THE DILEMMAS TO WORK

Although the dilemma language, as we have attempted to show, can be used to paint a broad stroke or a fine-grained picture of school life, it is still a pale effort that bypasses the intensities of feelings, pain and joy, anger and frustration, that are part of life's daily dramas at school. The dilemma language is not art – a deficiency it shares with other scientific constructions. However, even within the limits of its own terms, the dilemma language, like other languages, distorts and obscures as well as illuminates. Although if we use each dilemma as a separate lens we can, as we have suggested, portray a teacher's or a group of teachers' behavior and how it changes over time, using each dilemma as a separate lens distorts by fragmenting the integrated flux of classroom life. A teacher's every act signifies multiple meanings to them and to children.

Distorting fragmentation can, however, be reduced and a more holistic and unified portrayal of the teaching process can be constructed if teaching acts are viewed as a simultaneous resolution to multiple dilemmas. We have attempted to show in our exposition of many of the dilemmas how one dilemma may be taken with one or more of the others to trace the contribution of schooling to particular aspects of social reproduction and change. Because of our own central concern with equality we have most often considered how the *equal v. differential allocation* dilemma intersects with resolutions to others. In our language, any given pattern of behavior may be viewed as manifestations of the resolutions to several dilemmas. That some, perhaps most, of this 'coordination' may not be conscious and is rarely the result of coherent or logical plan, does not deny the intelligence and creativity that may be involved in the process. How given patterns of resolution are actually constructed by teachers is an empirical question we have not explored in detail. It is apparent, however, that some dilemmas are far more salient than others for some persons and groups, and their resolutions to these more salient dilemmas appear to influence their patterns of resolution to the others.

Will teachers change their patterns – coordinate and rationalize them more carefully if they become aware of the trade-offs implicit in their classroom behavior; both the trade-offs represented by each dilemma, and of the trade-offs among dilemmas? We focus on this question in Part Five. In Part Four we use dilemmas to analyze the schooling process in the British schools we visited.

NOTES TO PART THREE

Introduction

1 Brian Fay, in *Social Theory and Political Practice* (London: Allen & Unwin, 1975), provides a rationale for the development of a critical social science with which we find ourselves in substantial agreement. He argues that social science explanations must be 'rooted in the self understanding, perceptions and intentions of the actors involved' (p. 96). In this he acknowledges his agreement with the interpretive school. A second feature of critical social science, according to Fay, is that it recognizes 'that a great many actions people perform are caused by social conditions over which they have no control ... [and are] not the result of conscious ... choice' (p. 94). His third feature is that 'it ties its knowledge claims to the satisfaction of human desires and purposes (p. 95). We deal with Fay's first two features in Chapter VI, and the third feature in the introduction to Part Five and in Chapter X.

2 See n. 5, Chapter III.

Chapter VI

1 We draw our interpretations of George Herbert Mead from the following primary sources. *The Works of George Herbert Mead*, Vol. I, *Mind, Self and Society* (Chicago: University of Chicago Press, 1934); Vol. 2, *Movements of Thought in the Nineteenth Century* (Chicago: University of Chicago Press, 1938); Vol. 3, *The Philosophy of the Act* (Chicago: University of Chicago Press, 1936). None of the foregoing were written as a unified book; each was compiled and edited subsequent to Mead's death. The compiler-editors for each of the volumes, Charles W. Morris, Merritt H. Moore, and Charles W. Morris respectively, wrote useful introductions to each volume. For selected papers drawn from the foregoing see Anselm Strauss (ed.), *George Herbert Mead: On Social Psychology* (Chicago: University of Chicago Press, 1956). Other of Mead's writing include *The Philosophy of the Present* (Chicago: Open Court Publishing Co., 1932); 'Scientific method and the moral sciences', *International Journal of Ethics*, 33 (1923), 246. Interpretive works most useful to the writers include D.I. Miller's *George Herbert Mead: Self, Language and the World* (Austin: University of Texas Press, 1973); 'George Herbert Mead: symbolic interaction and social change', *Psychological Record*, 23 (1973), 294–304; Irving Zeitlin, *Rethinking Sociology* (Englewood Cliffs, New Jersey: Prentice-Hall, 1973). Other interpretive works include William H. Desmonde, 'G.H. Mead and Freud: American social psychology and psychoanalysis' in Benjamin Nelson (ed.), *Psychoanalysis and the Future* (New York: National Psychological Association for Psychoanalysis Inc., 1957).

The position in social science known as 'Symbolic Interaction' is often presumed to be synonymous with G.H. Mead's Social Behaviorism. The confusion is due in part to Herbert Blumer, a student of Mead's, who apparently coined the term Symbolic Interaction and who did not distinguish his position from the position he attributes to Mead. See I. Zeitlin, op. cit., pt 5 for a discussion of the significant difference between Mead and Blumer. For a discussion and statement of the symbolic interactionist position, see Herbert Blumer, *Symbolic Interactionism: Perspective and Method* (Englewood Cliffs, New Jersey: Prentice-Hall, 1964); Gregory P. Stone and Harvey A. Farberman (eds.), *Social Psychology Through Symbolic Interaction* (Waltham, Toronto and London: Ginn Blaisdell, 1970); Jerome G. Manis and Bernard N. Meltzer (eds.), *Symbolic Interaction* (rev. edn) (Boston: Allyn Bacon, 1972).

2 See n. 29 below for a short bibliography of our sources.

3 Portraying the social process in terms of 'interacting' categories does not avoid the distortions of western languages because it still reifies processes, conceptualizing social behavior in terms of entities of thought or consciousness, manifest behavior and social context. The passage from Georg Lukács's seminal essay, 'What is orthodox Marxism?', in Georg Lukács, *Marxism and Human Liberation* (New York: Dell, 1973), quoted in n. 37, clarifies this point.

4 David I. Miller, a student of Mead's and, in our view, a consistently reliable interpreter of his work, says it nicely.

Mead was first of all a naturalist. He contended that there is nothing supernatural about man or about what he experiences, and that reasons based on observation and experience can be given for the emergence of mind and for all so-called mental phenomena. The pragmatic thesis that mind and thinking can be explained only in terms of acts of adjustment involving social behavior and physical things acted on is a revolt against both dualism and idealism. [D.I. Miller, op. cit., 1]

5 We do not endorse the neo-Spenserian arguments of Edward O. Wilson, *Sociobiology, the New Synthesis* (Cambridge, Massachusetts: Harvard University Press, 1975). The fact that man is in nature does not mean that an argument from

Darwin depends upon accepting a jungle-like struggle in a state of nature. An argument from Darwin need not lead to a view that the existing social order is in some important measure the consequence of natural evolution and selection – thus, of course, making it quite unnatural, if not impossible, to tamper with the existing structure of society. For a concise overview of the sociobiology debate see C.H. Waddenton's review of Wilson's book in the *New York Review of Books* (7 August 1975).

6 See Miller, op. cit., ch. 1. See also S. Morris Eames, *Pragmatic Naturalism, An Introduction* (Carbondale: Southern Illinois University Press; London and Amsterdam: Feffer & Simon, 1977); Israel Sheffler, *Four Pragmatists: A Critical Introduction to Pierce, James, Mead and Dewey* (New York Humanities Press, 1974). In our view the dialectical aspect of Mead's thought is not accorded sufficient attention by Miller, Sheffler and Eames.

7 Mead places mind in nature in the following passage:

Darwin's hypothesis made it possible to deal with the formation of species in terms of natural causation. All that was needed for this was the hypothesis which Darwin assumed, namely, the infinite variation of young forms, the presence of far more forms than could actually subsist, a condition which brought about competition for existence. This seemed to be all that was necessary in order to account for the formation of the species themselves. Agriculture and the breeding of farm animals and of sport animals had indicated the very great pliability of the forms under the influence of selection. Nature seemed to provide such a selection in the competition for existence. The importance of these points of view . . . is that of the carrying-over of the mechanical sciences into the field of biology. Of course, it left vast stretches which could not be worked out; but it made such an assumption a perfectly legitimate hypothesis for the purposes of research. [George H. Mead, 1936, op. cit., 263]

8 Compressed and edited by the writers from ibid., 345–6, italics added.
9 Mead, 1938, op. cit., 6.
10 ibid., 68.

In so far, then, as the act reaches out beyond the future that is there and employs a revived part, it passes into a realm that is uncertain. Action that employs the past, acquired or inherited, in reducing that uncertainty from the standpoint of the result toward which the act moves, we call 'intelligent' in the most general sense of that word. Such intelligence, which is almost coextensive with life, far exceeds the domain of mind, but it marks the field within which mind operates. Nor is all of human intelligence mental. Not only do our inherited and acquired habits exhibit manners which do not disclose mental operations but a great deal of direct inference lies outside the processes ordinarily termed 'thinking'.

11 A. Schutz, 'The stranger' in A. Brodersew (ed.), *Studies in Social Theory* (The Hague 1964: Martinus Nijhoff), reprinted in Cosin, *et al.*, *School and Society* (London: Open University Press/Routledge & Kegan Paul, 1971).
12 Mead, 1934, op. cit., 152–7.
13 ibid., 155.
14 Mead, 1938, op. cit., 65–6, italics added.
15 Adapted from Morris's introduction to Mead, 1938, op. cit., xvi–xvii.
16 Adapted from Mead, 1938, op. cit., 3–7.
17 Mead, 1934, op. cit., 75–6, italics added.
18 ibid., 76.
19 ibid., 45.
20 ibid., 79, italics added.
21 ibid., 46.

22 Although in Mead's writing self-consciousness is sometimes used interchangeably with consciousness, in the following passage he distinguishes between them:

What we mean by self-consciousness is an awakening in ourselves of the group of attitudes we are arousing in others. It is unfortunate to fuse or mix up consciousness as we ordinarily use that term, and self-consciousness. Consciousness, as frequently used, simply has reference to the field of experience, but self-consciousness refers to the ability to call out in ourselves a set of definite responses which belong to the others of the group. Consciousness and self-consciousness are not on the same level. A man alone has, fortunately or unfortunately, access to his own toothache, but that is not what we mean by self-consciousness.

23 Mead, 1934, op. cit., 254.

24 ibid., 70.

25 Verbal language is not necessarily capable of representing the complexity of the phenomena or relations it attempts to capture. There are an infinite number of factually correct ways a physical object (a tree) or a process (a man walking) can be represented in words. Still, language is a reasonably dependable (though certainly not the only, nor always the best) way of making it possible that others will share ideas, feelings, images we have or had in mind. The reverse may also be true, that is, non-verbal gestures may convey meanings words cannot easily express. Non-verbal gestures (for example, visual arts, music, dance) are not to be taken as inferior to verbal ones, but qualitatively different from other forms of symbolic communication.

26 Mead, 1934, op. cit., 46.

27 ibid., 47. There is nothing in Mead's social psychology, incidentally, which implies human society inevitably will improve and progress. Neither progress nor extinction need to be taken to be inevitable. Mead himself appears to be far more optimistic about achieving social consensus than we are but both his optimism and our pessimism are irrelevant to the adequacy of this account.

28 Geoffrey Esland, 'Teaching and learning as the organization of knowledge' in Michael F.D. Young, Knowledge and Control: New Directions in The Sociology of Education (West Drayton: Collier Macmillan, 1971), 79–80.

29 For a short summary of the distinctions between various schools of Marxism see Brian Fay, Social Theory and Political Practice (London: Allen & Unwin, 1975), 92–3; and Richard P. Applebaum and Harry Chotiner, 'Science, critique, and praxis in Marxist method', Socialist Review, 46: July–August 1979. Our presentation of the Marxist perspective draws upon interpretations of Raymond Williams, Marxism and Literature (Oxford: Oxford University Press, 1977); Martin Jay, The Dialectical Imagination (Boston and Toronto: Little Brown, 1973); Georg Lukacs, Marxism and Human Liberation (New York: Dell, 1973), especially the essay, 'What is orthodox Marxism?'. Raymond Williams, 'Base and superstructure in Marxist cultural theory', New Left Review, 82 (December 1973) – reprinted in Roger Dale et al. (eds.), Schooling and Capitalism (London: Routledge & Kegan Paul, 1976). Schlomo Avineri, The Social and Political Thought of Karl Marx (Cambridge: Cambridge University Press, 1968).

Georg Lukács, History and Class Consciousness (Cambridge, Massachusetts: MIT Press, 1968); Melvin Rader, Marx's Interpretation of History (New York: Oxford University Press, 1979).

Our quotations from Marx are drawn from Robert C. Tucker (ed.), The Marx/ Engels Reader (New York: W.W. Norton, 1978).

30 A number of social theorists are working to provide a theoretical account of the social psychological relationships between individual social structures and forces. Jürgen Habermas, Knowledge and Human Interests (London: Heinemann; Bos-

ton: Beacon Press, 1972); *Legitimation Crisis* (Boston: Beacon Press, 1975). A number of writers acknowledge the compatibility of Marx and Mead. See, for example, Irving Zeitlin, *Rethinking Sociology* (Englewood Cliffs, New Jersey: Prentice-Hall, 1973); C.W. Mills, 'Language, logic, and culture', *American Sociological Review*, 4:5 (1939); Persell, *Education and Inequality* (New York: Free Press, 1977).

31 See Williams, 1977, op. cit., for a clarification of the meaning of productive forces. The meaning we and Williams attribute to this term goes beyond the narrower conception of industrial production of a material product to include the production of institutions, culture, and social and political orders.

32 In Marx's words, 'The tradition of all the dead generations weigh as a nightmare on the brain of the living', taken from 'Eighteenth Brumaire of Louis Bonaparte', quoted in Tucker, op. cit., 595.

33 Williams, 1977, op. cit., 85–7; Jay, op. cit., 54; Avineri, op. cit., 144–5 and passim. Applebaum and Chotiner, op. cit.

34 Tucker, op. cit., 595.

35 ibid., 115.

36 Lukács, 1973, op. cit., 23.

37 ibid., 24. Lukács stresses the continuous flux of this dialectical process as follows:

even the category of interaction requires inspection. If by interaction we mean just the reciprocal causal impact of two otherwise unchangeable objects on each other, we shall not have come an inch nearer to an understanding of society. This is the case with the vulgar materialists with their one-way causal sequences (or the Machists with their functional relations). After all, there is e.g., an interaction when a stationary billiard ball is struck by a moving one: the first one moves, the second one is deflected from its original path. The interaction we have in mind must be more than the interaction of otherwise unchanging objects. It must go further in its relation to the whole: for this relation determines the objective form of every object of cognition. Every substantial change that is of concern to knowledge manifests itself as a change in relation to the whole and through this as a change in the form of objectivity itself. [Lukács, 1973, op. cit., 113].

38 Williams, 1977, op. cit., 109. See Persell, op. cit., 9–11; Apple, *Ideology and the Curriculum* (London and Boston: Routledge & Kegan Paul, 1979), 21; Rader, op. cit., 41–3; Centre for Contemporary Critical Studies, *On Ideology* (London: Hutchinson, 1978) for references for and clarifications of this concept.

39 Williams, 1977, op. cit., 66; see Richard Lewontin, 'Marxists and the university', *New Political Science*, 1:213 (Fall/Winter 1979–80) for an excellent statement of how formal education supports this ideology.

40 Jay, op. cit., 75.

41 See Williams, 1977, op. cit., 66.

42 Persell, op. cit., 11.

43 Williams, 1977, op. cit., 110, stress added.

44 Williams, 1973, op. cit., 204.

45 Williams, 1977, op. cit., 110.

46 See Carl Boggs, *Gramsci's Marxism* (London: Writers' and Readers' Cooperative, 1976).

47 Williams, 1977, op. cit., 112–13. Paul Willis, in *Learning to Labour* (Westmead: Saxon House, 1978), utilizes these concepts in his analysis of the process of learning to labor.

48 'Marxism must abandon its traditional belief that the ideological superstructure [is] . . . a reflection of the socio-economic substructure. "The old question, what has objective priority . . . spirit or matter . . . is already meaningless as it is posed"' [quoted in Jay, op. cit., 72–3, from Marcuse's 'Berträge Zu einer

Phenomenologie des historischen Materialimus', *Philosophische Hefter* I:1 (1928)]. 'Both substructure and superstructure [interact] ... at all times, although ... under capitalism the economic base [has] a crucial role' [Jay, op. cit., 53]. Williams (1977, op. cit., 77) offers an explanation for why the concepts substructure and superstructure have so often been portrayed in a mechanistic relationship to one another.

49 Williams, 1977, op. cit., 88. See also Applebaum and Chotiner, op. cit., 95. In Jay's words, 'There is a reciprocal relationship between the totality or whole, and its moments' (Jay, op. cit., 54).

50 Applebaum and Chotiner, op. cit., 80.

51 Persell, op. cit., 1977, 8.

52 Lukács, 1973, op. cit., 29.

53 Avineri, op. cit., 134–49. Praxis is the Marxist term for 'man's conscious shaping of the changing historical conditions' (p. 138) that depend upon an adequate interpretation of the world (p. 137).

54 Carl Boggs 'Marxism and the role of intellectuals', *New Political Science*, 1:213 (Fall/Winter 1979–80), 7.

55 ibid., 13.

56 ibid., 14.

57 Avineri, op. cit., 143.

58 Mills, 1939, op. cit.; B. Roberts, 'G.H. Mead: the theory and practice of his social psychology', *Ideology and Consciousness* (Autumn 1977).

Chapter VII

1 For an alternative formulation of the control questions see Joseph C. Grannis, 'The school as a model of society', *Harvard Graduate School of Education Bulletin*, 12:2 (Fall 1967). Basil Bernstein, *Class, Codes and Control (Vol. 3) Towards a Theory of Educational Transmissions* (2nd edn) (London: Routledge & Kegan Paul, 1975), uses the concept 'framing' to refer to 'the degree of control teacher *and* pupil possess over the selection organization, pacing, and timing of the knowledge' [p. 89, our italics]. We confess to sympathy with Professor Douglas whom Bernstein claims 'even now says ... that she does not understand "framing" ' ' (p. 7). Does it refer 'to the strength of the boundary between what may be transmitted and what may not' (p. 88), which seems to imply how much control teachers and students have *vis-à-vis*, perhaps, the state; or to 'the specific pedagogical relationship of teacher and taught' (p. 88), which seems to imply how much control teachers have *vis-à-vis* students (paralleling more closely the control dilemmas as we formulate them). See also Bernstein, 'A brief account of the theory of codes' in the Open University's Educational Studies' Second Level Course Language and Learning Block 3, *Social Relationships and Language: Some Aspects of the Work of Basil Bernstein* (Milton Keynes: Open University Press, 1973).

2 A variation of this dilemma is implicit in a physician's treatment of patients. There is a pull, on the one hand, towards taking responsibility for and attending to a range of psychological and physical and socio-economic aspects of the patient's being, and, on the other, towards attending to the specific ailments of areas of specialization in which he/she has training and/or competence in diagnosis and treatment.

3 Any categorization of the realms of children's development obviously raises difficult problems. Some of these are dealt with below when we present the curriculum dilemmas.

4 Basil Bernstein, 'On the classification and framing of educational knowledge' in

M.F.D. Young, 1971, *op. cit.*, 48 defines the 'status' of a content in terms of the amount of time given over to it and whether it is compulsory or optional.

5 The significance of patterns of resolution to this dilemma for the development of capitalism is suggested by Stanley Aronowitz, *False Promises* (New York: McGraw Hill, 1973), 70.

6 See Nell Keddie, 'Classroom knowledge' in M.F.D. Young, op. cit., 145, for a graphic description of this process occurring in a classroom.

7 Bernstein (1973, op. cit., 68–9) raises the question of the 'degree of insulation between the everyday community knowledge of teacher and taught and educational knowledge'. The public–personal knowledge dilemma refers only to the relationship between children's everyday knowledge and 'school' knowledge.

8 George Dennison, *The Lives of Children* (New York: Random House, 1969); John Holt, *The Underachieving School* (New York: Dell, 1970), A.S. Neill, *Summerhill: A Radical Approach to Childrearing* (New York: Hart, 1950; London: Gollancz, 1962); Carl Rogers, *Freedom to Learn* (Columbus, Ohio: Charles Merrill, 1969). Roland Barth, one of the popularizers of English informal schools in the US, states his view of the stance of open classroom teachers on this dilemma in his claim that open educators believe, 'There is no minimum body of knowledge which is essential for everyone to acquire' ['So you want to change to an open classroom', *Phi Delta Kappan* (October 1971), 46]. See also our discussion of research on reading, Part Five, Chapter XI.

9 R.S. Peters, *Ethics and Education* (London: George Allen & Unwin, 1966), 54.

10 In R.S. Peters's words, 'The procedures of a discipline can only be mastered by an exploration of its established content under the guidance of one who has already been initiated' [ibid., p. 54]. Geoffrey Esland, in 'Teaching and learning as the organization of knowledge' in M.F.D. Young, 1971, op. cit., distinguishes 'everyday knowledge' from 'theoretical knowledge' (p. 92), suggesting everyday knowledge is non-theoretical. In our view, personal knowledge may be 'theoretical' or concrete. An example of personal knowledge which is implicitly theoretical is the Trukese knowledge of navigational theory as presented by Thomas Gladwin, 'Culture and logical process' in Nell Keddie (ed.), *The Myth of Cultural Deprivation* (Harmondsworth, Middlesex: Penguin, 1973).

11 Dewey and Mead both argue against this epistemological dualism. Dewey explicitly argues against conceptualizing teaching in terms of the corresponding pedagogical dualism of teacher v. learner-centered teaching – Dewey, *Experience and Education* (New York: Macmillan, 1963). Nevertheless, the very fact that Dewey devotes attention to this issue is an acknowledgement that many within the western tradition see the issue of what knowledge is relevant in terms of contrary and conflicting values and beliefs. It is, therefore, no surprise that this dualistic construction of knowledge and freedom makes its way into the 'generalized others' of teachers, and that teachers' behavior in some measure reflects these two simultaneously held commitments. Bernstein (1975, op. cit., 89) says there 'is another aspect of the boundary relationship between what may be taught and what may not be taught and consequently another aspect to framing ... the relationship between non-school everyday community knowledge of the teacher or taught *and* the educational knowledge transmitted in the pedagogical relationship'. We capture this relationship in the personal–public knowledge dilemma.

12 The reference here is to Harold Benjamin's witty, pungent, and in our view, under-appreciated, *The Sabre Tooth Curriculum* (London and New York: McGraw Hill, 1937).

13 John Dewey, op. cit., 23. The misunderstanding of Dewey on this point is common by his critics and many practitioners who claim to work within the progressive tradition. The activity-centered curriculum for some became an end in

itself rather than a means of entry into public knowledge. For a useful study of John Dewey's views on education see Arthur Wirth, *John Dewey as Educator* (Huntington, New York: Krieger, 1978).

14 This connection has been proposed by a number of writers. See Keddie, 1971, op. cit., for example.

15 This distinction resembles Joseph Schwab's distinction between syntactical and substantive structure; see, 'Structure of the disciplines: meanings and significances' in G.W. Ford and L. Pugno (eds), *The Structure of Knowledge and the Curriculum* (Chicago: Rand McNally, 1964).

16 Edward R. Mikel is completing a study of the resolutions to the knowledge dilemmas by several secondary-school social studies teachers at the level of classroom interaction, lesson and curriculum planning, and rationales that they offer for their curricular choices; *A Study of Social Studies Teachers' Conceptions of Knowledge and Knowing* (St Louis: Washington University, in process).

17 Esland, 1971, op. cit., 75. Esland's contribution to the M.F.D. Young collection, op. cit., is in part a detailed analysis of what, in our language, is the knowledge as given–knowledge as problematic dilemma. The nature of Edward Fenton's inquiry-oriented history curriculum, developed in the 1960s at Carnegie-Mellon University, clarifies the distinction between the given–problematic and content–process dilemmas. The curriculum emphasizes knowledge as process, focusing on alternative ways history has been interpreted, but it does not deal with the problematic nature of all modes of historical analysis and interpretation. A criticism that has been leveled against the problematical position is that at its extreme, its relativism leaves us without any criteria for determining whether one view is truer or more dependable than another. We do not think the criticism is well-founded. The argument that taking knowledge as problematic need not lead to relativism is presented by Georg Lukács, *Marxism and Human Liberation* (New York: Dell, 1973), and, of course, Habermas; see Part Five, introduction, n. 2.

18 Jules Henry, *Culture Against Man* (New York: Random House, 1963).

19 Bernstein, 1975, op. cit., 97. Bernstein acknowledges that his concepts, classification and framing, cannot analyze specific contents, that is, deal with the ideological basis of knowledge. We address this problem through the dilemmas, knowledge as given v. knowledge as problematical, and common culture v. sub-group consciousness.

20 The choice of language for the dilemmas was dependent in part upon the level of generality and specificity that would be useful for our audiences. It would be possible to include in the list of dilemmas Bernstein's formulation: knowledge as collection v. knowledge as integrated or unified. We presently regard this tension as a special case of the *knowledge as given v. knowledge as problematical* dilemma; the pull, on the one hand, being towards treating areas of knowledge as having strong, distinctive and legitimate boundaries and the pull, on the other, towards seeing such distinctions as provisional and somewhat arbitrary. We treat this formulation of Bernstein's in part as a particular case of the *knowledge given–problematical* dilemma because fundamental to the latter is the issue of whether boundaries between subjects are socially constructed. One significant potential consequence of a teacher's pattern of resolution to this dilemma may be on the students' inclination to connect knowledge to social reality. (See Bernstein, 1971, op. cit., 58). One of the arguments often heard from the left is that it is the segmenting of the social process into parts that mystifies people about the true nature of society. Thus when social analysis is segmented into philosophy, history, sociology, political science, its power for critical analysis is attenuated.

21 Bernstein's concepts of weak and strong classification focus our attention on the

degree of insulation between contents (1975, op. cit., 88). These concepts also capture a part of the holistic–molecular dilemma.

22 Dennison, op. cit., 163.

23 Stanley Aronowitz, op. cit., 78, describes this as follows:

In public schools, reading is typically taught through repetition of atomized pieces of information that are accorded differential status in the knowledge hierarchy and are arranged arbitrarily according to conceptions of child development that assume the progressive character of learning capacity.

The theory of linguistic competence implied by almost all current reading programs in schools is sharply disputed by Noam Chomsky and others who have developed a more rationalist theory of language learning. . . . If Chomsky . . . is right in his assertion that the role of the schools can only be to provide a conducive learning environment within which the deep structures of language embedded in individuals can be developed to their greatest potential, then the current emphasis of schools on segmented, conditioned-reflex, and associative methodologies for teaching reading may be irrational and consequently destructive to learning to read . . . (H)is assertion provides a clue to the reasons why children become restless in school when inevitably subjected to these methods.

24 This issue is dealt with in more detail in Chapter XI.

25 This is the approach advocated by Carl Bereiter and Siegfried Engelmann, *Teaching Disadvantaged Children in the Pre-School* (Englewood Cliffs, New Jersey: Prentice-Hall, 1966).

26 Robert Dreeben, 'The contribution of schooling to the learning of norms', *Harvard Educational Review*, 37:2 (1967).

27 See Jeffery Galper. *The Politics of Social Service* (Englewood Cliffs, New Jersey: Prentice-Hall, 1975). The child as client perspective is parallel to the banking view of education and knowledge as represented by Paolo Friere; see, *Pedagogy of the Oppressed* (New York: Seabury Press, 1974); *Education for Critical Consciousness* (New York: Seabury Press, 1974). The latter was published under the title *Education: The Practice of Freedom* (London: Writers' and Readers' Cooperative, 1976).

28 There are numbers of portrayals of this, for example, Jonathan Kozol, *Death at an Early Age* (Boston: Houghton Mifflin, 1967); Gerry Rosenfeld, *Shut Them Thick Lips* (New York: Holt, 1971); Gerald E. Levy, *Ghetto School* (Indianapolis: Bobbs Merrill, 1970).

29 See, for example, Sara Lawrence Lightfoot, 'Politics and reasoning: through the eyes of teachers and children', *Harvard Educational Review*, 43:2 (May 1973); Eleanor Burke Leacock, *Teaching and Learning in City Schools* (New York: Basic Books, 1969).

30 John Dewey, 1963, op. cit., 47–50, makes the case for transformational resolutions to this dilemma.

31 There is ambivalence within western societies about the particular capabilities and deficiences of age-cohorts throughout the life cycle and not surprisingly about what kinds of authority, power and responsibility should be limited by age at both ends of the life cycle. Psychological developmentalists are continually redefining for us the 'natural' capacities and capabilities of various ages, while social and economic changes raise questions about how the age gradations should be treated. For example, employment patterns and changes in technology surely relate in some way to views of the appropriate age for retirement and/or of the desirability of extending the school-leaving age. The courts confront the dilemma in its most general form, when deciding whether or not to 'certify' a juvenile offender as an adult, the legislature, when setting the age for conscription, defining voting qualifications and age or mandatory retirement. Just as persons in the socially-

constructed category of 'retirement age' or 'senior citizen' are virtually excluded from the workplace regardless of economic or social standing, so too are children regularly excluded from certain forms of institutional life and their rights and privileges or participation carefully circumscribed. There are forces in the US toward assuring that young persons have rights and responsibilities similar to adults; yet the press toward treating children in ways that are consistent with their unique nature persists and is reflected in the daily activities of teachers and other adult members of the society.

32 This view is argued by many British and American progressive educators. See, for example, Susan Isaacs, *The Children We Teach* (London: University of London Press, 1963; New York: Schocken Books, Inc., 1971); John Dewey, *The Child and the Curriculum* (Chicago: University of Chicago Press, 1956).

33 Samuel Bowles, in 'Unequal education and the reproduction of the social division of labor' in Martin Carnoy, *Schooling in a Corporate Society* (New York: David McKay, 1972), writes: 'The various socialization patterns in schools attended by students of different social classes do not arise by accident. Rather they stem from the fact that the educational objectives and expectations of both parents and teachers . . . differ for students of different social classes' (p. 52). This widely repeated generalization has been subjected to limited empirical investigation, that is, we do not have much detailed understanding of how teachers treat children of various social classes differently in different schools or within the same classroom. The equality dilemma provides one way to formulate 'close in' inquiries into questions of schooling and equality.

34 See Part One, Chapter I. For a more complete discussion see A.H. Halsey (ed.), *Educational Priority, Vol. 1 Problems and Policies* (London: Department of Education and Science and Social Science Research Council, HMSO, 1972).

35 To quote Justice Holmes:

The standards of the law are standards of general application. The law takes no account of the infinite varieties of temperament, intellect, and education which make the internal character of a given act so different in different men. It doe not attempt to see men as God sees them, for more than one sufficient reason. In the first place, the impossibility of nicely measuring a man's powers and limitations is far clearer than that of ascertaining his knowledge of law, which has been thought to account for what is called the presumption that every man knows the law. But a more satisfactory explanation is, that, when men live in society, a certain average of conduct, a sacrifice of individual peculiarities going beyond a certain point, is necessary to the general welfare. If, for instance, a man is born hasty and awkward, is always having accidents and hurting himself or his neighbors, no doubt his congenital defects will be allowed for in the courts of Heaven, but his slips are no less troublesome to his neighbors [or to his teachers] than if they sprang from guilty neglect. His neighbors accordingly require him, at his proper peril, to come up to their standard, and the courts which they establish decline to take his personal equation into account. [Quoted in Charles P. Curtis Jr and Ferris Greenslet (eds.), *The Practical Cogitator* (Boston: Houghton Mifflin, 1953): source: Holmes Collected Legal Papers, pp. 669–70]

36 The manifestations of the *allocation* and *deviance* dilemmas in four classrooms has been studied by Naida T. Bagenstos in her unpublished PhD dissertation (Washington University, 1975).

37 Patrick Lee and Nancy B. Groper, 'Sex role culture and educational practice', *Harvard Educational Review*, 44:3 (August 1974).

38 This dilemma can be considered from a number of vantage points. It has some affinity with Bernstein's distinction between consensual rituals and differentiating

rituals (1975, op. cit., see ch. 'Ritual in education'). From a Marxist perspective, the common culture pull is towards transmitting the hegemony of capitalist ideology, and the sub-group consciousness pull towards the development of class consciousness.

PART FOUR
INTERPRETATIONS OF THE SCHOOLS

INTRODUCTION

In Part Four, we use the dilemma orientation and language to analyze the schooling experience we portrayed in the narrative in Part Two. In the first section (Chapter VIII) we use the sixteen dilemmas to describe and compare schooling patterns using material drawn from the narrative and on occasion from our experience in US schools. In Chapter IX we use the language and orientation to probe into some of the origins and consequences of schooling patterns in these schools, thereby showing how the dilemma orientation may be used to inquire into complex questions of the role of schooling in the life histories of individual persons, and in the history of the culture and society. Both chapters should be seen as tentative, and in places speculative, a consequence of the facts that we did not set out to conduct systematic inquiries on these issues, and we did not have the dilemma language in hand to sharpen the focus of our studies and guide the gathering of information.[1]

VIII PATTERNS OF RESOLUTION

The analysis of patterns of resolution in the schools is organized in terms of the three sets of dilemmas. We compare Mrs Martin's dominant and exceptional patterns of resolution to the patterns of a number of other teachers at Port, Castlegate, Heathbrook and several other schools, and to patterns we have observed or have experienced in the United States. We conclude with some observations on the nature of formal and informal methods.

THE CONTROL DILEMMAS

Realms

Mrs Martin controls closely those realms of the children's intellectual development represented by the 'accordion card' tasks and her reading scheme which, in her classroom, are the 'basics'. She monitors these basics far more closely than the non-basics – arts and crafts, music, dramatic play, etc. – the afternoon activities. We see, for example, how carefully she sets daily standards for quantity and quality of children's work in maths. A child must complete each accordion card task and may not move to another until she puts a 'tick' on the child's work or otherwise indicates approval. She also keeps a record of children's mastery of what she considers to be basic skills or concepts.

Relative to her next-door colleague, Mrs Eden, Mrs Martin exerts control over a wider range of realms. Although Mrs Eden provisions for arts and crafts and maintains a well-outfitted Wendy house, she does not take the same pains as Mrs Martin to set up these environments and keep track of children's participation in them. Note, for example, how Mrs Martin encourages Mary to become integrated into the hospital playgroup. Mrs Eden rarely 'drops in' to the Wendy house for a chat, nor does she take time at the end of the day to show noteworthy art to the entire class. Instead, she often devotes her afternoon energies to the realm of language development, hearing children, particularly the 'dimmer' ones, read.

Compared to the Castlegate teachers, Mrs Eden and all Port infant teachers maintain *more* control over the non-intellectual realms. Mrs Paynter, for example, treats the arts, creative play, construction work and social development more as extras – as rewards for work in the basics well done rather than as activities that are significant in their own right. Children at Castlegate who have completed the basics may shift (Mrs Martin would say 'wander') from one activity to another with a teacher usually taking notice only if a child shifts too often or lies 'fallow' (that is, appears not to be busy).

Mrs Martin's control of educational diet in the non-basics, though more extensive than other teachers at Port or at Castlegate, is looser than the Heathbrook teachers'. Diet – that is, range of planned educational experiences – in the non-basics at Heathbrook appears to be very loosely controlled, almost hit or miss, since the children choose a 'commitment' each week from an array of options (sports, art, science, social study, music). However, if we examine control of diet over the course of the school term rather than by week, we find that diet is tightly controlled. No child is permitted to lie 'fallow'. There are roughly the same options available over the term and repeated choice of an option is frowned upon and, on occasion, vetoed by a teacher. In this way Heathbrook teachers make certain all children engage in the full range of non-basic activities during the term, and once having 'chosen' an activity, the children experience considerable teaching control over standards, operations and time.

The English primary teachers we studied – with the exception of Mr Edgar and the Highrock teachers – appear to resolve the whole child–child as student dilemma with a greater emphasis on whole child than their American counterparts. For example, they generally exerted closer control over social development and peer relationships. (This responsibility is sometimes given over to counselors in US primary schools.) Compared to our American experience, children in all the classrooms, with the exceptions noted, were given far greater officially sanctioned opportunity to work with others, that is, to develop social relationships, in basics as well as non-basics. Mrs Martin's hospital was purposefully designed to give children opportunities to converse and cooperate. It is a strong pull in Mr Scott toward the realms of social development that underlies is willingness to allow Steven to chat with his friends rather than do his maths. The teachers at Castlegate also arrange a great many opportunities for the children to develop social skills through cooperative activity – the café, the Wendy house, playing board games, etc. As Mrs Hollins told us, however, she feels she is forced to choose between helping children gain experience managing social relationships – in the café – and helping them learn to read, and, painfully, she most frequently chooses the latter.

Meal times in the English schools we visited also reveal a greater whole child emphasis. The family style of serving food, the prayers and the generous length of time allotted for dinner reflects a broader concern for the well-being of the child than the child as student resolutions of American school cafeterias – where the goal is to feed as many children in as short a period of time as possible.

Mr Sprinter exhibits a pattern of resolution to the realms dilemma that stands apart from the others. His control of time, operations and standards is quite similar for all realms of development, although his requirement that children over the course of a year learn particular maths concepts is a vestige of patterns found in other classrooms. And it is not only that his concern for the development of the intellectual realm is approximately equal to his concern for the other realms, but his definition of the intellectual is much broader, more integrative with the others. Indeed, it was far more difficult in his classroom to classify any particular task as 3R or non-3R, a distinction that, in spite of some confusion over 'topic work' and 'painting', teachers and children (even the very youngest, after a few terms of school) made in all Castlegate, Heathbrook and Port classrooms.

How are resolutions formulated differently for different individuals or groups of children? At all schools, in spite of different populations, in general, a whole child emphasis was more commonly directed at those children considered 'clever' in terms of the 3Rs, though there were obvious exceptions and emphases varied greatly. Differential treatment of this sort was barely perceptible in Mrs Martin's room: there is no required 3R or remedial work for anyone 'dim' or 'clever' to finish while others are ngaged in non-basics during the afternoon as there is in Mrs Eden's room, and in Castlegate and Heathbrook classrooms. However, even in Mrs Martin's room those who are quick at the 3Rs (the 'top' group) have more opportunities than others to engage in non-3R work. In the morning, for example, Elaine is often free to talk with other children and make choices outside of the accordion cards and reading scheme; Samuel and David virtually never. And as David and Samuel move into Mrs

Eden's class they will find that, because they complete the required 3R work more slowly than the rest, they will have to continue it during afternoon choosing time on most days, thus regularly receiving far fewer opportunities for developing other realms than those who are more successful at 3R tasks.

Time control

At first glance children in most of the classrooms we portrayed appear to have a large measure of control over their time as compared with classrooms in the US. Rarely do all children engage in the same activities at the same time – which is the pattern we see in Mr Edgar's room. The children are almost always free to chat, and even to 'mess about' within limits prescribed by 'good manners'. While completing their morning tasks, there was relatively little of the 'time's a' wastin' mentality that is so evident at both Castlegate and Highrock. At Port, as at Heathbrook, there are almost always an extra few moments for a personal encounter. Mrs Eden, as she stands by the door to Mrs Martin's classroom, takes the time to say a few pleasant words to Maria about her news rather than waving her away because they were already late for prayers. Children wait patiently for Mrs Martin's attention at her desk, a pattern that is also evident in Mrs Newhouse's room. Rarely did school events begin *precisely* on schedule or did teachers chastise children who were a moment or two late to class, or a bit slower in responding to teachers' questions or calls for order.[1]

However, close examination reveals a subtle, complex and tight pattern of control over time for the basics (however defined) as compared to other activities. Mrs Martin exercises some degree of control over *begin* time in the basics by her expectation that the accordion cards and reading scheme tasks be completed each day by noon, although the children have within that requirement considerable control over *begin* and some control over *duration*. Her time control in the non-basics is looser relative to basics. Control over begin time is virtually absent in the non-basic realms (excepting physical education, prayers and a few other activities). Duration control of most non-basic activities – Lego, bricks, educational games, sand table, plasticine, play hospital – is entirely up to the child. Because the number of tasks to be completed is not tightly prescribed for the afternoon, control of work rate remains with the child.

Resolutions at Castlegate reveal even more marked differences in time control of basics v. non-basics. Each child at Castlegate does 'news' and maths (and sometimes one arts or crafts activity) as a member of a group, and at a specified time, and the child continues until dismissed by the teacher – with exceptions made for the diligent or clever ones. In contrast Mr Scott's patterns of resolution in the basics more heavily emphasizes child-control of time than do Mrs Martin's. Children in his classroom have, except for a half-hour given to reading and a quarter-hour devoted to 'mechanical' maths, a great deal of control over *'duration'* and *'begin'* for the basics. Over the course of the week he exerts considerable control of time, but it is control more analogous to that afforded a salaried executive than to an hourly wage-earner. Time, *begin* and *duration*, for the non-basics at Heathbrook are more controlled than in *any* of the infant classrooms. (This is the same pattern of time control that is being introduced by Mr Nigel to the Port Juniors.)

The resolution to the time dilemma in all these settings may be distinguished from Mr Edgar's classroom where there is officially a heavy emphasis on teacher control of *begin* and *duration* for the 3Rs and practical activities. However, while there are few periods of officially sanctioned time control by children, there is a continuous level of unofficial child control of time. At least one-third of the class has a lot of time on their hands, though the requirement that they sit in one place and face forward limits their choices to engaging in solitary reflection or whispered conversations.

How do teachers control time differently for different children? Attention to Mrs Martin's exceptional modes reveals she is more likely to control more closely the time of children who are unwilling or unable to succeed at school tasks. Children like Samuel and David rarely have the 'luxury' of tuning out of any realms (but particularly the 3Rs). To insure the intellectual growth of the 'deviants', Mrs Martin 'tails' them constantly, controlling their *begin* time ('Samuel, have you done your news?'), rate and duration by generally prescribing (according to the child's table assignment) enough 3R accordion card tasks to fill their mornings and keep them working faster than they would if left to their own devices. 'Top' children like Elaine, because they can usually finish the prescribed tasks, are freer to work at the rate they choose. The differential treatment of children at Castlegate follows a pattern similar to Mrs Martin's. Those children who have most control of time in the basics at Castlegate are those judged to 'require no watching' (that is, can be trusted) and who are not 'dim' (they are not always the most 'clever'). In addition, thirty additional minutes of time for the 'bottom' groups at Castlegate and at Heathbrook are under the close control of remedial reading teachers. In contrast, the 'dim' children in Mr Edgar's room have *most* control of their time – they are allowed to daydream or to sit in the back and engage in continuous unofficial transactions while the time of the 'Elaines' is consumed with answering Mr Edgar's questions.

Operation control

As with time control, the teachers exert closer control over operations in the 3Rs than over operations in other activities, again with the exception of Mr Sprinter. Mrs Martin controls operations in a number of the accordion card activities by specifying a sequence of tasks or a set of 'job' or 'activity' cards, and by monitoring not only children's understanding of the concept, but also their ability to use the required procedures. She shows Tracy how to write the numbers and how to line up tens and units columns; and monitors her operational understanding of the maths concept and her use of the maths activity cards and 'apparatus' in conjunction with the number book. Only after Tracy has completed two cards and Mrs Martin has watched her performance, placed a tick in the child's number book, and made a notation in her record book, does she allow the child to proceed. The complexity of Mrs Martin's pattern of control over operations and her reflexive adjustment of control to the characteristics of individual children may be seen in her system of writing the 'news'. She controls the form of the operations – children write their news in a way that she thinks is appropriate to their level of competence (trace, copy or write) – but control of the content (*what* they write) without exception resides with them.[2]

For most afternoon activities in Mrs Martin's classroom, operations are more loosely controlled – how children build, play in the hospital or at a game are largely left to them. However, Mrs Martin's snowflake-making table represents a form of operations control over 'practical' work. Through the selection of materials and tools Mrs Martin provides control over operations (pencil-tracing of different triangles, cutting around the tracing, symmetrical mounting on black or gray paper, etc.). Again, we find exceptions. Samuel cuts free-hand trees unhampered and is even encouraged to do so. Mrs Martin exerts a similar indirect form of control over children's painting by controlling paint density, colors, size and condition of brushes and setting clear standards for using the entire surface of the paper.

The emphasis in Castlegate teachers' patterns of resolution to this dilemma varies in several respects from Mrs Martin's. The Castlegate teachers control the basics somewhat more tightly. For example, rather than insisting children control the content of their news, Castlegate teachers frequently provide children with 'starters' (photographs, phrases) and, in some situations, specify the particular sentences to be copied. However, Mr Scott, Mrs Martin and the other Port infant teachers, and the Castlegate teachers exerted far *more* control over operations in the basic subjects (even in narrow Skinnerian terms, in the sense of controlling, sequencing and specifying intermediate operations) than Mr Edgar, Mr Jerrid at Highrock or any of the other 'chalk and talk' teachers.

Castlegate teachers also maintained far less operations control over the 'practical' subjects than Mrs Martin. What transpired at the carpenter bench is a good example – except when one of us took responsibility it was a place where children, left to their own devices, would saw off the corners of a fragment of a wood board, pound a few nails to provide a superstructure for their 'boat', and then leave. Mrs Hollins and other teachers were aware of the pattern but, to their regret, felt children's heavy needs in the 3Rs left teachers virtually no time to control even minimally operations in these activities. The art easels and Wendy houses were also generally left unmonitored. (Note the exception of the daily prescribed arts or crafts activity which was heavily controlled.) At Highrock we see extremes in the control of non-basics – either very tight control over particular activities to turn out a standard arts or crafts product or none at all.

Mr Sprinter again provides contrast. His pattern revealed the relative absence of transformational operations control in other classrooms. For example, he recognized the girls at the snail observation table had drawn some faulty conclusions because of the confusing way they set up their observational records. He resisted control over their operations, believing that these children would discover their own confusions when they attempted to calculate the speed with which snails move. He watches constantly, not to assume control, but for the opportune time to wander by, should the girls discover that they are ready for his help, a discovery that was not made during our observations. He was nearby when the boys constructing the cable station were ready for his help in understanding how pulleys are used to reduce force. Such transformational patterns represent not less, but qualitatively different control. The transformation to mutuality in resolution could also be seen in Mrs Martin's

185

classroom as she works collaboratively with children, particularly in the afternoons. For example, as she and a child together puzzle how to design the way wheels can be affixed to a cardboard lorry and then cut the tires from a cardboard tube, locus of control resides with both, rather than with teacher or child.

Control of standards

Mrs Martin's pattern of resolution to the standards dilemma shows a heavy teacher-control emphasis in the 3Rs, particularly in maths and handwriting. During encounters with children at her desk she simultaneously sets and monitors standards (and controls operations and time as well) by indicating to children whether they are ready to begin the next task; for example, she decides whether Brian has practiced enough 8s or is required to do more. And though Brian's friend may finish Brian's 8s for him and Mrs Martin may on some occasions accept them as Brian's, she is as likely to ask him to produce an 8 before her eyes, and in this way to maintain standards control.

However, her pattern of standards control for the news and reading the normal reader is frequently transformational. She is unlikely to press a child to do better in these activities, though she will commonly do so for other writing and virtually all mathematics tasks. She appears to expect children to do their news and read in order to satisfy a standard she and the child have in common – that of doing their very best. We were struck repeatedly by the fact that her patterns of resolution for writing the news are more similar to those for the non-basics than for other 3R activities. For example, she suggests to a child that she might want to fill in some of the white spaces in her painting and, Mrs Martin says, 'she [the child] comes to see for herself how much nicer it looks'. We infer from this statement that Mrs Martin views the standard setting, in this case, in transformational terms. It is probably worthy of further investigation to discover whether, as it appears, transformational modes of standard setting are far more exceptional in mathematics as compared to reading and writing in all classrooms. Both Mrs Newhouse and Mr Scott, in collaboration with their headmasters, set maths standards – number of pages or tasks completed or number of responses to maths facts per unit of time – and there are few hints of children setting standards in maths, or of transformational standard setting, for example, a child striving for a personal standard of understanding probability, or of solving a mathematics problem in 'base 2'.

At Castlegate, teachers control standards more tightly in a *wider* range of 3R work than one finds in Mrs Martin's and other Port infant classes. The contrast is particularly noteworthy when considering patterns of standards setting for the news. Castlegate teachers commonly pass judgment: 'You can do better', 'Write one more line'. Transformational standard setting occurred more regularly at Castlegate during the process of 'hearing' children read. The children seen to take pleasure from showing to adults or other children their ability to take meaning from print, but this enthusiasm was much rarer in writing news and virtually non-existent in maths.

Again, it is the children who are less successful at 3R school tasks who are most likely to have standards set and maintained for them. Mrs Martin tells David – 'You can do better'. The patterns of resolution in Castlegate's remedial class stand in sharp contrast to the more frequent transformational standards set for reading in the regular classrooms. The children who were sent for remedial reading were given a reader where the possibilities of extracting meaning from print were minimal, and the remedial reading teacher set standards for them in terms of calling words and collecting as large a cache of word cards as possible, and completing each day as many pages in the reader as they could so that they would be rewarded with the status symbol of a *Janet and John*. Standards for reading at Highrock in all classrooms, not only in the remedial class, from the limited data we have, appeared to be a version of what occurred in the Castlegate remedial program.

We have portrayed patterns of resolution to the standards dilemma in terms of the locus of standards -- in the child, in the teacher, or in both. We have alluded to, but not focused on, the content of the standards – what forms of knowledge and ways of knowing and learning are implicit in the standards that are set. These questions may be answered by an analysis of teachers' resolutions to the curriculum dilemmas to which we now turn.

CURRICULUM CONTROL – THE CURRICULUM DILEMMAS

Patterns of resolution in the language curriculum

In Mrs Martin's classroom the daily activity of writing the news which includes personal and generally pleasant child and teacher encounters at Mrs Martin's desk, is a significant part of the children's initiation into the world of the written word. The entire process, drawing a picture, discussing it with the teacher, choosing one or more sentences, is, as we have indicated, more frequently than any other 3R activity characterized by transformational modes. The simultaneous attention to different levels of skill and interest and the common expectation that all can and should write one or two sentences daily whether by tracing, copying or using a dictionary, represent a fusion of each child unique with children have shared characteristic modes. The learning of conventions of written language to express one's personal concerns and interests weds public to personal knowledge. As the children listen to one another gathered around Mrs Martin's desk while she helps each individually, the news activity is at once an individual and a social learning experience. In writing the news, there are also frequent transformational resolutions to the holistic–molecular dilemma. Particular skills, the printing of letters, spacing of words, letter sounds, are shaped and practiced, but in the context of their relationship to the whole. The writing of the news is also often a transformational resolution to the motivation dilemma, as the child's and the teacher's motives are joined.

Relative to writing the news, reading the reader in Mrs Martin's room is more extrinsically motivated and more responsive to the public knowledge perspective. The content of the readers is not related to the particular personal interests of individual children – they do not choose the book, it is chosen for them by the teacher – and all go through the same sequence of readers, with the exception of remedial students.

Every child in Mrs Martin's classroom every day also engages in a wide variety of molecular, public knowledge tasks to develop language literacy – the memorizing of flash cards, the writing-readiness and fill-in-the-word exercises specified by the accordion cards (though the emphasis in these tasks is on *words* as parts rather than *sounds* as parts). However, these activities are clearly less important in Mrs Martin's eyes than the relatively more holistic and intrinsically motivating activities of reading the reader and writing the news. It is also, we think, highly significant that in contrast with American classrooms, such molecular activities are never labeled 'reading' by her or the children.

What are some of the differences between Mrs Martin's patterns of resolution to the curriculum dilemmas in teaching basic literacy and those characteristic of Castlegate teachers? The willingness of Mrs Paynter and Mrs Carter to provide the ideas for their children's news is one marked difference. It represents the greater separation for Castlegate children of personal from public knowledge, a separation that becomes a chasm at Highrock. Though we have much evidence that the Castlegate children have many thoughts and feelings they could, with help, transfer to writing – a father who 'combs his hair lovely and goes out and gets drunk' – these are only rarely represented in their news. Now and again, there is a fusion of public and personal knowledge as Anthony, considering whether his parents would be sorry if he dies, writes in his news 'my mum and dad came to my cross'. Most often, however, Castlegate teachers assume they must provide topics for children to write about. Nevertheless, writing the news at Castlegate represents a heavier personal knowledge emphasis than the copying of teachers' sentences from the board that, according to Mrs Hollins, was characteristic of Castlegate prior to her arrival. Castlegate teachers also generally play out molecular modes more often than does Mrs Martin. The children spend a longer time with sight vocabulary and sounds before they are deemed ready for a 'reader', and more than a fifth of the children in each class experience patterns of resolution with the remedial reading teacher that emphasize molecular modes quite heavily.

Reading to the teacher from readers at Castlegate more frequently represents an intrinsic motivation mode than does writing the news. The infant children at Castlegate, as at Port, cherish the short period of intimate contact with their teachers, even though the story itself has not been chosen by and may not greatly interest them. However, though the material in the readers to some degree bridges the gap between personal and public knowledge for children at Port, the stories are far more discrepant from the Castlegate children's experience. Nevertheless, the way the basal reader is used (reading individually and chatting with the teacher, teaching those phonemes a particular child needs as identified by the teacher as she listens to the child read) reflects a far stronger emphasis on transformational resolutions to the personal–public, motivation and standards dilemmas as compared to American elementary teachers. More commonly, the American teacher who employs a basal reader expects children to read the story *in order to* do a workbook exercise, and frequently will not allow the child to read another story until the molecular workbook exercises are complete and correct. Skill mastery via workbook is made primary.

Mr Scott's and Mr Sprinter's resolutions to the motivation, the holistic/molecular and personal/public knowledge dilemmas in the language and reading curriculum are, in comparison to teachers at Castlegate (and many other infant and junior teachers we saw), more consistently transformational. Though we have no indication how these teachers would teach beginning reading, both exhibited patterns of resolutions that emphasize individuals gaining personal satisfaction from taking meaning from print. Both work with children to help them find books which are both challenging ('not beneath their capacity') and personally interesting. ('If you begin a book and it doesn't catch your interest, it is time to find another.')

Distribution of patterns of resolution in the language curriculum

How are patterns of resolution to the curriculum dilemmas distributed among children within Mrs Martin's and other teachers' classrooms? Mrs Martin tells us:

I think their minds are very live [when they first come to school] – they want a challenge – they look at a book and want to know what the words say. This business about a child not being ready to read until he's six – I think it's a lot of rubbish. Some children are ready at three. They don't find it very difficult and if they do find it difficult, I don't push them. The trouble lies, of course, in trying to teach a child to read who obviously is not capable of doing it and pushing them on. That's the only thing that I am against.

For Mrs Martin children share an attitude toward learning to read: 'They want a challenge . . . they want to know what the words say', and they also share the characteristic of having 'live' minds. On the other hand, children differ from one another in that some children (a very few in her classroom) 'find it [reading] difficult' at the same time that others are 'ready'.

How does she allocate knowledge and ways of learning differentially to those who 'find it difficult' and those who are 'ready'? The differences are, in her room, subtle, but prefigure differential treatment of what passes for knowledge and learning in the vast majority of classrooms. Children whom Mrs Martin considers 'ready' are those who most quickly memorize written words, and/or have acquired the molecular skills of decoding (without systematic instruction), and who are motivated to use them. They are the first to receive the *Janet and John* and the higher status associated with it. Those children who are deemed not ready are those who, for one reason or another, cannot easily retain the dozen sight vocabulary words prerequisite to receiving a normal reader; they will, within the first $3\frac{1}{2}$ to 4 to 5 weeks of entering school, find themselves out of step with 'normal' progress. These are the children whom Mrs Martin (and all the other teachers, with the exception of Mr Sprinter) come to consider 'not clever' or 'dim'.

The learning experiences to which these 'slower' children are subjected are more molecular, extrinsically motivated and separate personal from public knowledge more completely. For example, though all children experience the transformational resolution implicit in writing the news, some children (Samuel, David, Brian) spend a somewhat greater proportion and a longer period of time on the more molecular task of memorizing words out of context, and, if this fails, reading in a 'reader' that controls vocabulary in terms of structurally similar words (for example, cat, hat, mat). The stories constructed with this limitation are more likely to be inane (cat sat on the mat . . .), barely meaningful let alone interesting. These children also experience more extrinsic push than others as they are constantly reminded to 'get on with it'. In addition, Mrs Martin's choice of classroom organization and activities and her accepted treatment of knowledge and knowing are probably more appropriate for developing literacy in some children than others. The individual learning emphasis that is built into her reading scheme may not be appropriate for Samuel who may, for example, have been better served by a more heavily learning as social resolution. Also, given his religious affiliations – he is a Jehovah's Witness – the public knowledge represented by the reader is more likely to be completely divorced from his personal knowledge than for the others.

In Mrs Martin's classroom we see the outlines of differential patterns that will become increasingly distinct as children advance in school. Although Mrs Martin makes relatively few distinctions among children, advancement in her classroom is significant because Mrs Eden, from the beginning, stratifies children by tables based on her and Mrs Martin's estimate of the normal rate of progress. Most children like Samuel, over the next few years, will spend more and more time being 'remediated', by being subject to more molecular resolutions (using more molecularized readers, attending special reading sessions with Mr Nigel, Mr Bolton or the remedial reading teacher at Castlegate). They will experience more extrinsic, child as client modes, and the public knowledge will, for them, be more distinctly separated from their personal lives.[3]

In contrast virtually all children in Mr Scott's class, no matter what their reading skills, spend equal amounts of time each day in the holistic and intrinsically motivated task of reading a book they have chosen themselves – though the bottom readers at Heathbrook are also 'remediated'. Mr Sprinter exerts control over the time of David, who is performing inadequately, requiring that he write for an hour on several consecutive days. But, rather than giving David a set of molecular tasks to perform or using extrinsic modes (offering

191

physical or material rewards or punishments), Mr Sprinter sits with the child, giving him full attention, exposing him to a transformational resolution to the child as person–child as client dilemma.

Non-basics

What passes for knowledge is curricular areas outside the 'basics' and how is it transmitted? Public knowledge in the non-basics in Mrs Martin's class is transmitted primarily during the afternoon,[4] through role play in the hospital, arts and crafts, and building activities. Transformational resolutions of the motivation, and personal–public knowledge dilemmas are more frequently seen in these activities than in her morning work periods. During these afternoon activities there are also more likely to be transformational modes of teaching maths and language literacy – (for example, children read the patient list in the hospital, learn colors and shapes at arts and crafts and how to measure volume at the sand table). Mrs Martin shows little concern that all should learn any particular 'content' about hospitals. However, whatever children do learn – about how X-rays work, or how one is admitted to a hospital – is gained holistically, arises initially from and is sustained by intrinsic motivation, and is integrated with their personal knowledge through 'play'. She justifies the hospital environment in part by the view that some public knowledge about hospitals is or may become personally significant to children by helping them cope with what is often a frightening experience. Her resolutions in these non-basics resemble Mr Sprinter's, although he plays out the patterns during the entire day and for more realms. Both provision their classrooms generously – Mrs Martin provides costumes, salves, bandages, etc.; Mr Sprinter has a 'magic cupboard', printing press, terraria, always some new planned addition to the environment to bring children to the flashpoint. Both resolve the knowledge as content–knowledge as process dilemma with emphasis on the latter. Mr Sprinter does not ask the girls to read about snails until they have observed carefully and have done some thinking on their own.

Patterns of resolution for topic work in virtually all junior classrooms, more often than not, emphasize molecular, extrinsic, public knowledge, knowledge as content, individual learning and knowledge as given. These resolutions are common in Mr Edgar's classroom for virtually all subjects and reach their apogee in his question and answer sessions. If any relationships are drawn in class between the 'facts', Mr Edgar does it rather than a child; his emphasis on public knowledge is exemplified in his failure to capitalize upon the firsthand experience of several children who had been to France (even though the class was studying that country), and in the discussion about erosion and crop rotation with no references to the real world examples that could be found within two miles of the school. The motivation in these sessions is almost entirely extrinsic, and though the scene is obviously social, social learning is virtually never encouraged by the teacher. Mrs Newhouse's lackadaisical treatment of topic may be seen in part as an inability to achieve the transformational resolutions of Mr Sprinter, and an unwillingness to use extrinsic motivation to get children to accumulate, through topic work, content that she herself acknowledges would not be integrated into their personal knowledge.

Mr Sprinter is the only teacher who plays out knowledge as problematical modes to any significant degree though he rarely does so explicitly. By failing to treat learning as an activity where somebody 'decides for you what is important' – by refusing to define 'reading [as]... more important than music' he is implicitly raising questions about the value of traditional school expectations. We have no evidence of Mrs Martin stimulating children to question taken-for-granted knowledge. We do not, for instance, find her asking if sick children are better off at home than in a hospital, whether prayers are proper within schools, any more than we see Mr Edgar encouraging children to question why it is that Mexico and Canada are generally taken to be part of the 'New World' while Australia is not. The patterns of resolution in this classroom and in this school are uniformly and heavily weighted towards treating knowledge as given rather than problematical, a pattern replicated in the majority of primary classrooms we have visited in England and the US.

Summary

The child as person–child as client dilemma is a way of characterizing overall patterns of resolutions to the curriculum dilemmas. All teachers represented a combination of opposites, for example, at times treating children as members of categories, keeping a dispassionate distance; at other times treating them in a way that acknowledged the teachers' common bond of humanity with children. The child as person orientation we saw not at all in our brief visit at Highrock. In Mr Edgar's room the common bond is indicated in his asides, affectionate pats and frequent before and after class 'chitchats' about events in children's lives or happenings in the village. In contrast, Mr Sprinter usually deals with each child as a client and a person simultaneously, a unity that occurred less frequently at Port and Heathbrook and less frequently still at Castlegate. Castlegate teachers often express doubts as to whether some children have *any* interests, and at times speak of the children as 'them', offspring of parents with whom they have nothing at all in common. 'There is intelligence to be found', says Mrs Hollins, indicating the improbability of this event (and, given the school's definition of intelligence, she is making an accurate estimate). Teachers of the poorer children express their social distance from the children in their more extrinsic, molecular patterns and their emphasis on public knowledge that reflects their presumption that the children have fewer social experiences to draw upon than middle-class children.

PATTERNS OF CONTROL OVER BROAD SOCIETAL MEANINGS: THE SOCIETAL DILEMMAS

Childhood and sanctions

In general, English infant and junior teachers relative to American teachers we have seen (except at Highrock) put greater emphasis on both *ad hoc* application and childhood unique modes of resolutions. We see this emphasis on childhood unique in Newton, Port and Castlegate infant teachers as they nurture children in symbolic ways that link family to school experience – the birthday celebrations, dinner time, allowing siblings to sit with one another during assemblies, in the ever present home corner or Wendy house, the pains taken to provision the classroom with water, sand, paint, blocks and crafts. Similar emphasis may be found in American kindergartens, but resolutions appear to shift abruptly with children's entry into first grade. There is also evident in these schools strong pulls towards the continuous or preparation for adulthood resolutions – the frequent reminders, particularly for some, to 'get on with it'; the press toward defining normal progress in terms of the 3Rs presumed to be the *sine qua non* for success in the job market. Given the common assumption that the schools exist to prepare children for the adult world, it is not surprising that primary teachers' patterns reveal strong child continuous emphases. What was surprising to us as Americans was the relatively greater frequency of childhood unique modes in virtually *all* classrooms we visited, including many formal

194

classrooms, extending throughout the infants and into the early junior years.

Subtle shifts to childhood continuous patterns are evident as the children approach and pass to the juniors. Mrs Martin's spontaneous distribution of sweeties represents a childhood unique mode; but in Mrs Eden's hand distribution of sweeties is almost always a form of extrinsic motivation, a reward for good school work. However, tendencies toward childhood unique persist in upper infants and the juniors even among the chalk and talk teachers, for example in Mr Edgar's frequent personal touches with the children, his willingness to overlook conversation, his lack of moral indignation when children share answers – in American terms, 'cheat'. He and many other teachers whose style resembles his are more tolerant of children's foibles than are American teachers.

The somewhat stronger childhood continuous emphasis at Castlegate than at Port is indicated by the greater amount of time and concern Mrs Hollins and her teachers devote to preparing for and teaching the basics and their tendency to forgo involvement in the childhood pleasures of the café, the Wendy house, and the arts because of a deeply felt urgency to get children ready for junior school. Evidence that qualities usually associated with childhood are cherished or respected at Highrock is conspicuously wanting

Mrs Martin's resolutions, though in the main alternating from a continuous (more frequent in the mornings) to a unique emphasis (more frequent in the afternoons), are also often transformational. These were the occasions when future and present orientations were one – when she and a child would look at a painting together and discuss the merits of its composition, work together on a project, authentically engage in role play together at the hospital. At her desk in the morning there were also times, usually associated with news and chats about reading, when the mutuality of concern for understanding and successful accomplishment transcended the adult–child orientation.

Mr Sprinter's pattern is more consistently transformational in all school activities – basics and non-basics. He deliberately seeks to erase some of the distinctions between childhood and adulthood by redefining both. He explains he is eager for children to spend time observing the natural world because 'sitting and looking [is] the greatest strength kids have that we don't have'. In this comment he implies that he wants to extend the 'natural' capacity of children to be keen observers into adulthood rather than only helping the child develop adult characteristics. Like Mrs Martin, this transformational resolution reflects respect for the powers and capacities usually associated with childhood. But only Mr Sprinter explicitly identifies them as human, not merely childhood, capacities.

The treatment of rule-breaking in the schools we visited parallels the childhood resolutions. In brief there were far more instances of *ad hoc* application of rules than in the US classrooms we know. In Mrs Martin's room there were frequent reminders, but only one recorded instance of punishment (withdrawal of playtime), and for every rule or expectation there seemed an exception: Samuel was allowed to play during work periods, a child would clean up for another or swot another now and then. A similar pattern was evident in Mr Edgar's classroom, where as many as two-thirds of the children engaged in unofficial activities during formal lessons, but were rebuked only on occasion and rarely punished.

The incident of Colin running home illuminates the playing out of the competing claims of this dilemma at Port, and suggests that though there are limits to the *ad hoc* application, there is disagreement among teachers over where the limits should be drawn. For Mrs Carpenter, leaving school without permission crosses the line. For Mrs Newhouse, the case warranted an *ad hoc* application of sanctions. The fact that Colin was quite angry, in her opinion, ruled out even the necessity of an 'apology', and though she was angry at Colin, she did not invoke the police power of the state.

At Castlegate, though there was more punishing of rule-breakers – children were on occasion restricted to their classroom for fighting – it appeared that treatment of 'deviants' was also frequently very much an *ad hoc* affair. Mrs Lawton overlooks Anthony's temper tantrums because of 'trouble at home' (though other children experiencing 'trouble at home' may not be overlooked). Mrs James punishes, never in the cause of equal justice, but only when in her view the child was 'beyond kindness'. We do not have sufficient information to characterize with any confidence the differences between patterns of resolution to this dilemma at the schools we studied, nor how these resolutions are distributed among different groups or individuals, that is, whether particular categories of children are regularly treated on an *ad hoc* basis or in terms of the equal justice claim.

Sub-groups and common culture

We were able to distinguish four 'sub-groups' in the classrooms we visited: poor children, immigrants, females and the 'cheeky ones', that is, consistent violators of school norms. However, we failed to record sufficient data to analyze in detail how this dilemma was played out differently for each of these groups. We could see in Mrs Martin's class the seeds of an emphasis we saw repeated in most classrooms on the 'English' common culture, rather than on sub-culture or multi-cultural resolutions. The common culture mode is explicit in the daily prayers or assemblies and also in prayers before dinner. It is English law that all children say Christian prayers. Mrs Martin's treatment of Samuel, a Jehovah's Witness, is an example. There is no thought that the prayer ritual might be adjusted, much less abolished, because he cannot participate.[5] Being 'English' appears to imply something different than being 'an American', the former being a far more restricted category than the latter. Apparently the fact that one is native born is not a sufficient criterion for being English. 'Non-whites', regardless of parents' place of birth, were often referred to as immigrants, 'West Indians' or 'Asians'. The common culture press is also seen in the treatment of sex differences. It was striking to us as Americans that teachers expected boys and girls to strip unself-consciously to their underwear for physical education, unmindful of sex differences.

Common culture modes of resolution also dominated Castlegate; we saw no evidence of an attempt to emphasize any positive aspects of working-class life or culture. This was apparent when we compare Castlegate teachers' frequently expressed cultural deficit views of children and parents (which included a few West Indian children) with the frequently heard respect for the culture of the Asian (but not the West Indian) children at Newton. Several of the children at Castlegate were also of oriental origin but no teacher ever took any special note of this.

Equal v. differential allocation

How patterns of resolutions are distributed among children and groups of children has been discussed in terms of each of the dilemmas. We here summarize these analyses. Teachers' patterns of resolution to a number of the dilemmas differ according to how quickly individual children master a particular set of tasks. These tasks are primarily the ones teachers use to define success at 'reading'. As we have shown, for children who do not demonstrate mastery of a dozen or so sight words within four to five weeks, Mrs Martin shifts her patterns of resolution slightly. Her control is somewhat more complete, learning more molecular and extrinsic, the division between personal and public knowledge more pronounced, and the opportunities open to children for developing realms other than basics more restricted than for the more successful children. The 'slower' children in short become increasingly treated as clients – as collections of deficiencies it is the teachers' responsibility to overcome. The failure of these children is defined arbitrarily since memorization of words is not, of course, the only way to teach children to decode printed symbols. It is merely the first step in *her* sequence (which resembled many reception teachers' reading schemes). These variations in patterns of resolution, though evident within the first week of school, are not, however, as starkly drawn as in American schools where there is often stratification by 'reading group' after the first several weeks of school.[6] As the children pass from reception to higher classes these differences in patterns that are based on attribution of native ability become more distinctly seen. In most of the classes, those children who have difficulty meeting the school's standards are subject to shifts of resolution that are more striking than the shifts detectable in Mrs Martin's classroom. The exceptions should be noted. The chalk and talk teachers like Mr Edgar respond to these 'slower' children quite differently – they often allow children to tune out, to exert more control over their own time than the other children, so long as they face forward most of the time and whisper softly.

PATTERNS OF RESOLUTION AND 'INFORMAL' OR 'OPEN' EDUCATION

The terms 'informal' and 'formal' and others used as synonyms – progressive, open, traditional – have been value-laden words in the so-called Great Debate in England and the increasingly bitter public controversy over 'back to the basics' and 'accountability' on the other side of the Atlantic. Proponents of informal education often associate it with freedom, child-centeredness,[7] priority on creative expression, rejection of traditional distinctions between school subjects, and continue to argue that informal methods make a positive contribution to the solution of many of our pressing educational and societal problems. Conservative detractors, increasingly vocal, portray such methods as a source of the problems, as contributing in significant measure to a loosening, if not a total abandonment, of standards in basic subjects, placing the emphasis on psychological well-being to the detriment of intellectual development, pandering to immediate interests of children rather than developing in them respect for tradition and authority.[8] Leftist critics sometimes take another tack; they portray progressive methods as perhaps well-intentioned, but just one more liberal-social democratic delusion that contributes to the maintainance of the status quo.[9]

Despite their ambiguities, the labels formal/informal as commonly used in the schools we visited, do in some general way distinguish two sets of teachers, between Mr Sprinter, all the infant teachers at Port, Castlegate and the majority of infant schools we visited, the Heathbrook Junior and Port 'team' teachers, on the one hand, and the teachers at Highrock, and Mr Edgar, on the other. Teachers considered 'informal' by the teachers and heads we met do as a group organize learning in ways that are patently different from those considered 'formal'. However, it is only in dealing with the extremes that this division does not present insurmountable problems. The gamut of differences in approaches among teachers can be more accurately distinguished using the dilemma language. There is clearly a wide *range* of patterns that teachers and heads commonly associated with informal, and a range they associated with formal. In relative terms, what were called informal methods in the schools we studied may be characterized as patterns of resolution where there is greater teacher control over more realms of the child's development, generally tighter teacher control of time in the basics, but more child control over begin and duration in the non-basics. Informal teachers also exerted far tighter control over operations and standards in the basics than was evident in the more formal settings. A number of these claims contradict many commonly held notions about the differences in the two types of teaching.[10] With respect to transmission of knowledge, there was, in informal classes, less separation of personal from public knowledge, greater reliance on holistic learning, more emphasis on intrinsic motivation and on each child unique modes of resolutions. There was, in general, a stronger child as person orientation. With respect to the societal dilemmas, there were more frequent childhood unique modes in 3R and non-3R activities in informal settings. And what have been called transformational resolutions were more frequently exhibited in these settings as well.

On the other hand, it is essential to recognize that the differences between the two styles are in many cases merely differences in emphasis on particular dilemmas. For example, all teachers used extrinsic motivation but it tended to be a more exceptional mode (except for a few children) in informal classrooms. The emphases on molecular learning and children have shared characteristics were implicit in all teachers' behaviors, but heavier, particularly in the basics, in more formal settings. differences between formal and informal teachers regarding patterns of allocation, and sanctions are difficult to characterize simply. Our information is limited but it appears that there is a tendency in informal classrooms for a greater number of children to receive a somewhat more equal share, perhaps with the very 'clever' receiving somewhat less and the slightly 'backwards' more. However, there appear to be no sharp differences between informal and formal teachers' patterns of resolution to the common culture, *ad hoc* application, knowledge as problematical and learning is social v. learning is individual dilemmas, although the few places where we observed a heavy emphasis on learning is social were in informal settings.[11]

Finally, a note on Mr Sprinter's resolutions. He was not intensively observed, so a detailed analysis of the relationship between his more transformational intentions and his day in and day out practices was not conducted. However, even on the basis of several days' observation it was clear that his resolutions are, in spite of superficial resemblances, as distinctly different from Mrs Martin's and Mr Scott's as resolutions of the latter two are from Mr Edgar's.

Our intent in this summary is merely to show in what way the language can be used to talk about how classrooms are similar to and different from one another. We want to stress that we are not claiming that the patterns we found in the settings we studied are necessarily linked to the common distinction, formal v. informal. A thorough study of the relationship between these variations and the attributions of formality–informality that we have speculated upon would require, among other things, more systematic, longer term observation, the gathering of data using the dilemmas to sharpen and focus observations, and a group of teachers that includes a higher proportion considered formal than we had in our study.

Whatever may be the merit of using the common terms formal and informal, they do, as we have shown, bypass and obscure many distinctions among teachers. There is nothing new in this point. The problems associated with describing schooling in terms of bipolar or tripartite categories, such as democratic–authoritarian, direct–indirect, or more recently, traditional, informal and mixed, has been noted repeatedly over the years.[12] Division of the world into progressive v. traditional (Left v. Right) has long been a useful handle for those with political axes to grind and this is unlikely to change. However, the wide differences between the resolutions of Mr Sprinter, Mr Scott, Mrs Lawton, Mrs Martin and Mrs Newhouse should alert us to distortions that are created by categorizing teachers into two or three or half a dozen mutually exclusive types. The recognition of such differences among teachers is, however, important only if they have differential effects upon children. What connections might there be between different patterns of resolution, what children learn, and social transmission and change? It is to this question we now turn.

IX PATTERNS OF RESOLUTION AND SOCIAL CHANGE: AN EXPLORATION

How do the dilemmas represent the connections between everyday school life and social and cultural reproduction and change, or, in the language of social science, between the micro and the macro? Our answer is in three parts. We show how the dilemmas may be used, first, to examine the meanings children take from teachers' actions; second, to explore the origins of teachers' actions in their histories and the situation; third, to inquire into the relationship of the meanings children take from schooling to social stability and change. These questions have been explored by many social researchers over the decades.[1] Our purpose in these analyses is not to contribute original or definitive answers to these problems but *to demonstrate how the dilemma language* (and the general approach it represents) *may be used to penetrate some of the uncertainties and confusions that surround these questions.*

Mrs Martin tells Cheryl, 'I think you are now ready for your *Janet and John.*' In the subsequent weeks, we see her tell several children who had mastered the sight vocabulary in the readers that they are 'ready', and she gives them their 'normal readers'. On a given morning she may say 'Andrea' or 'David, you haven't read yet', reminding them to come to her desk so she can listen to them read from their readers. [summarized from our field notes]

Meaning arises and lies within the field of the relation between the gesture of a given organism and the subsequent behavior of this organism. [George Herbert Mead]

We assume as fact that persons take meaning from everyday experience. To consider some familiar examples, as Mrs Martin gives *Janet and John* readers to children who demonstrate to her satisfaction that they can perform a particular set of operations, and, through her words and other gestures, indicates they are now 'ready', they take from her the generally accepted definition of what it means to be *ready* to advance to a higher status position in the classroom group. As children hear her call the names of those who have not 'read' today, though many children have read cereal boxes, the traffic signs and, most significantly, may have read to her their own 'news', from such acts they take her meaning of 'read' – reading the school reader. As they experience the sequence of events that leads to receiving their *Janet and John* and come to know their location in the sequence, they take the school's definition of how clever or dim they are relative to others. One must not, we think, in efforts to understand schools' contribution to social continuity and change, discount the possible impact of such events which occur during children's first encounters with a public institution and an authority figure whom many initially call 'mum'.

The children will, of course, continue throughout their lives to revise the meanings they have taken from Mrs Martin's classroom, as they are told for example, by other teachers, in other situations, subtly or directly, that they are or are not 'ready' for higher-status educational activities. However, the views they develop as they meet with Mrs Martin in compulsory sessions daily over the course of ten months, will quite likely survive in some form, as part of their 'generalized other'.

Our formulation of the problem commonly posed as 'the effects of schooling' is: what meanings do children take from teachers' patterns of resolution to the dilemmas of schooling, and how do these meanings become transformed as they engage in other experiences – in classrooms and elsewhere? [2] Teachers' patterns of schooling, as we have shown, may be described in terms of both dominant and exceptional modes of resolution. This fact is of central significance to our analyses. As teachers through these patterns of resolution play out the alternative and often contradictory meanings of the culture, they transmit these contradictions to children. Studying these contradictions and their interplay as they are transmitted via schooling is more complex and difficult than examining only the dominant patterns and meanings. However, it provides an alternative to analyses that portray teachers' beliefs and patterns of behavior as static and simplistic and looks at classroom effects in terms of a unitary set of meanings transmitted to children.[3] Such analyses can only account for how schools reproduce the society, they cannot conceptualize the possibilities in the schooling process for social transformation.

THE CONSEQUENCES OF PATTERNS OF RESOLUTION

Meanings related to the quality of work

Dominant and exceptional modes of resolution to the dilemmas of schooling may be seen as transmitting to children contradictory views of how much satisfaction they can expect in their workaday lives. Children at Port begin to make a distinction very early between 'work' and those activities done voluntarily with pleasure. We interviewed seven of the younger children in Mrs Eden's class, the most recent arrivals from Mrs Martin's class. Lisa's rhyme catches their sentiments. When asked 'Can you describe your work?' she chants:

> readin', writin', 'rithmetic
> put 'em together, they make you sick.

The idea that school work can be pleasurable, related to one's interests, does, however, persist among Mrs Eden's children. They express diverse views about whether jigsaws, bricks, painting, model building, all things they enjoy doing, are work or play. Many are uncertain about how to categorize painting. Some say writing the 'news' is sometimes work, sometimes play. Others identify something as work if 'it is hard', as play if 'it is easy', 'if you can choose it', or 'if you can do it the way you like'. The children also perceive that as they move up to the upper infants and to junior school, work will get 'ever so hard'. Several believed, 'if you don't work [in the juniors] you'll get a smack'. Many studies have suggested that by the time these children reach adulthood most will have all but abandoned the idea that work can be personally meaningful, though some will expect to be able to control and create in their working lives.[4]

We noted an emphasis on the childhood unique, holistic and intrinsic motivation modes and the fusing of public and personal knowledge by Mrs Martin and (to a lesser extent) in Castlegate teachers. In these classrooms 'reading' means *taking meaning from print*, reading a *book*. Even though the books are 'readers', chosen by the teachers, reading is from the start a holistic activity, not a set of fragmented reading skills exercises. These patterns of introducing reading appear to transmit a conception that school work can be satisfying and personally meaningful. The differences in resolutions between Port and Castlegate infant teachers, however, are probably significant. Children at Castlegate experience more teacher control over time and operations, more use of extrinsic motivation, fewer fusings of personal and public knowledge, and less attention to realms outside a narrow range of the intellectual. Particularly in light of the resolutions they will experience at Highrock, we surmise that relative to Port, Castlegate children are less likely (assuming such differences continue) to look for personal meaning from school work and to expect meaningful, pleasurable work in their lives as adults, and are more likely to take as given that pleasure at school can only be experienced at playtime and, analogously in one's adult life, during one's leisure time.

We have pointed out that as the children pass through Port, the emphases in teachers' patterns of resolutions shift towards greater teacher control of time, operations and standards. Motivation becomes increasingly extrinsic – set in terms of rewards for the number of pages or problems completed – and certain tasks are increasingly detached from children's interests (for example, topic). We suspect that as a result of these shifts children's expectations change – and as they approach the final year at Port they are increasingly likely to think of work in school and perhaps in the adult world as onerous, joyless, something done for others, to be avoided if possible. They come to a view, which they take for granted, that alienated work is the inevitable concomitant of school and social life. However, some resolutions, particularly in the earlier years of primary school, though more exceptional in later years, will have likely transmitted quite contradictory meanings. Although 'topic' for most may have become a ritual of transliterating public knowledge from encyclopedias, for some it remains an opportunity to pursue a serious interest, to integrate public with personal knowledge. 'Reading' in Mr Scott's, Mr Sprinter's and the greatest majority of infant classrooms, remained reading a book – a holistic, intrinsically motivated activity. Morning work in the basics provided some opportunity for Port and Heathbrook juniors to control their own lives and to engage in activities of intrinsic interest to them. Such modes, though increasingly infrequent as one ascends in years, never disappear entirely, thus they may remain as seeds of expectations that autonomy and satisfaction in work are desirable and possible.

In sum, we take as problematic but likely that children who have experienced more frequent holistic, intrinsic, personal fused with public knowledge modes, and are treated as unique (rather than as having shared characteristics), as persons rather than as clients, will, as adults, more strongly sustain expectations, perhaps subconscious, that work can and should be meaningful. These expectations will no doubt be tempered, perhaps deeply buried, during subsequent years by encounters beyond the primary school which convey that one should not expect to express or develop one's capabilities in one's work, nor to exercise much control over one's own daily activities. They will, however, live on in the consciousness of Mrs Martin's children long after they have forgotten the particulars of life in her classroom, perhaps to be evoked at some future time when an opportunity to work towards changes in working conditions presents itself in later life.

We have indicated how everyday schooling activity may convey contrary and ambivalent expectations that work in adulthood can and will be satisfying and meaningful, and that differences in teachers' patterns of resolution may convey differing expectations to different individuals or groups of children. Social stability depends in some measure upon widely shared views that some more than others have the right to engage in autonomous and meaningful work and to receive the monetary rewards and/or higher status that are attached to such work; that particular forms of work deserve higher status – and greater financial reward; and that particular individuals are qualified to work at these valued occupations because they possess superior capacities and/or talents.[5] We turn now to a consideration of how such notions might be transmitted in school: what might be the relationship of patterns of resolution to children's acceptance of a particular form of social hierarchy, and of the allocation of particular individuals to positions in this hierarchy.

Meanings taken about school knowledge, hierarchy and status

Respect for those who have certificates, diplomas and degrees that testify to mastery of school knowledge is by no means universal. Yet even those who question the legitimacy of conferring status on the basis of knowledge as it is defined by schools are not likely to be completely free of the notion that there is a significant relationship between economic success, school success and individual merit.[6] Almost everyone, at least to some extent, comes to respect school-legitimated public knowledge and those who are its masters, and to nurse doubts about the legitimacy and value of non-school-based knowledge and experience. Though perhaps not a necessary concomitant in our society, respect for school knowledge is often accompanied by learning to discount one's own personal knowledge (the housewife who says after raising several children, 'I don't know anything', or the experienced teacher who insists she knows nothing about learning).

There is no question that in modern industrial societies the jobs one gets that require official certification that one is educated in the basics (for example, so many O and/or A levels, diplomas or university degrees) are, in general, more highly valued in the marketplace. The rates of un- and underemployment of skilled practitioners in the creative arts and crafts, particularly those without school credentials (with a few highly visible exceptions, sports, entertainers, etc.) attest to this. We will, using fragments of data, speculate on how teachers' patterns of resolution transmit views of worthwhile knowledge and legitimate or merited status.[7] We will consider first how teachers transmit to children what realms and forms of public knowledge are more worthwhile than others.

Teachers transmit that the *basics* are most worthwhile by controlling them more tightly and by more frequently utilizing extrinsic, molecular resolutions in their transmission. When Mrs Martin and the Castlegate teachers control and set standards, divorce personal from public knowledge, molecularize the learning process in the basics more regularly and rigorously, and monitor their performance more closely than for other realms, they appear to be communicating that 'basics' are most important to them and the society than other 'activities'. Yet this meaning is to some degree contradicted by the obvious care that Mrs Martin and the infant teachers give to the non-basics (the arts, dramatic play and social development). In her classroom a cleverly built Lego ship or a lovely painting are publicly treated as deserving of as high a status as a child's demonstrations of wizardry in maths or reading. Juniors in Mrs Newhouse's classroom probably receive ambivalent notions of what areas of knowledge and knowing are of most worth. We see how Mr Nigel and Mrs Newhouse accord status to maths by their public praise and their close controls over the quantity of pages successfully completed. But Mrs Newhouse, to a degree we rarely see in other junior teachers, controls and sets standards for creative writing and originality in drawing. Her tendency to leave control of 'topic' to the children and her reliance entirely upon intrinsic motivation for this activity probably conveys to most children that knowledge of society, people and nature is lower-status knowledge. The virtual absence of control over many of the 'non-basic' realms at Castlegate, as compared to Mrs Martin's and Mrs Newhouse's classes, probably conveys to Castlegate children the greater conviction that arts and crafts and other 'practical' activities are of little value compared to the 3Rs.

Patterns of resolution also communicate to children ambivalent notions of what *forms* of knowledge (as opposed to realms) are most worthwhile and of how worthwhile school knowledge is in general.

For example, we indicated Mrs Martin's *relatively* stronger emphasis on transformational public/personal knowledge and molecular/holistic modes, intrinsic motivation, child control of time and the uniqueness of each child, as compared to Castlegate teachers and to many American teachers. This constellation of resolutions may convey to a higher proportion of Mrs Martin's children that school knowledge is worth possessing for its own sake. As children progress through school, however, many will experience increasingly resolutions that resemble Mr Edgar's heavy emphasis on extrinsic motivation, knowledge as content, and public divorced from personal knowledge. As a consequence many children may come to define school knowledge (and public knowledge in general) as 'facts' that one can recall in response to disconnected questions. They may come to believe that 'knowing the facts' is what education is about. The roots of skepticism of the value of such knowledge are detectable during Mr Edgar's Sicily lesson.[8] In spite of the intensity of hand-raising many tune out. What we may be seeing is the origin of the near total disdain for school knowledge that Paul Willis identified in a group of working-class boys who were completing secondary school and entering the world of work.[9] However, the widespread concern of juniors at Port and Heathbrook to 'forge ahead' by completing as many pages of maths as possible, and the intensity of hand-raising by over a third of the class in an effort to deliver answers to Mr Edgar's questions suggests that the respect for school knowledge as defined by Mrs Newhouse, Mr Scott and Mr Edgar strongly endures in many, probably most, children. Even some who openly disdain Mr Edgar's questions consider the successful answerers the 'brains'. As adults, many of the children, perhaps including the disinterested in Mr Edgar's class, will press their own children to work hard in school, to learn 'Sicily' and 'flax'.[10] Although many children may come to feel kindly about Mr Edgar, he may in his own way have sown some seeds to skepticism, planted doubts about the relevance of school learning of the serious issues of living. Patterns at Highrock may also nurture disdain for school knowledge but it is unlikely to be tempered by kindly feelings toward teachers or school authorities. Mr Sprinter's resolutions that emphasize holistic learning and transformational personal/public knowledge and control may also convey to some children skepticism about the social or personal value of school knowledge that is granted high status by other teachers, and/or they may reject what Mr Sprinter represents as valued knowledge and embrace views Mr Sprinter attributes to most of their parents: that their children 'should be good at maths –

good at writing and good at reading . . . handwriting as well'.

These patterns not only transmit what sorts and realms of knowledge are more important than others, but a belief that those who most easily and successfully learn school knowledge are worthy of higher status. How early this process begins is suggested by the children's discussion about who is in the 'bottom' of Mrs Martin's class. Of course the process of assigning status on the basis of school knowledge (like the development of all meanings) has roots in the outside culture as well. This is indicated by some children assuming that the tables are ranked according to cleverness in spite of the fact that Mrs Martin assigns children (with very few exceptions) to tables on the basis of age. However, the seeds of hierarchy are nourished by her resolutions as well. Mrs Martin withholds readers from children until they have memorized a set of 'sight' words. This pattern, as we have suggested, conveys that some children are more clever than others. And, we suspect, children come to believe that 'cleverness' is a wholly inborn attribute of the child rather than a reflection of what has been socially defined as valued knowledge.

After a term, Samuel, who probably shares some of his parents' ambivalence about school's values (they are Jehovah's Witnesses), and David have 'fallen behind'. They do not (cannot, or have no interest to) retain the dozen or so words they need in order to obtain the normal reader. When these children who are 'not reading' enter Mrs Eden's class, often a term later than their age mates, they will be placed at work tables not on the basis of age (a deficiency that everyone eventually overcomes) but solely on the basis of the speed with which they have demonstrated mastery of the valued tasks in the 3Rs. Subsequent teachers will no doubt contribute to these children's notions that they are less deserving of status by allocating other symbols of success differentially on the basis of their success at reading as defined and taught by the teachers. Many of these children will eventually come to terms with what Jules Henry calls the 'essential nightmare', the fear of failure, as they resign themselves to the bottom of the heap.[11] The vast majority of the others who observe this process do their school work with varying degrees of enthusiasm, in part, to save themselves from David's and Samuel's fate.

The areas of the curriculum that are differentially controlled and monitored by teachers also likely affect children's notions of who merits high status. Virtually all the infant and many of the junior teachers provide more opportunities in the aesthetic, social and physical realms than is common in the American classrooms we know. However, the range of realms included in the curriculum of the English primary classrooms is less likely to accord status to a potential social scientist, physicist, creative thinker or automobile mechanic than to a writer, mathematician, stenographer, accountant or athlete. And the range of realms accorded status is narrower in the school attended by the poorer children. Thus children such as Anthony (in Mrs Lawton's room at Castlegate), who appear to be highly talented in the arts or sciences but have moderate interest in the narrow range of the 3Rs, which his teacher and the teachers at Castlegate generally take such pain to control, will likely have more limited opportunity for recognition as compared to children in Mr Sprinter's, Mrs Martin's or Mrs Newhouse's classrooms.

The irony is that those children who fail at those tasks that are taken as meriting high status will experience resolutions that are increasingly molecular, extrinsic and devoid of personal meaning. They will also receive *fewer* opportunities to engage in activities that might develop 'non-basic' talents. As the gap between their spoken language and the language of the readers becomes even wider, these 'dim' children will, we suppose, become increasingly disinclined to engage in school tasks and, as a result, will likely confirm teachers' and classmates' low regard for their abilities.

Let us not assume, however, that socialization to accept the prevailing status hierarchy is uniform, that there is a perfect correspondence between resolutions and the dominant notions of status in the society at large. There are the exceptional modes of resolution. The talented artist *is* given high recognition by Mrs Martin, Mrs Newhouse and several others. We assume that these more exceptional modes transmit some respect for those talented in realms of knowledge and experience beyond the basics, and that these teachers may in some measure contribute to a greater willingness of some of these children to question the definitions of high-status knowledge that prevail in the society when they become adults.

Meanings related to autonomy and collectivism

The ideology of the common school includes the promise that attendance will develop students' capacities to the fullest, empower them to think for themselves and to become masters of their own fates within the limits of the rights of others. Yet many critics of schools have argued that, contrary to the promise, schooling encourages passivity and acquiescence, and contributes to feelings of personal inadequacy and powerlessness.

210

How do differences in patterns of resolution affect persons' capacities and will to control their lives both in the present and in their lives as adults? Whatever the school's role, persons in western societies have come to possess complex and paradoxical conceptions of their own autonomy and powerlessness, and these conceptions are unequally distributed among social classes. The part that social experience, both within and beyond the school walls, contributes to the development of these conceptions remains largely unexplored. Though the problem is obviously a complex one – since later school experiences and experiences outside schools likely have very significant force – we suggest that early schooling patterns may have important consequences. Patterns implicit in the teaching of literacy, for example, are likely to affect the extent to which children use literacy to increase personal control. The emphasis in Mrs Martin's patterns of resolution as she introduces children to the world of the printed world on intrinsic motivation and transformational personal/public and molecular/holistic modes, the close control over operations adjusted to some degree to the uniqueness of each child, may convey to children that literacy is something that is *for them*, that reading can illuminate and thus give them personal power over their world.[12] Will children for whom learning to read means gaining immediate power to communicate important ideas feel differently about the promise of schooling and the power of public knowledge than those for whom reading means submitting to the molecular tasks of others? And what are the immediate (as well as long-range) effects of these attitudes toward schooling on how well children learn to read and thus on the power they derive fròm literacy? Furthermore, will those children who have been socialized by parents to expect some autonomy over their actions and/or to be suspicious of teachers, be more resistant to schools' efforts to teach reading in a molecular fashion?

The molecular, content-oriented, public knowledge emphases in Mr Edgar's classroom (and other classrooms with similar patterns) likely convey to many children that the traditions of public knowledge offer few answers that will help them direct the course of their lives. The result may also be fundamental doubts both about one's own and others' power to understand. In contrast, Mr Sprinter's and Mr Scott's patterns would, we think, convey optimism that public knowledge enhances personal power. What is more, if knowledge is treated as given rather than problematical, then the disillusionment that may follow from the failure of school knowledge to help persons make sense of their reality may throw into question the usefulness of all school-transmitted public knowledge. In short, too heavy an emphasis on knowledge as given, on public separated from personal knowledge and on knowledge as content, by planting doubts in children about the general usefulness of public knowledge, may feed anti-intellectualism among certain groups of children that they may carry into adulthood. And though extreme patterns of teacher control, extrinsic motivation, molecular learning and public knowledge such as those at Highrock may result in oppositional stances towards schooling, learning and authority, as Paul Willis shows in his study, such oppositional stances do not in the long run empower children, as long as they must live in a society which rewards success at school and conformity to societal norms.

Resolving the childhood dilemma predominantly in terms of either extreme we suspect conveys a sense of powerlessness to children. On the one hand, a heavy emphasis on the childhood unique mode may convey the notion that there is a clear line between adult and child rights, and thus result in a reluctance directly to confront authority that may carry into adulthood. On the other hand, an extremely strong childhood continuous emphasis probably conveys to children that their interests and rights as persons will be disregarded, also conveying a sense of powerlessness.[13]

We also suspect that the predominance of knowledge as given over knowledge as problematical resolutions that appeared to us to characterize virtually all classrooms (except Mr Sprinter's), communicates that knowledge is a true reflection of the social world as it is. Children who virtually always experience knowledge as given patterns may be less likely to question the decisions or the legitimacy of those in power or the prevailing social arrangements, or to see that any set of social norms including classroom rules, having been made by human agency, can be undone.

How patterns of resolution are distributed may communicate conceptions of autonomy and powerlessness differentially to children. For example, resolutions to the control and motivation dilemmas that are patterned according to a child's mastery of a certain set of 3R tasks may convey as natural that those who succeed at such tasks merit greater autonomy – that the capacity for self-control is legitimately related to a particular set of talents. Because Mrs Martin grants all children some control, she may be contributing to children's views that all are capable of self-control. At the same time, the fact that some children are assumed to require more extrinsic motivation and teacher control than others, may communicate that some persons, more than others, must accommodate themselves to control by more knowledgeable authorities. Resolutions that provide greater autonomy to those who finish their work correctly or quickly, that more frequently treat knowledge as problematic for the 'clever' children (by giving more open-ended questions to those who advance more quickly in the readers) may empower a particular set of children more than others.[14]

The nine- and ten-year-old children in Mr Sprinter's classroom make few distinctions between work and play, and they take far greater control over their classroom lives than children who experience more common patterns of resolution. Yet Mr Sprinter's patterns are rare and it is not likely that he will, in one school year, transform the meanings children have taken from previous teachers. The long-term effects of uncommon patterns during a single school year (or two or three during one's formal schooling) are interesting to contemplate and deserve close study.

While many writers have studied the effects of schooling on the development of autonomy, power and powerlessness, less attention has been paid to how 'social skills and attitudes that lead to altruism, cooperation, and social responsibility'[15] are or are not fostered by classroom life. It is likely that patterns which emphasize each child unique and child as student, though they may convey to some children subjective feelings of autonomy, and develop socially-valued academic competencies, may also foster competitive, egoistic, and atomized social relations over what Elizabeth Cagan calls the more 'collectivist' values. She also argues that altruistic and cooperative behaviors do not 'arise spontaneously. . . . (They) must be deliberately cultivated (and require) . . . structures and adult interventions different from those that appear to enhance personal freedom.'[16] In our terms greater teacher control over moral and social realms (whole child), and greater emphasis on shared characteristics of children (rather than on their uniqueness) and social learning are likely to convey more cooperative values. Mr Sprinter's patterns of resolution more consistently reflected these emphases than the other teachers we observed. However, only in a Rudolf Steiner school in the Netherlands did we see patterns that are likely to contribute to the development of generalized social responsibility and collective participation. Cagan also argues that unless 'collectivist education . . . (is) self consciously oppositionist . . . not only will this effort fail, but it may be subtly transformed into a means of increasing conformity to existing social institutions and arrangements'.[17] In our terms, a knowledge as problematical emphasis is necessary if collective values are not to eclipse values of autonomy and personal power.

213

ORIGINS OF PATTERNS OF RESOLUTION

How can teachers' schooling behavior be explained? We have, in Chapter VI, sketched our answer to this question in terms of Meadian and Marxist concepts. Here we show how formulation in terms of the dilemma language adds precision and concreteness to this question.[18] We formulate the problem: what in teachers' social biographies and in the history of the institutions, the society and the culture, together with the present set of circumstances, shapes teachers' resolutions to the dilemmas of schooling? The tentativity of these explorations must be underscored since we made no systematic effort to gather evidence on teachers' histories or the institutional setting.

Mrs Martin's patterns of resolution may be seen as the playing out of contrary 'pulls' *within*, and pressures in the situation that push *upon*, her. These contrary dispositions, as we have argued, although they are experienced individually, are social, that is, they are conflicts of the society and culture as well as of her personal biography. She internalizes them throughout her life and they act upon her in the present to shape her view of the alternative possibilities.

The dilemmas in teachers' social histories

Individuals, including teachers, throughout their lives, take from experience and continuously adjust their conceptions of what is valued knowledge, what is a fair allocation of status and other social resources, how much control they and others have over their own lives and destinies, etc. The meanings teachers take from experience during their schooling, from their formal training at college or university, during their careers as teachers in encounters with children, administrators and parents, in their lives as citizens and parents from the countless events in their personal and social histories, continuously affect their patterns of resolution and their views of the desirability and practicality of resolving differently the dilemmas they face as teachers.

We have some fragments of data that suggest the broad range of social experiences that are represented in Mrs Martin's patterns of resolution. Her parents in the 1930s, she tells us, brought her up to believe, 'You must'. Children were expected to do without question what adults required of them. These views were not unlike those of her professional peers at her initial teaching post. She told us that, according to her experience, encouraging children rather than controlling them 'is not very general in English teachers'. She also told us of support for an alternative perspective – 'that one should teach through encouragement' – which was predominant among the infant teachers at Port when she joined the staff. Over time she incorporated their perspectives: 'I've learned a lot since coming here – Mrs Carpenter and Mrs Eden have taught me quite a lot.' She comments on how her own experience as a parent also affected her classroom patterns. 'If John [her son] says no, I appeal to his sense of justice. Then I give up – I don't make it a matter of principle.' These fragments suggest that Mrs Martin's views about control of children have been shaped over her lifetime, in her roles as child, parent, teacher, and that the views that have been presented to her in these roles were not coherent and consistent with one another.

We did not ask many questions of teachers about their own schooling as children and adults. However, it is possible that Mrs Martin's alternating responses to equal v. differential allocation, for example, in part reflect the perspectives of courses she studied in English history and political economy, where, perhaps, the modes of resolution were primarily knowledge (and society) as given (that is, that implicitly if not explicitly, portrayed honesty and hard work as the foundations of the English Tradition), rather than modes that treated as problematical English history, society and social structure. Perhaps a course in child development, that portrayed atypical children in terms of their deficits (a common culture view) rather than as socially and culturally different (a sub-group view), has contributed to her treatment of Samuel's problems as 'in him' rather than in the ways the generally accepted Church of England orientation of the school might be affecting his will and capacity to accept school knowledge. Her readiness to give more time to some rather than others and the nature of her resolutions during that time may even have been affected by a course that posed questions about whether, or took as given that, children like Samuel deserve help in overcoming deficiencies for which they are not responsible.

We suspect it would also be illuminating to explore the links between her patterns of resolution to the dilemmas and other aspects of her social experience, growing up in a mining town, coming of age in English society as a woman during the Second World War years, living as a wife of a working-class man. We would be curious to know, for example, how aspects of her personal and social history have affected the greater emphasis on childhood unique resolutions that she shared with many other English primary as compared to American teachers.

We do not wish to imply that Mrs Martin is pawn to these prior experiences – indeed, she could not be, given the conflicting dictates implicit in her experiences. Rather, from what she tells us, it is reasonable to conclude that some of her patterns of resolution are, in part, outcomes of reflections (either in the recent or distant past) upon her social experience. Mrs Martin at several points explicitly referred to this process of reflection when she discussed her parents and traced for us the history of the shifts in the way she has come to organize schooling experience for children.

Institutional influences in teachers' dialectics

It is not only teachers' previous social experiences that, with or without reflection, are represented in their patterns. Features of the present situation – the perspectives of others, peers, parents, children, administrative superiors and the organization and physical structure of the school itself – play a part in the dialectic of dilemma resolution. For example, Mrs Hollins's preferred patterns are very clear in Castlegate teachers' resolutions. All of the teachers and Mrs Hollins attest to this (happily). Recall that Mrs Hollins told us how she shaped her teachers' patterns:

I started out by approving of what they were doing . . . I said, 'I like what you're doing, . . . there are some interesting things going on. I wonder if you could keep your activities going.' . . . I sat with them and (talked) with them. And that's how we got this free writing established in one room . . . by sitting with the children myself and seeing that they all had a book . . . and had a pride in it . . . and didn't copy just a piece off the board.

Mrs Martin's patterns coincide rather closely with those of the deputy, Mrs Carpenter, who is nominally head of the infant department, Mr Nigel (who has been headmaster but a short time), and resolutions encouraged by LEA advisors. Their views are 'in' her patterns of resolution in the sense that they legitimate her patterns, as Mrs Calthorpe's do Mr Sprinter's. Though Mrs Martin tells us that she formerly taught in schools where 'heads like to see them actually sitting down all the time', her present headmaster supports her patterns. In our interview, Mr Nigel says,

[In] 'class' teaching the children did their sums on the blackboard and the bright ones finished and that was it. . . . Those children that were slow struggled on until they'd finished . . Traditional teaching was time-tabled. . . . The children would . . . look up and say, 'OK, it's writing time'. Various subjects, perhaps art, suffered greatly under this system. . . Say they'd got a special story they wanted to write. . . . Who's to worry what they [the children] do in the afternoon if they work in the morning – you have to worry about parents too. You can justify the [free choice] afternoon for individual fulfillment [if you have] 'tool making' in the morning.

We infer from this and from the shifts in patterns he is trying to effect in the junior teachers, that Mr Nigel favors patterns of resolution to the control, motivation and unique/shared characteristics dilemmas that are congruent with Mrs Martin's. Had he specified or implied support for greater emphasis on public knowledge, teacher control, child as student, molecular and extrinsic modes, she would have 'found it very difficult'. Mr Nigel's perspectives and behavior also play an important part in Mrs Newhouse's patterns of resolution. She told us, 'I've always wanted to teach informally . . . Mr Nigel encouraged me quite a bit'.

But why does Mr Nigel favor these moderate and gradual shifts in teachers' patterns of resolution? Again, our data are limited. He did tell us that he moved from an initial teaching post in a 'fairly progressive school' to a place where 'they were certainly very, very traditional'. However, he reports, he was unclear about his own views until he became deputy headmaster under Mr Bolton at Heathbrook. 'I think working with Ralph was my training as a headmaster . . . he interested me in education through thinking very carefully.' Mr Bolton's views are thus in a very real sense in Mrs Martin's and in Mrs Newhouse's patterns of resolution. The congruence of Mr Bolton's preferred patterns with Mr Nigel's and Mrs Martin's on the standards and the realms dilemmas are suggested in the following piece from our interview with him:

The way I see it is to make sure that the teachers know that you've got to have certain standards in the school, that the children get up to those standards that you want them to reach before they go up to [the local comprehensive school], but at the same time, that must not be all they know of it. Because I think that in addition to sending out children who are good at reading and competent at mathematics, they've also got to be well-adjusted . . . but you don't get well-adjusted children unless you get children who are competent at mathematics and reading; hang-ups come from the fact that they can't read, I think. And then we've also got to provide a place which is pleasant. And again you see this is all part of it, to make sure you've got well-adjusted children with a pleasant atmosphere in the school.

Policies of the LEA may also be seen as contributing to Mrs Martin's and Mrs Newhouse's schooling patterns. Mr Nigel was one of three candidates on the LEA's list for head teacher of Port because, in the words of an LEA official, 'He was considered an agent of change'. It appears that it was conscious policy somewhere in the LEA to put such persons forward. According to the LEA official, he saw Mr Nigel's task 'to introduce new curricula and some new methods to the junior school where . . . a few as usual were ready for change . . . and others were not necessarily ready'. The ideal set of teaching resolutions for this LEA official, in his words, was 'skills coming through all the other work' but, he added, 'only after having taught for five years or so is one able to do this successfully'. If teachers cannot manage such integration they should 'make some minimal work requirements'. The LEA offical's expectations for Port under Mr Nigel are to encourage child as person resolutions, 'to get teachers to be on the side of the kids', *and* to manifest patterns of organization that are 'conscious, not anarchistic', by which he means close teacher monitoring of 3Rs. The Director of the LEA in which Castlegate is located discussed with us his priorities, and also expressed preferences for patterns of resolution that appeared to be closely congruent with those of Mrs Hollins. It is in this sense that the resolutions of LEA administrators are – through their head teachers – 'in' the classroom teachers' patterns.

Though the influence of the administrative structure and incumbents of administrative roles is not complete, it is considerable. At the time of our study persons within the two local education authorities in which the schools we studied were located were consciously, through the nomination of individuals such as Mrs Hollins and Mr Nigel to headship, changing teachers' patterns of resolution toward greater emphases on child control, personal knowledge, holistic, individualized learning and intrinsic motivation. We had little evidence of administrative influence direct (for example, through use of power of appointment) or indirect towards shifts in resolution to the common culture or equality dilemmas. It was policy in one of the LEAs to encourage knowledge as problematical and process resolutions in nature studies, arts and maths through the programs of the teaching centres, and roving primary-school advisors (these episodes have not been included in the description of the schools), but we found no efforts, direct or indirect, to encourage greater problematical or process emphases in the areas of political and moral education, or in the study of history and society more generally. Nor was there strong press by any of the administrators for the more transformational patterns of Mr Sprinter. The officials in the LEA to whom we talked, and all head teachers, emphasized that teachers must maintain control, set standards, teach the 'basics', and maintain 'balanced' patterns. (This, one must recall, was during the heyday of informal education.) As we have argued, teacher's patterns at Castlegate and Port did come to more closely resemble the patterns desired by the LEA authorities.

We see in each of the schools evidence of administrators' initiatives upon teachers' patterns of resolutions. However, their power is limited by the situation, which includes the life histories of those they attempt to influence. For example, the views that many in England, including Castlegate teachers, hold about the working-class poor will likely mean that some Castlegate teachers may never emphasize personal knowledge and intrinsic motivation to the extent desired by Mrs Hollins. Given his professional and personal life history, Mr Edgar is not likely to develop patterns that are congruent with Mr Nigel's, though there is some evidence of shifts in the directions preferred by the headmaster. Mrs Newhouse's changes may be attributed in part to her own decision to shift her resolutions toward those preferred by Mr Nigel.

The children also carry their social histories into the classroom and affect teachers' resolutions. To take one example, Port children, in the words of Mrs Martin, 'come in awe' to her class or, as Mrs Newhouse puts it, 'the [Port] children have manners'. No child we interviewed at Port, even Colin, the school 'troublemaker', could conceive of 'telling off' a teacher. We surmise that a significant contribution to the greater tendency of Port teachers to emphasize child control modes relative to Castlegate is their confidence that the children will do what they are asked willingly, without being overseen by an adult. Children came to school ready to trust teachers, and they are trusted by them.

When Castlegate children begin school they probably bring with them more ambivalent views of school and teachers. Many are from the start suspicious and remote and are more likely to have among their ranks a number who are positively hostile. These attitudes are no doubt reflexive – at least in part – to the condescension they or their parents detect in teachers and in other governmental officials they have encountered, health officers, nursery school teachers, etc. In addition, there is a greater gap at Castlegate between the children's personal knowledge and the public knowledge of the schools than at Port. We surmise that these differences in children's attitudes and experience affect stronger emphasis on molecular, extrinsic, teacher control modes and the more restricted focus of the curriculum at Castlegate relative to Port. By the time Castlegate children encounter Mrs Carter and Mrs Paynter in the third-year infants they will experience resolutions forged in response to children whose initial antipathy to school work has likely intensified in response to the patterns of resolution they have encountered since they entered school. The foregoing portrayal of the careers of poor children in school exemplifies what we mean when we say that schooling patterns are forged reflexively: differences among children based on their out-of-school experience and created by the situation affect teachers' patterns of resolution. These patterns at the same time intensify characteristics ('dim', 'apathetic') persons presume exist.[19]

Institutional arrangements and physical features of school buildings are also 'in' teachers' resolutions. The size of Mrs Martin's and Mr Sprinter's classroom (they are large in contrast to most of the rooms at Castlegate and Mr Edgar's) make it easier for teachers to grant children control of their own time, given the inevitable greater physical movement of children and the necessity for easy access to learning materials that accompanies child control resolutions. That these teachers are responsible for 30–35 children simultaneously strengthens the pull toward teacher control – because of the obvious difficulty of dealing with the variety of activities and responses that would be the inevitable result of allowing them more control over their own time. The size of the classroom also affects the degree in which a teacher will treat children as members of categories, as similar to one another, as does the age-governed division of children into grades that is characteristic of schools in industrialized nations.

SPECULATIONS ON THE RELATIONSHIP OF PATTERNS OF RESOLUTION TO SOCIAL STABILITY AND CHANGE

We have argued that teachers both transmit the society from one generation to the next and influence its transformation. We offer the dilemma language as one way to formulate questions about the part particular patterns of schooling play in this process. We have shown that the sixteen dilemmas may be used as a language to describe patterns and to inquire into the origins and consequences in terms of meanings which students take from teachers' actions. In the concluding paragraphs of Part Four we speculate on how the differing patterns of resolution and the meanings children may be taking from these resolutions affect the children and the society in which they will live as adults. Our speculations will focus on how patterns may affect continuity and change in the relationship of knowledge, status and autonomy.

As we have argued above, children may take as given from

teachers' patterns of resolution the ideology of liberal capitalism – that control, high status and meaningful work are allocated to those who most successfully incorporate that knowledge which is most valued by society and that, because that knowledge is not only most valued, but also truly valuable, the allocation is just. But we have argued that children also take from these same patterns (from the more exceptional modes of resolution) alternative meanings as well, for example, that talents and skills less valued in society – e.g., less marketable talents in creative and performing arts – are nevertheless of great value and that all persons of diverse levels and kinds of skills and abilities deserve opportunities for meaningful work and autonomy.

In order to know the consequences of teachers' patterns of resolution for social continuity and change, we would need to inquire into the connections between the meanings children take from schooling and other social experiences,[20] and the realities of the world they confront as adults. We do not know what the society at the turn of the millenium will be like for children schooled in the 1970s and 1980s – to what extent, for example, those who have mastered the valued knowledge will reap the benefits implicitly promised by teachers as they resolve the dilemmas of schooling. There are many social analysts who believe that if present trends continue, the productive systems of Britain and the US will require, over the years, fewer and fewer individuals who are highly skilled and literate. Stated differently, the probability of material and social rewards for adults who have succeeded in school may continue to decline.[21]

Our analysis of patterns of resolution at Highrock and Castlegate suggested that the Castlegate patterns are more likely to convey expectations for autonomy and meaningful work than are patterns at Highrock, and that Mrs Martin's and Mr Scott's patterns likely convey stronger expectations for autonomy and meaningful work than do those of Castlegate teachers. However, virtually all the teachers' resolutions are significantly similar in that they likely transmit an expectation that possession of particular realms and forms of knowledge will earn future social status. In our view, even the fairly limited expectations transmitted to Castlegate children are discrepant from what appear to be the realities that many of these children will likely face as laborers and service workers. However, the greater expectations for autonomy and meaningful work transmitted by teachers such as Mr Scott and Mrs Martin to children at Heathbrook and Port may be as discrepant from the realities of these children's futures as are Castlegate children's more limited expectations from their own future lot. Patterns that convey meanings which will be contrary to the realities of the future job market and the political and personal life these children will experience in adulthood may promote social unrest. That is, when children as adults see that the mastery of school knowledge brings neither status nor power, their consciousness of these 'false promises' [22] may, under some circumstances, evolve into social discontent. However, the predominance of the knowledge as given resolutions, particularly in the areas of the school curriculum that deal with moral and political development will, we surmise, act as a counterforce to the development of persons who will become social critics. Thus, at the same time that teachers plant hopes for social status through school knowledge that will be to some extent disconfirmed by future experience, they are also likely conveying that the social order is to be taken for granted, thus accepted without criticism.

Ironically children who have experienced patterns of resolution that prepare them not to expect status and autonomy in exchange for incorporating the realms and forms of knowledge valued at school may accept uncritically a general social evolution toward more meaningless work and individual powerlessness so long as those who are certified as deserving of high status continue to receive the rewards they have come to expect. However, in the event that social opportunities for the most 'successful', the 'good students', are also severely limited, the unsuccessful, along with the successful ones may become agents for social change – progressive or reactionary. [23] At the very least they may become more likely to endorse or press for resolutions to the dilemmas of schooling that differ from those they experienced as students. However, in our view it is likely that only those who have had substantial experience with knowledge as problematical resolutions (in school or elsewhere) who are likely to respond to the discrepancies between their expectations and the realities of their lives by questioning the legitimacy of the relationships between knowledge, status and power that prevail in the society, and to press for changes in these relationships.

Mr Sprinter's transformational patterns may be seen as both in and out of step with the direction society is moving. It may be, as we have speculated, that his patterns transmit to his students expectations for personal autonomy and meaningful work which likely will go unfulfilled for many. On the other hand, his patterns also implicitly convey that much of the 'high-status' school knowledge presumed to be significant by teachers such as Mr Edgar is irrelevant or trivial. Thus he may be preparing children to accept what may be the future reality – a world where the 'school knowledge' most people accumulate will gain neither status nor worldly goods. Teachers like Mr Sprinter would have to emphasize more heavily than he does a problematical perspective on the relationship of knowledge, status and autonomy for us to have confidence that his patterns convey to children the capacity and will to be critical of society; that is, to become agents of social transformation.

In summary, teachers' patterns of resolution may be seen as both a playing out, and a perpetuation, and at times a redirection of social contradictions. However, as the children who experience schooling grow to adulthood the alternatives they see and experience and their responses to them will be affected by their own previous social experience of which schooling has been one part. The significance of the meanings they have taken, and as adults will transmit to others, can only be understood when considered in the context of the times, which cannot be wholly predicted. One can only assume that children who have been schooled to expect to engage in meaningful work and to act autonomously, and to see knowledge as problematical rather than given, will be better prepared than those who have not, to become social critics in societies where opportunities for autonomy and meaningful work are limited, and will be more likely than others to engage in socially transforming activities. And, without a problematic and critical stance towards society, many may take what is, as inevitable – thus accepting without opposition existing inequalities and their own failure to achieve financial success or personal happiness.

The connections we have sketched in this chapter are offered not as certainties, but to show how the dilemma language of schooling may be used to formulate and investigate the relationships between consciousness, behavior and the social context past, present and future that are 'in' individuals in the moments that they act. Practitioners who engage in action without a consideration of these connections will likely have little chance of achieving intended outcomes. How the language may be used by practitioners and researchers to examine the dialectical relationship of human consciousness to the schooling process and to social reproduction and change is the subject to which we now turn.

Introduction

1 We, for example, had collected many and quite detailed descriptions of intellectual and cognitive tasks in language and reading curricula, relatively fewer in maths, and fewer still for arts, crafts, sports and music. Similarly, because we had not anticipated an effort to analyze origins and consequences of teachers' schooling patterns, we did not ask teachers much about their social histories nor make any effort in this area to be systematic in our conversations with children.

Chapter VIII

1 At about the time we had first recorded this observation in our field notes, we overheard a conversation in our local pub that suggested a parallel to the world of work. Several young persons who worked in what they called an 'American' factory in a nearby town complained about the rigorous adherence to a time clock. . . . 'We're actually expected to work 'til 5 on the nose.'

2 See n.5, Chapter IV, for further examples of how operations control is adjusted to individual differences by Mrs Martin's use of the 'accordion cards' and through her reading scheme.

3 Dennison's *The Lives of Children* (New York: Random House, 1969) is a nicely written account of the schooling of children, many of whom have failed in other schools, where the emphasis is on holistic learning, intrinsic motivation, and the fusing of personal–public knowledge and, frequently, other transformational resolutions.

4 Other times are during prayers and story time.

5 In contrast, at a workshop for US teachers presented by one of the authors, a teacher discussed her efforts to adjust her art projects so they would fall within the realm of what is acceptable to the families of Jehovah's Witnesses. We note this, not to indicate that these differences in resolutions are necessarily characteristic of teachers in the two countries, but to suggest how teachers may resolve this dilemma differently from one another.

6 See Ray Rist, *The Urban School: A Factory for Failure* (Cambridge, Massachusetts: MIT Press, 1973), for a graphic portrayal of this process occurring in an American kindergarten in St Louis, Missouri.

7 See the discussion in Part One, Chapter I.

8 See C.B. Cox and A.E. Dyson, *The Black Papers on Education* (London: Davis Poynter, 1971), sec. 2 'Progressive education' op. cit.; Neville Bennett, *Teaching Styles and Pupil Progress* (London: Open Books, 1976); Paul Copperman, *The Literary Hoax* (New York: William Morrow, 1978) for other versions of this view of progressive methods.

9 See Sharp and Green, *Education and Social Control: A Study in Progressive Primary Education* (London, Henley and Boston: Routledge & Kegan Paul, 1975).

10 See Roland Barth 'So you want to change to an open classroom', *Phi Delta Kappan* (October 1971); Carey and Liza Murrow, *Children Came First* (New York: American Heritage Press, 1971). Our portrayal also differs significantly from Basil Bernstein's portrayal in terms of the dichotomy visible v. invisible pedagogy; see, 'Class and pedagogies: visible and invisible' in Bernstein, *Class, Codes and Control (Vol 3) Towards a Theory of Educational Transmission* (2nd edn) (London: Routledge & Kegan Paul, 1975) and Bennett, op. cit.

11 We visited a Rudolf Steiner school in the Netherlands that fits the stereotype of a more formal classroom (for example, whole class instruction), with strong *learn-*

ing as social resolutions. Conversely, as Elizabeth Cagan points out, in 'Individualism, collectivism, and radical educational reform', *Harvard Educational Review*, 42:2 (May 1978), many of the 'radical' educational reformers of the 1960s and 1970s, particularly Americans, expressed little concern for the learning as social emphasis. Indeed, they press for highly learning as individual resolutions. 'Mastery learning', currently in vogue in the US, represents almost exclusively learning as individual coupled with knowledge as given modes.

12 See Richard C. Anderson, 'Learning in discussions: a résumé of the authoritarian-democratic studies', *Harvard Educational Review* 29:4 (1959), 201–15.

Chapter IX

1 See Part One, Chapter II; Part Five, Chapter XI.

2 With respect to how subsequent schooling experience may affect the meanings children have taken from primary schools, the English situation is most striking, because of the abruptness of shifts in patterns of resolution between those junior schools that are 'informal' and the greater formality of the secondary schools. Bernstein comments upon this discontinuity in 'Class and pedagogies: visible and invisible' in Bernstein, *Class, Codes and Control (Vol. 3) Towards a Theory of Educational Transmissions* (2nd edn) (London: Routledge & Kegan Paul, 1975). In Davies's words, in *Social Control and Education* (London: Methuen, 1976), according to Bernstein, the new middle class will 'want visible secondary school pedagogies for their children to consolidate what the primary school has "located" and opened up' 130.

3 This is one of the most frequent and, in our view, only partly justified criticisms of the Marxists; Samuel Bowles and Herbert Gintis's *Schooling in Capitalist America* (New York: Basic Books, 1976). See n. 5, Chapter II. Criticisms of Marxist and non-Marxist theorists of schooling for postulating an exact correspondence between schooling and society (for being 'functionalist') are increasingly frequent (see n. 34, Chapter II). Our conceptualization of teacher activity in terms of dominant and exceptional modes and our recognition of the possibility that teachers may resolve the dilemmas in minded and autonomous ways is our attempt to avoid deterministic forms of analysis. See Chapter VI above.

A number of researchers have recognized the contradictions conveyed to students through schooling. See, for example, David K. Cohen and Marvin Lazerson, 'Education and the corporate order' in Jerome Karabel and A.H. Halsey (eds), *Power and Ideology in Education* (New York: Oxford University Press, 1977); and Dreeben, 'The contribution of schooling to the learning of norms', *Harvard Educational Review*, 37:2 (1967).

4 Discovering empirically the extent to which adults expect to engage in meaningful work is complicated by at least two problems. First, though many researchers, on the basis of empirical studies, conclude that workers are satisfied with their work, for example, Robert Blauner, *Alienation and Freedom: The Factory Worker and His Industry* (Chicago: University of Chicago Press, 1964), other researchers attribute such conclusions to the research methodology and to the fact that when work has been organized according to the dictates of corporate capitalism over several generations, workers no longer have a point of reference from which to judge their work as meaningless, degrading or inappropriate for their capacities. See Harry Braverman, *Labor and Monopoly Capital* (New York: Monthly Review Press, 1974); Rosabeth Kanter, *Men and Women of the Corporation* (New York: Basic Books, 1974), 161ff, and n. 25, p. 315; Aronowitz, *False Promises* (New York: McGraw Hill, 1973); Henry, *Culture Against Man* (New

York: Random House, 1963). As Marcuse states in 'The concept of essence', 'Individuals raised to be integrated into the antagonistic labor process cannot be judges of their own happiness.' [Quoted by Jay, *The Dialectical Imagination* (Boston and Toronto: Little Brown, 1973), 59]

A second problem in assessing the degree to which adults expect meaningful work is that expectations are, or appear to be, changing. One strand of research suggests that the demand for control and meaning at work is increasing at the present time; see Rosabeth Moss Kanter, 'A good job is hard to find', *Working Papers for a New Society* (May/June 1979).

A number of researchers have hypothesized how schooling experience reproduces in the young differential expectations for meaningful work — cf. Samuel Bowles, 'Unequal education and the reproduction of the social division of labor' in M. Carnoy (ed.), *Schooling in a Corporate Society* (New York: David McKay, (1972); Henry, op. cit.; Aronowitz, op. cit., ch. 2; Bernstein, 1975, op. cit.). See also Jeff Henderson and Robin Cohen, 'Capital and the work ethic', *Monthly Review* (November 1979). Paul Willis's *Learning to Labour* (Westmead: Saxon House, 1978) is an excellent recent study of this problem, though he deals little with what actually occurs in classrooms. But what Karabel and Halsey, op. cit., pointed out in 1977, in reference to conflict theorists' explanations for the correlation between scholastic achievement and social class, applies to this issue as well. We still find ourselves 'in the position of pointing to the schools as the source of the problem without being able to specify what it is about them that is responsible' (p. 44).

5 These 'widely shared views' are, in Marxist terminology, ideology (see 'Dialectical materialism', Chapter VI above). For discussions of the importance of ideology to the perpetuation of capitalism see Persell, 1977, op. cit.; Rader, *Marx's Interpretation of History* (New York: Oxford University Press, 1979); Boggs, *Gramsci's Marxism* (London: Writers' and Readers' Cooperative, 1976), Apple, *Ideology and the Curriculum* (London and Boston: Routledge & Kegan Paul, 1979). Apple writes,

In understanding these hegemonic relations we need to remember something that Gramsci maintained — that there are two requirements for ideological hegemony. It is not merely that our economic order 'creates' categories and structures of feeling which saturate our everyday lives. Added to this, must be a group of 'intellectuals' (like educators) who employ and give legitimacy to the categories, who make the ideological form seem neutral (p. 11).

See also John Rawls, *A Theory of Justice* (Cambridge, Massachusetts: Harvard University Press, 1971), who advances the modern version of the social contract theory as a rationale for granting privilege to a meritorious élite only if they act in the interest of those who have a disproportionably small share of social goods and benefits.

6 See Richard Sennett and Jonathan Cobb, *The Hidden Injuries of Class* (New York: Random House, 1972), for an analysis that captures the contradictions in adults' conceptions of the legitimacy of the allocation of status and the opportunities for mobility in the United States today.

7 Although there has been little *empirical* research based on extended classroom observation that focuses directly on how schooling transmits these notions, there has been much thoughtful and useful primarily theoretical work, including that of Pierre Bourdieu, Basil Bernstein (see Chapter II); papers collected by Michael F.D. Young, *Knowledge and Control: New Directions in The Sociology of Education* (West Drayton: Collier Macmillan, 1971); Geoff Whitty and Michael Young, *Explorations in the Politics of School Knowledge* (Driffield, Yorks.: Nafferton

Press, 1976); Nell Keddie, 'Classroom Knowledge', in Young, 1971, op. cit.; Sennett and Cobb, op. cit.; Aronowitz, op. cit.; and Apple, op. cit., include relevant empirical work though none explores these questions empirically in much depth.

8 As John Tulloch suggests (in 'Gradgrind's heirs: the quiz and the presentation of "knowledge" by British television' in Whitty and Young, op. cit.), the popularity of TV quiz shows in the adult world suggests that there are many who have accepted Mr Edgar's definition of knowledge. However, the ambivalence of the working class toward the value of school knowledge is suggested by Tulloch's analysis of differences among quiz shows. Tulloch suggests British quiz shows of the 'Sale of the Century' type, which focus directly on the cash value – not the intrinsic worth or status – of knowledge, and pose questions that are easily answerable, reflect (as well as contribute to) the disdain that members of the working class feel toward 'school knowledge' as they have experienced it.

9 Willis, op. cit.

10 In James Herndon's marvelously funny and engaging *How to Survive in Your Native Land* (New York: Simon & Schuster, 1977), 'flax' is used as a symbol of school knowledge that is isolated from personal knowledge.

11 Jules Henry, op. cit. Roy Nash, 'Camouflage in the classroom', *New Society*, 447 (22 April 1971) suggests that they will, in fact, learn to prefer this position as 'people want to have their expectancies fulfilled' (p. 249).

12 These relationships are discussed in different terms by a number of others. See particularly Paulo Freire's *Education for Critical Consciousness* (New York: Seabury Press, 1973), and *Pedagogy of the Oppressed* (New York: Seabury Press, 1974). Willis, op. cit., and Aronowitz, op. cit., also consider these relationships.

13 Our analysis may be contrasted with that of Martin Hoyles who, in *Changing Childhood* (London: Writers' and Readers' Publishing Cooperative, 1979), makes a case for the liberating consequences of a greater childhood continuous emphasis: 'Children can be loved without being separated off as if they were a different species. It is with particular regard to work, sex, and politics that we deny children their humanity' (p. 6). What we are arguing is that each emphasis in the dilemma (as in all the dilemmas) may have paradoxical consequences. A *childhood unique* emphasis could result in giving children a more prolonged experience in developing their full capacities, insulated from the needs of the labor market, or it could result in segregating children as different beings from adults, thus encouraging social and communication barriers based on age. Similarly, a *childhood continuous* focus may, as Benn ('School is bad, work is worse', *School Review*, 83, 1 Nov. 1974) suggests, merely habituate children at an early age to the adult world of work. The conditions under which either consequence is likely to occur depend perhaps in part on the particular configuration of the pattern of resolution to this dilemma and on patterns of resolution to other dilemmas. Bernstein recognizes such potentially paradoxical consequences when he writes, '(G)roups with radically different ideologies might find themselves supporting integrated codes' [1975, op. cit., 12]. Horkheimer, and his colleagues of the Frankfurt School, expressed the same idea when they claimed that '[a]ll cultural phenomena expressed the contradictions of the whole including those forces that negated the status quo. Nothing, or at least almost nothing, was solely ideological' [Jay, op. cit., 55].

14 This discussion parallels Bowles and Gintis, 1976, op. cit.

15 Cagan, 'Individualism, collectivism, and radical educational reform', *Harvard Educational Review*, 42:2 (May 1978), 228.

16 ibid., 241.

17 ibid., 244.

18 M.F.D. Young (op. cit., 6) formulates the question as follows: '[T]he direction of research for a sociology of educational knowledge becomes to explore how and why certain dominant categories persist and the nature of their possible links to sets of interests or activities.' From Williams's perspective (see *Marxism and Literature*, Oxford: Oxford University Press, 1977), one might ask, from 'a whole possible area of past and present meanings ... (why) certain meanings and practices are selected for emphases and certain other meanings and practices are neglected or excluded' (p. 115). See also Persell, op. cit., 14.

19 This explanation for why poor children do poorly in school, and fall increasingly farther 'behind' middle-class children the longer they remain in school parallels the position taken by the critics of the cultural deprivation thesis, for example, William Labov, 'The logic of nonstandard English' in Frederick Williams (ed.), *Language and Poverty* (Chicago: Markham, 1970); Joan Baratz and Stephen Baratz, 'Early childhood intervention: the social scientific basis of institutionalized racism', *Harvard Educational Review* 40:1(1970) 29–50; Murray L.Wax and Rosalie Wax, 'Cultural deprivation as an educational ideology' in Eleanor Leacock, *The Culture of Poverty: A Critique* (New York: Simon & Schuster, 1971); Herbert Ginsberg, *The Myth of Cultural Deprivation* (Englewood Cliffs, New Jersey: Prentice-Hall, 1972). The culture of poverty perspective is well represented by Martin Deutsch, 'The disadvantaged child and the learning process' in A.H. Passow, *Education in Depressed Areas* (New York: Teacher's College Press, 1963).

20 The dilemmas, probably with some reformulation, could be used to conceptualize the process of parenting. One might then be able to formulate questions about the relationship of patterns of resolution of parents and teachers to children's meanings and, ultimately, to the problem of social continuity and change. Using the dilemma approach it is possible to, in Williams's words, 'identify common features in family, school, community, work, and communications', and also to capture the 'contradictions and unresolved conflicts' between these institutions (1977, op. cit., p. 118).

21 These trends have been suggested in a number of places including Heilbronner, *An Inquiry into the Human Prospect* (New York: Norton, 1974); Aronowitz, op. cit.; Braverman, op. cit.; Persell, op. cit.

22 This is a reference to the title of Aronowitz's book, *False Promises*, op. cit.

23 See Karabel and Halsey, op. cit., 70, and the works of Bourdieu, for discussions of the increasingly contradictory position of the middle classes under corporate capitalism as these are related to schooling.

As discussed earlier (see Chapter VI) one must also consider the tendency for oppositional elements to be incorporated into the dominant culture. See Williams, 1977, op. cit., 23–5.

PART FIVE
ENGAGING IN CRITICAL INQUIRY

INTRODUCTION

In this, the final part of the book, we show the uses and discuss the broader implications of the dilemma orientation and language. Chapter X focuses on the uses of the dilemmas for guiding critical curriculum inquiries by teachers (and other educational professionals and citizens) and for examining the problems of teacher education in universities and colleges and directions for curriculum and structural reforms. Chapter XI returns to the question we raised in Part One: what can schooling researchers contribute to a clarification of the present educational debates and problems and alternatives for action? We briefly recapitulate criticisms of Jencks's well-known *Inequality* and other 'black box' studies that purport to make a statement on the social and political significance of the schooling process without an examination of the process itself or of its consequences on human consciousness. We close with a critique of research in one curriculum area, reading and language development, and illustrate how the dilemma language may be used to formulate systematic, collaborative and critical inquiries by teachers and university researchers on curriculum questions.

Overview of the purpose, process and method of critical inquiry

For a cogent statement of the purpose of critical inquiry we return to C. Wright Mills's *The Sociological Imagination*. In the first chapter, entitled, 'The promise', he writes:

We have come to know that every individual lives from one generation to the next, in some society; that he lives out a biography, and that he lives it out within some historical sequence. By the fact of his living he contributes, however minutely, to the shaping of this society and to the course of its history, even as he is made by society and by its historical push and shove. . . . No social study that does not come back to the problem of biography, of history and of their intersections within a society has completed its intellectual journey.[1]

Critical inquiry is both an intellectual journey and a deliberated effort of persons to shape their society and the course of its history. It is at once practical and theoretical; situational and universal. It rests on a naturalistic assumption consistent with the views of George Herbert Mead and a number of critical theorists: that persons are both products and creators of their own history. To survive they are continuously active, working to satisfy their purposes and desires but within a world that has formed their consciousness and shaped the circumstances of their lives and daily work, the constraints and possibilities. Critical inquiries seek to examine the origins and consequences of everyday behavior, to illuminate internal and external constraints and the widest possible set of alternatives for future action. As teachers and others engage in critical inquiry they '*objectify*' themselves in the sense that, for some moments at least, they suspend personal involvement,[2] and see their present purposes, desires and acts in history, as they might be seen by others, past and contemporaneous. They deliberately seek to *dis*orient themselves from the perspectives they have taken as normal, given, natural, by searching out viewpoints on their own and others' acts and circumstances heretofore not at all or little understood, perhaps long rejected or distorted.

Critical inquiry may be seen as an effort to free person (intellectually) in so far as is possible, 'not only from the domination of others, but from their domination by forces they do not understand or control'.[3] It may also be understood as a form of therapy in the root sense of 'clarifying one's knowledge of self'.[4] Its intention is to liberate persons from mindless activity by bringing to consciousness how behaviors draw 'upon resources and depend upon conditions of which [we]. . . are unaware or which [we]. . . perceive only dimly'.[5]

Seeing one's present behavior, understanding rather than rationalizing its origins, examining its consequences, and developing the necessary knowledge and skills to change it are not at all easy, of course. Explanations for the tendency to distort and rationalize as persons engage in self-analysis vary greatly, but there is little disagreement that it is difficult to see ourselves objectively – that is, as others might see us from the perspectives of different times, cultures and personal and social histories. Nor is there much doubt that the process of self-study can evoke anxiety and defensiveness. Surely most of us, to some extent, have vested interests in seeing our actions, and projecting to others an image of ourselves as rational, intelligent and compassionate. Thus, critical inquiry may be liberating, but it is also likely to be threatening since it requires re-evaluation of one's taken-for-granted, often long-used, sometimes comfortable behaviors which may be acceptable or even admirable in the eyes of peers and/or superiors. Such inquiries are transformational in that they could lead by increments to a major reorientation to one's work, political activity and culture. For these reasons, it is likely that persons, to some degree, are tempted to sidestep or resist such inquiries.

What are the principles of the method of critical inquiry? Because it seeks to clarify alternative possibilities for addressing human purposes and desires of persons in situations, critical inquiry must (1) *be cast in terms that do not distort the experience and knowledge of persons acting in the situations*. As it seeks out alternative possibilities, disorienting them from their present viewpoints, concerns and purposes, it transforms persons by leading them to a greater and deeper understanding of the origins and consequences of their acts and of the situations in which they find themselves. Since no person or group of persons can be assumed to have greater capacity for detaching themselves from their own interests and desires, critical inquiry (2) *must be conducted without coercion, direct or implicit, on the basis of equality of regard, that is, without any presumption that some persons' perspectives are more valid or less distorted than others*; (3) *critical inquiry thus also requires active involvement of the persons in the situations under study*. Finally, because critical inquiry seeks to help persons see their own situation and alternatives for action from others' perspectives, because of the high probability of distortion when human interests and concerns are implicated, and because help and support and collaboration may be required for engaging in new courses of action, (4) *critical inquiry is most successful if pursued in a group, with persons of similar and quite divergent perspectives who have a common interest in clarifying the alternative possibilities in the situation*.

The process of critical inquiry then requires of persons

the capacity to shift from one perspective to another – from the political to the psychological; from examination of a single family to comparative assessment of the national budgets of the world; from the theological school to the military establishment; from considerations of an oil industry to

231

studies of contemporary poetry. It is the capacity to range from the most impersonal and remote transformations to the most intimate features of the human self – and to see the relations between the two. Back of its use there is always the urge to know the social and historical meaning of the individual in the society and in the period in which he has his quality and his being . . . to grasp what is going on in the world . . . as minute points of the intersection of biography and history.[6]

X   CRITICAL INQUIRY: TEACHERS, SCHOOLING PROFESSIONALS AND CITIZENS AS CRITICAL INQUIRERS

How the dilemma orientation and language may be used for practical inquiry by teachers, other professionals and citizens is the focus of this chapter, with an effort in the closing pages to suggest implications of our more general arguments for reforming pre-service and in-service programs for teachers.

The position that is implicit in the recommendations and suggestions in this and the concluding chapter is that teachers, like all others, must be involved as fully equal partners in the critical inquiry process. There is a presumption among educational administrators, researchers and segments of the public, that teachers, particularly teachers of younger children, do not have the capacity for engaging in inquiry. Because of its implications for critical inquiry, we begin with a brief examination of this presumption.

Many administrators, intellectuals, educational researchers and others in the business of knowledge transmission, take for granted that teachers are less reflective than themselves and the implicit or explicit corollary that teachers should therefore be guided by or subject to the wills or authority of these persons. In both the UK and US there has, over the decade, been a number of efforts to improve schooling through various means that would hold teachers accountable to school administrators who in turn must answer to the appropriate educational or political authority. Although the intention of advocates of such efforts (most notable in the US in state-sponsored or monitored minimal competency testing programs) is primarily to raise standards, the effect is to centralize authority and thus to reduce the scope of teacher autonomy. These efforts contribute to the redefinition of a teacher as a low-level civil servant whose responsibility it is to implement the policies and programs devised by others. Whatever the intention of those who continue to press for such schemes, their effect is to discourage the exercise of critical intelligence by teachers, a move which runs contrary to the principles of critical inquiry which we have argued in support of above. Because schooling is a face-to-face encounter between teachers and their students, to change in any substantive way the nature of this encounter requires that *teachers* behave differently. And because teachers' day-to-day schooling behavior *cannot* be entirely controlled from above, teachers themselves must engage in critical inquiry if we expect schooling to be conducted intelligently.

The position we take is, of course, based on the assumption that as a group teachers are as capable of understanding schooling and engaging in reflective action as others in the educational hierarchy, including researchers and professors of education. The view of teachers as something less than knowledgeable, rational and complex in their thinking is sometimes explicit in the writings of educational researchers and often implicit in educational policies and programs of schools, school districts and governments, particularly in the US. It is a view assumed in many research and development (R & D) efforts and in the various state programs in the US for closely monitoring teachers' performance through the practices of scientific management (known in the language of contemporary administrative science as management by objectives).

Since this less than complimentary view of teachers has some standing as scientific truth in the educational research community, we briefly examine it as presented in two well-known books, *Schoolteacher* by Dan C. Lortie, and *Life in Classrooms* by Philip Jackson. Lortie's study of the occupation of teaching, though it includes many useful insights, portrays teachers as a group as less rational and knowledgeable than others who have university or college training. Lortie argues, 'The preparation of teachers does not seem to result in the analytic turn of mind one finds in other occupations where members are trained in colleges and universities.' [1] Further, '(T)he absence of a common technical vocabulary limits a beginner's ability to "tap into" a pre-existing body of practical knowledge.' He adds, 'Haller [a colleague] analyzed my interview tapes ... and found a very low proportion of words which are not commonly used; since the interview dealt with teaching, it should have elicited a technical vocabulary.' [2]

Philip Jackson's *Life in the Classroom*, a study that is often regarded as a modern classic of 'qualitative' research in education (that is, research based on interview and observation) also concluded that teachers are less than full professionals, as evidenced by their 'tendency to rely on spontaneous expressions of interest and enthusiasm of their students rather than on scientific or objective measures' and by their 'conceptual simplicity'.[3] He writes, 'Not only do teachers avoid elaborate words, they also seem to shun elaborate ideas.' Jackson cites an 'uncomplicated view of casuality' and 'an intuitive, rather than a rational, approach to classroom events' as aspects of teachers' conceptual simplicity,[4] and claims that teachers tend towards an 'unquestioning acceptance of classroom miracles'.[5]

Neither Professors Lortie nor Jackson are unsympathetic to teachers. Both explain teachers' purported lack of intellectual rigor in a variety of ways – because they are at the bottom of a hierarchical system, are unable to control licensing of their own profession, receive poor professional training and so on. But the implication can hardly be missed. Though they may possess the 'soft' human virtues of patience, understanding and idealism, and the quality of mind that enables them to put up with what Jackson calls the 'daily grind' of dealing with children or adolescents for six or more hours a day, teachers are low on the hard virtues, the capacity to engage in rigorous scientific and disciplined thinking as true professionals. Though it is widely presumed that experts in flute playing are flutists, Professors Lortie and Jackson and many professional educationalists assume that the experts in teaching are not the teachers but scientifically-trained administrators, or educational scholars who study schooling scientifically.[6]

We are especially wary of 'scientific' attributions of irrationality leveled at low-status groups. It is probably not coincidental that the traits these researchers attribute to teachers resemble those attributed to low-status, historically-oppressed groups in society – racial or ethnic minorities, working-class poor. We should recall in this regard that the largest numbers of teachers, particularly of younger children, are women.[7] The quotations offered by Philip Jackson to support his simplicity of thought hypothesis can easily be interpreted as teachers' proclivities to view their schooling problems more contextually than educational researchers.

Although Lortie studies the recruitment and socialization patterns of teachers, their career and work rewards, and what teachers say about teaching – using information 'gathered in interviews which encouraged respondents to talk at length in terms of their conceptionalization of the teacher's world'[8] – he does not study what teachers actually do in classrooms. His failure to collect systematic information on teachers' classroom activities and how teachers construct and justify these activities does not, in our view, permit

235

him to draw conclusions about how rational, analytic or simple-minded teachers are as they actually perform their profession. Lortie attributes teachers' failures to share their knowledge with each other to the absence of an appropriate technical vocabulary. Is it not shallow, if not arrogant, however, to assume that the measure of persons' professionalism is their use of technical language?

This rather uncomplementary perspective on the capacities and knowledge of teachers is often shared by teachers themselves, as well as by parents and the public at large. The reasons, of course, are complex. They may be found in the hierarchical structure of the schools and the generally lower regard for practical activity that is evident among intellectuals, particularly academics. We also suspect that the academics' views of practical knowledge are transmitted to teachers during their professional education. Many teacher educators contribute to teachers' views of themselves as inferior professionals by their assumption that prospective and in-service teachers need to master the languages and categories of psychology and social science, thus conveying to teachers that the knowledge and concepts of non-teachers is a greater source of wisdom than their own powers of critical inquiry and their practical knowledge gained from experience. Many teachers, of course, often recognize that higher status is afforded to knowledge possessed by educational researchers and professors, but they may not themselves respect that knowledge and may in fact see it as unworldly, unrealistic or a joke.

In sum, there is no convincing evidence that as a group, sociologists, deans of schools of education, school superintendents or LEA officials, are more or less likely to be knowledgeable, fallible or astute in their understanding of schools and schooling than teachers. There is no evidence to support the contention that educational scholars are more detached or dispassionate than teachers, or less likely than teachers to overlay their personal and political preferences upon their observations or judgments. There is, however, ample evidence that government officials, LEA officers, and educational researchers often fail to grasp the complex, intellectual and social problems of daily school life. It is, therefore, necessary for anyone who presumes to influence teachers, to seek teachers' knowledge and perspectives, work with them closely in ways that foster respect for one another's experience, acknowledging one another's areas of partial and gross ignorance.

THE INQUIRY PROCESS

Teachers, other educational specialists, and citizens may begin a critical examination of schooling practice out of a conviction that all behaviors which are taken for granted should be subject to scrutiny from time to time, or perhaps out of a desire to anticipate future problems so as not to be caught off-guard by circumstances or events. Usually, however, one begins a critical inquiry because a problematic situation – either clearly defined or vaguely felt – has arisen. In this latter case, members of these groups may face a common problem but each may define it differently. For example, a parent may attribute his child's truancy to a teacher's demeaning views of the intellectual abilities of his child; the teacher may see it as the consequence of the parent's disinterest, or antagonism toward school, confounded by unavailability of appropriate materials or staff; an administrator may explain it in terms of the failure of a teacher to command respect and maintain standards. There are also times when groups or individuals face problems that appear to be of no immediate concern to others – a parent upset by her child's anxiety about going to school, a teacher uncertain about how much pressure to put on a failing student, a head teacher puzzled about whether and/or how to confront the teacher of a particularly boisterous class.

The purpose of the inquiry, for teachers and non-teachers, is to enable them to engage in reflective or minded action, that is, to chart a course of action with awareness of the realities that constrain and the likely consequences of the alternatives open or that they might create. Engaging in this process requires that each of the participants render as problematic what they have been taking for granted about what is happening in classrooms, the origins of the schooling activities and their consequences upon children and the society both in the immediate and longer range future. Using the dilemma language, then, to structure critical inquiry involves an examination, from the widest possible range of perspectives, of *present patterns* of resolution, *alternative possibilities*, the *consequences* of present and alternative patterns, the *origins* of present patterns and of proposals for alternatives. A critical search for alternatives is not complete if it does not include development of skills and knowledge needed by teachers to alter their schooling patterns. The latter we call *craft knowledge*. We offer in the next few pages a format for analyzing schooling in terms of these realms of inquiry; the realms are stated as questions in Table 3 and the reflexive relationships among the realms are portrayed in Figure 7.

Table 3 Realms of inquiry for analyzing schooling[9]

    I What are my *present patterns* of resolution?

   II What *alternative patterns* are desirable and possible?

  III What are the *consequences* of present and/or alternative patterns in terms of meanings transmitted to children?

  IV What are the *origins* – socio-biographical, historical and structural – of:
      (a) present patterns (my own as teacher, or those prevailing in a school classroom)?
      (b) the alternative patterns?
      (c) the discrepancy between the present and the alternative patterns?

   V What knowledge of *craft* is necessary in order to change my patterns of resolution?

We first illustrate the *reflexivity* among the five realms and then discuss some of the complexities of conducting investigations within each. Though we cast our discussion of the process of critical inquiry in terms of a single teacher, we believe that the inquiry process will be furthered if it is undertaken by a group of teachers, perhaps with the participation of non-teachers. Indeed, how schooling is conducted is also the proper concern of educational professionals other than teachers (heads, curriculum specialists, researchers, teachers' educators, etc.), parents and citizens. Since the intent is to see schooling from the perspectives of others, the inquiry will be advanced, at particular stages, by including persons of diverse viewpoints and backgrounds. We have had limited experience with the use of this format and we anticipate that further explorations will reveal additional possibilities and problems.

REFLEXIVITY OF REALMS, AN ILLUSTRATION

Each of the five realms bears a reflexive relationship to all the others – that is, in the course of inquiring into any one realm, each of the others will become problematic. For example, a teacher may face a problem of several boys who are inattentive and antagonistic during reading time. She may initially define the problem as one of control, and her inquiry may begin with an examination of her present patterns of resolution to the control dilemmas during 'reading time'. Perhaps her analysis of her present control patterns reveals that she maintains tighter control over boys than girls, and that she intervenes less frequently and more sympathetically in social relationships among the girls that are carried on during reading period. At this point she may examine the origins of the differential treatment, perhaps uncovering her assumption that boys require closer control than girls; analysis may disclose that this view began to develop as she was growing up in a family of obedient daughters and assertive sons. She may also find that the origins of this pattern are not

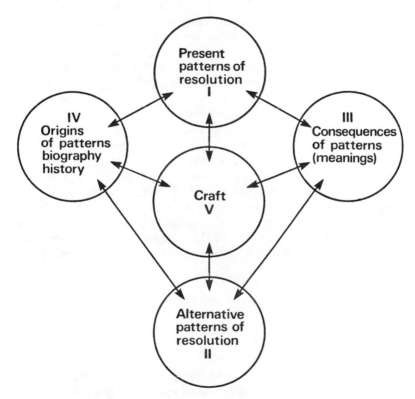

Figure 7 Reflexive relationships among the realm of inquiry

exclusively in her history, but are fed by the contemporary situation – that is, she controls boys more closely because many appear to her to be unreliable, unproductive and disruptive when left to work on their own.

Her analysis of the origins of her behavior may lead in a number of directions. She may alter her control pattern to give the boys more control over time and operations based on her 'discovery' that her differential treatment may be based as much on prejudgment as on the behavior manifest by these particular boys. The consequences of shifting more control to the boys may, however, be an increase rather than a decrease in the boys' inattentiveness. After an assessment of the consequences of her altered patterns, she may attempt to redefine the problem. Perhaps she will conclude that shifting patterns in other instructional areas or other patterns of reading instruction may solve the problem. Her awareness of the ways she resolves the control dilemmas differentially for boys and girls and her developing awareness of the origins of these patterns may lead to an inquiry into how her present patterns of resolution to some of the curriculum or societal dilemmas also vary according to gender. Does she generally emphasize intrinsic motivation more heavily for girls than for boys? Does she tend to relate to girls' personal experience more easily than to boys'?

As she engages in these inquiries, she may begin to question the assumptions she has been making about the meanings not only the boys, but all children, have been taking from her present patterns (or may be taking, or are likely to take from her present effort to alter her patterns). She might consider, for example, the effects on girls as well as boys were she to set up a special shelf of books that are more likely to fuse the boys' personal knowledge with public knowledge or were she to set aside time for designing projects of intrinsic interest to boys. Would the consequence of these particular shifts accentuate gender differences? Will this 'affirmative action' for boys rectify or compound the problems?

Any change she contemplates requires that she possess requisite craft. She may investigate what other teachers do to involve boys in taking greater responsibility for their own work without encouraging sex segregation and inappropriate gender distinctions. Perhaps her explorations of craft knowledge will lead her to develop over time a reading program that is less dependent upon standardized tasks and more responsive to everyone's interests, not only the interests of the boys. As a result of developing this aspect of craft, she may come to observe and converse with children more proficiently.

This may, in turn, sharpen her awareness of the meanings children take from other patterns of resolution and encourage her to look more closely at the origins of these other patterns.

This hypothetical account of a critical inquiry illustrates its ongoing reflexive quality. Teaching from this perspective becomes a process of continuous exploration and change of one's patterns of resolution, an unending search for alternatives.

INQUIRY IN EACH OF THE REALMS

The range of questions one may pose in each of the five realms is presented in Table 4. A critical inquiry can be directed at *overall* present or anticipated future patterns within each set (control, curriculum, societal). This *overall* analysis could be likened to an aerial photograph. Not many details are visible, but the general configuration of the terrain is distinct. However, if teachers intend to focus on changing particular aspects of the overall configuration, they will

Table 4 Range of questions in each of the five realms of inquiry

Realms of inquiry

Dilemma

I–II What are *present/alternative* patterns?

III–IV What are *origins*/consequences of present/alternative patterns?

V What *craft* knowledge is used/needed for present/alternative patterns?

	Overall		In a given subject or area		For a given child or category of children	
	Dominant	Exceptional	Dominant	Exceptional	Dominant	Exceptional
Control						
Curriculum						
Societal						

need to examine in detail some subset of patterns of resolution. This may entail comparing present (or anticipated future) resolutions in different subjects or activities (for example, basics v. non-basics) in particular topics *within* a given subject (for example, how patterns of resolution in a unit on the emergence and demise of the English Commonwealth differs from those in a unit on more recent British history, perhaps the recent history of Northern Ireland), or in different types of school sanctioned or arranged educational experiences (school trips, field trips, homework, athletics). One might instead find it more relevant to focus an inquiry on how present or alternative patterns are (or could be) distributed to particular individuals or groups of students. (Do and should children talented in the arts have more or less control over operations in art activities than less talented children?)

One may conduct a range of inquiries in the origins and consequences realms. What are or what do I presume are the overall meanings taken from my present patterns or from the alternative patterns I am considering? What are or might be the meanings taken by a particular set of children or from resolutions in a particular activity or subject? How did I come to emphasize molecular patterns in all the areas I teach? Why are my patterns more molecular in maths than in art?

Finally, a range of inquiries may be made in the craft realm; for example, what craft knowledge do I need in order to shift to patterns that are more problematic overall, or that are more problematic in the social studies?

It is probably obvious that a full investigation within each of the realms of inquiry is beyond human possibility. It is necessary *to direct inquiry selectively* pursuing those answers one needs in order to engage in practical action as constrained by physical resources, energy and the immediacy and seriousness of the problems. Figure 7 and Table 4 may be seen as maps to help us to locate ourselves and to see how any particular inquiry fits into the broader picture, and to remind us what regions and directions remain untraveled.

I–II *What are present/alternative patterns?*

An effective way of beginning to identify one's own patterns is to compare them with the patterns of others. The process of comparison may be undertaken by reading about or observing, directly or on film, others' teaching, and what they say about it and by comparing others' dominant and exceptional patterns with one's own.[10] One's own experiences as a student may also serve as points of reference.

Inquiry in this realm may proceed, individually or with others, by posing the following sorts of questions: Do I (or does a teacher or group of teachers) teach reading more molecularly than art? Do I control the 'dim' more closely and/or differently than the 'clever' or provide more problematic experiences for the 'clever' than for the 'dim'? What modes do I tend to emphasize in maths v. reading? How do the patterns implicit in the way I teach initial reading compare to the way I was taught to read? How problematical were my college history courses compared to the emphasis that is implicit in my own resolutions? How do I (a high-school art teacher) resolve the whole child dilemma differently from you (a primary-school art teacher)? Under what conditions do each of us become involved in realms of development beyond the artistic sphere? How do my patterns compare to those of eighteenth-century school marms or masters? Through these types of inquiries teachers become aware that they, like others, are drawn to some extent by each pole of each dilemma, and that they have characteristic – though changing – patterns of resolution, which though similar also differ from the patterns of others in their own school and culture, and from those of other times and cultures as well.

Observations by others of one's own teaching patterns will at some point be a necessary part of the process of clarifying one's own resolutions because of the difficulties of seeing one's own action from the perspective of others. Special and difficult problems are, however, created if the others are persons who have not had similar teaching responsibilities and/or are in positions of authority or with whom there is not mutual respect and trust. Perhaps the most effective way to identify one's own dominant and exceptional patterns accurately is to have the benefit of the observations of others on oneself. However, because respect, confidence and trust are so crucial, one may probably most safely begin inquiry in this realm by comparing one's own perceptions of one's own behavior to the behavior of others and moving slowly to the point of having others observe oneself.

In the course of comparing their own patterns with others', teachers will likely begin to see alternatives to their own practice, and perhaps to anticipate shifting some of their present patterns. The teacher whose reading program consists primarily of molecular exercises with holistic tasks such as 'free reading' relegated to half an hour a week, may decide to shift to a more holistic emphasis as a result of awareness of alternatives, provided she knows the necessary craft (how to keep records, etc.). However, awareness of alternative patterns will not, in itself, necessarily result in change. Changes in patterns will often require inquiry into other realms.

III–IV *What are the origins/consequences of present/alternative patterns?*

A considered decision to shift or to maintain one's patterns must involve an examination of the meanings that are transmitted by present patterns and may be transmitted by anticipated changes. For example, teachers may consider what meanings children take from a pattern of resolution that requires children to work 'on their own' in maths and reading, but emphasizes social learning in art and construction activities by encouraging children to work together. Answering these questions involves examining both long- and short-range consequences which are often both complex and paradoxical, and social research can make only limited contributions to their clarification. To examine more immediate consequences teachers will need to be researchers themselves, engaging in reflexive (and reflective) action, shifting patterns of resolution and examining the consequences. A teacher might, for example, decide to emphasize holistic modes in reading and language activities for a given period of time, and look at changes in children's attitudes toward reading, perhaps focusing on differences among particular sorts of children. Or a teacher may work for several weeks to help children set their own standards in creative writing and see whether some or all begin to write more imaginatively, fluently and eagerly. The most crucial skill for this phase of inquiry is the ability to make correct inferences about the meanings children are taking. This requires teachers to develop the art of conversation with children. To hypothesize about long-range consequences of shifts in emphasis, teachers must consider the relationship of macro to micro, of their daily behavior to social continuity and change.

Though teachers may sometimes shift patterns after considering the meanings children take from present or alternative patterns, inquiry into the origins of patterns (and, where relevant, why there is a discrepancy between actual patterns and those they aspire to) will usually be necessary for lasting and significant shifts in patterns of resolution to occur. This realm of inquiry may be seen as an examination of the intersection of biography and history. It might involve an examination of such questions as what are the influences upon one's present or desired patterns of the unique factors in one's upbringing (family structure, sibling position, etc.); the changes in society and culture one has lived through, or one's professional history within particular schooling institutions. As a result of inquiry in this realm teachers might discover that their patterns of setting standards differentially for boys and girls in physical education is rooted in their histories as members of a culture that expects male children to possess greater physical endurance, agility and strength.

Involved in this realm of inquiry is an examination of the reasons for discrepancies between actual and desired patterns. To clarify this question teachers must consider to what extent their views that their present patterns are shaped by outside forces over which they have little or no control are justified, and to what extent their views of the difficulties involved in shifting patterns are rationalizations for an unwillingness to risk administrators' or parents' displeasure (or worse). For example, it is at this point that teachers may begin to question their acquiescence to district (LEA) requirements with which they disagree, and to consider what alternatives may be open, including active participation in professional organization, unions and other political bodies in order to have greater voice in the establishment of local and national educational policies and priorities.

Procedurally, debating with others preferred patterns of resolution is a good way to identify, make explicit and hold up for scrutiny implicit ideas or views about the meanings children take from alternative patterns of resolution, and the origins of these views. Teachers may discuss the following sorts of questions: What difference does it make if one gives equal time to each reading group or more time to the 'low' group? Why do I allocate my time this way? Is this pattern really a response to district policy – especially when others allocate time differently – or am I rationalizing my own mindless pattern? Is a greater emphasis on the problematical in history really of value? Of what value? How has my more 'given' emphasis been encouraged by the history courses I have taken as a student, or by the economics of the publishing industry?

V Craft knowledge

The problem in this realm of inquiry is to develop a course, or a set of schooling activities that realize desired shifts in patterns of resolution. Though a teacher may want to change a pattern of resolution, change is not possible without the appropriate craft knowledge. Constructing this craft knowledge is complex since the search is for curricular activities that satisfy not only the desired emphasis in one or two dilemmas, but simultaneously embody a constellation of desired patterns. For example, a teacher may want to shift to a reading program that puts greater emphasis on holistic learning and intrinsic motivation and to do this she may devise a scheme whereby children read books of their own choosing. An analysis of this activity may, however, suggest that learning as social and teacher control over standards are sacrificed. The craft problem, then, may become how to construct a reading program that at once puts greater emphasis on social learning and control of standards while maintaining the desired emphasis on intrinsic motivation and holistic learning.

Little is known about how craft knowledge of teachers develops, how to encourage its growth, at what point in a critical inquiry it is most fruitfully pursued.

We have some evidence that teachers learn their craft largely from one another. Mrs Martin credits her two infant-teacher colleagues with helping her master the craft involved in conducting a decentralized classroom. Mrs Hollins clearly plays an active and crucial role in developing her teachers' craft by offering suggestions at the appropriate moment, and by modeling the appropriate behaviors as she visits their classrooms. Mrs Newhouse's effort to develop a more individualized maths program flounders without Mr Scott's proficiency in maths and his knowledge of how to keep track of children's mastery of maths concepts, and how to teach four- or five-minute lessons on particular maths concepts to several children at a time. Although use of books and other media may be very useful for the development of craft, this process is greatly enhanced if teachers have the opportunity to observe and talk to one another regularly about the craft alternatives they are searching for in order to realize their intentions.

Finally, in our experience, the development of a craft depends upon the practitioners' pride and pleasure in their work. In Bertrand Russell's words:

Skilled work, of no matter what kind, is only done well by those who take a certain pleasure in it, quite apart from its utility either to themselves in earning a living, or to the world through its outcome.[11]

EDUCATIONAL ADMINISTRATORS

The term 'administrator', as used here, refers to all who occupy a place in the schooling hierarchy equivalent to or higher than teachers and do not (or rarely) teach. Their work is to provide facilities, materials, services, leadership and/or to represent the interests, as they interpret them, of the local community or the public at large. With the exception of the head of the LEA (the director or super-intendent) and the school head (or principal), most of the persons who occupy such roles (the inspectors, advisors, supervisors of teachers, coordinators of curriculum services and/or teachers' centers, school counselors, psychologists) are out of the public eye. Still further from public view are the civil servants within governmental educational bureaucracies, who work under a specific or general mandate from a legislature, from another public body, or from persons higher in the hierarchy. They provide information and oversee or develop evalua-tion procedures and research studies, etc. Some of these roles within educational bureaucracies carry with them the legal right to mandate policy change, while others carry only the power to advise and recommend alternatives to officials who have the mandate. However different the roles, they have the same professional goal – directly or indirectly to influence the way teachers conduct schooling, or, in our terms, how teachers resolve the dilemmas.[12] Though we confine our discussion here to how the language may be used by heads or advisors many of our comments apply also to other administrators in the local and national educational bureaucracies (and in North America, state or provincial bureaucracies).

School head teachers are the chief administrative officers of rela-tively large establishments (generally several hundred and in larger secondary schools several thousand students). As managers of these organizations they are responsible for the physical structures, resources, staff recruitment, relations among staff and students, and maintaining the confidence of the public and the schools' governing bodies that the primary goal of the organization, educating students, is being satisfactorily pursued. The foregoing is not a full accounting of the head teacher's responsibility, only some indication of their 'managerial' functions.

Many heads also think of themselves as teachers or 'educators' in the root sense of the word – being responsible for leading persons from a narrower to a broader perspective, in our terms, for encourag-ing the community, the school staff, and others in the bureaucracy, to question the patterns of resolution, normally taken for granted, and helping each of these groups to see schooling in terms of the concerns and interests of others.

School heads' conceptions of the capacities of teachers (and of parents and the public at large, etc.) will affect the extent to which they embrace the 'educator' role, and how they perform their mana-gerial functions. What general approaches may heads take? We

247

outline three possible emphases, not to exhaust the possibilities, only to point out the issues of control that face heads in their relationships with teachers and the public, and the various ways the dilemma language may be used.

1. Heads may take as their primary responsibility the shaping of teachers' patterns of resolutions to the political, social and cultural preferences of the community, a segment of the community, or its governing board, as they see or interpret them. From this perspective the role of the administrator is the 'head' of teachers in the literal sense that they do the thinking for teachers. As is most often the case in physicians' relationships with nurses, these heads may see themselves as more qualified than teachers to make difficult moral choices and decisions, although they may recognize that teachers do, of necessity, resolve many dilemmas as they arise in the classroom. Administrators who see their role in this way may use the language of dilemmas to inquire into teaching practices in their schools, and to specify to teachers the range of patterns of resolutions and the shifts in emphasis they desire.

2. Heads may see their role as enabling teachers to resolve the dilemmas with as little interference from outside as possible. Teaching at its best is, from this perspective, a highly developed art, and the heads' role may be likened to that of patron of the arts: protecting the teacher-artist from the tyranny and banality of popular opinion. The administrators' problem from this point of view is to understand the teachers' intended patterns of resolution and, in so far as possible, to remove obstacles that hinder the development of the art of teaching within their schools.

3. Heads may see their primary role as educator: to raise questions about preferences of the community and of teachers, which are normally taken for granted, and to assist a search for alternatives; in other words, to encourage critical inquiry. Heads who take this view see themselves as first among equals, their special leadership responsibilities flowing from their experience as teachers, their (presumed) ability to initiate and sustain critical inquiry, and the delegation of authority from the public to insure the coordination and coherence of the educational programs internal to the school and throughout the schooling sequence. Heads who see their role in this way may use the dilemma language to facilitate critical inquiry among teaching staff, and among staff and parents.

The heads in the three English schools we studied in depth illustrate the three emphases. Mrs Hollins at Castlegate was the physician, prime expert in all schooling matters, curricular and organizational. Through the power of her intellect, her skills in human relations, and her knowledge of teaching, she, with the consent of her staff, over a period of years influenced teachers' patterns of resolutions to the point that every teacher to a greater or lesser extent manifested the overall patterns she preferred. There were, to our knowledge, no discussions among staff where they considered alternatives to the patterns of resolutions she fostered.[13] Mr Nigel at Port revealed two approaches: with respect to the infant teachers he was patron of the arts; his stance towards the junior teachers resembled that of Mrs Hollins. He actively attempted to shape the resolutions of the 'team' but he did not specify resolutions. Rather, he limited himself to structural changes, for example, setting up the team organization, introducing new maths programs, providing new resources (library, TV).

Among the three heads, Mr Bolton at Heathbrook came closest to the educator orientation. In spite of the authoritarian-father image he projected to children (and sometimes to teachers) he encouraged, often provoked, continuous examination of the current patterns of schooling which were taken for granted in Heathbrook. How should the basics be integrated into other school subjects? Which curriculum activities should be required? Which children should be given more opportunities and why? Such questions were discussed in staff meetings each week, sometimes at great length. He placed a high value on teachers who raised questions about accepted resolutions and on occasion allowed teachers to institute changes he did not fully endorse. However, he maintained the prerogative of the head, vetoing, though only rarely, some modes of resolution preferred by the faculty as a whole.[14] In dealing with parents he took the patron of the arts position, making every effort to convince them that professionals know best, thus insulating teachers from parents' preferences and concerns.

CITIZENS AND PARENTS

The relationship between schools and the public is obviously a complex subject. We comment briefly on the place the dilemmas may play in establishing communication between teachers, heads and parents. (There are parallels to the problems of communication between many segments of the public and educational officers at other levels; for example, between lay governing boards and superintendents, between business and labor leaders and school heads, between citizen groups and government educational officials, etc.)

Commentaries on practices in both countries generally confirm our own experience in US and English schools: teachers and heads generally try to restrict parents' influence on how teachers will resolve the dilemmas.[15] Parent–teacher conferences and parent –teacher meetings are for the most part conceived by the professionals as one way conduits for providing parents information about, and mustering support for, the professionals' prevailing or preferred patterns of resolution. Teachers and heads rarely solicit parents' perspectives on how existing patterns of resolution may be affecting their own children's growth or how shifts in emphasis might better serve them. Just as teachers could be seen as experts *vis à vis* administrators and researchers so, too, could parents be seen as prime experts in matters relating to their own children. Most parents abdicate their role as expert, even though many may have regrets, and may have experienced intense anger and pain in relationship to their children's schooling experiences.

A basic assumption of the common school is that the public has a legitimate right to influence the process of schooling of *all* children. But to exercise this right intelligently citizens and parents – if they are not to be manipulated by the professionals – must have an understanding of schooling. Some will raise the fear that to bring such troublesome questions to the fore will embroil staff and community in such intense political controversies that the schooling of children will be left unattended. Indeed, there have been instances on both sides of the Atlantic when political heat reached such an intensity that the quality of the educational experience of the children was virtually forgotten. In our experience these instances are almost invariably characterized by a history of neglect by the professionals, teachers and administrators of the deeply felt concerns and interests of the parents and the children. The dilemma language is one way for citizens to engage in inquiry with one another and with professionals about possible and desirable changes in schools. The language may be used to clarify the confusion hidden in debates over 'basics', 'discipline', 'progressive' v. 'traditional', 'racist' or 'sexist' teaching. An examination of schooling using the language will not erase conflict, but it may illuminate areas of agreement, help parents and professionals to formulate clearly their differences, and provide a way of structuring inquiries into assumptions underlying present resolutions and desirable and possible alternatives. Understanding the perspectives of others is a precondition for developing patterns of resolutions that take into account the rights and interests of parents, children and all others who have an interest in the futures of our children and of the society in which they live.

THE DILEMMA LANGUAGE AND TEACHER EDUCATION

In 1905 Henry Adams, man of letters, descendant of a patrician family that influenced the course of the American Revolution and the early years of the Republic, reflected upon his life that spanned the years when America grew from a confederation of commercial, agrarian states, to the emerging giant of industrial capitalism. What, Adams asked, prepared him for the enormous social and political transformation he witnessed, that accompanied the invention of the means to generate and direct energy for human use in ways that were unimaginable in his youth? Although he did not discount entirely his experience as a student and later as a professor at Harvard College, he concluded that his years in formal schools were least educative. Of his years as a student, he said that on the whole it was a 'negative force', and some of it 'befogged his mind for a lifetime'.[16]

Adams's autobiography is a dramatic reminder not only that formal schooling and education are not one and the same, but of how little is understood of how persons become educated. Little in the professional literature clarifies how teachers acquire the capacity for critical inquiry; how, for example, Mr Sprinter and Mrs Hollins have come to be masters of their craft, astute observers of children, sensitive in some measure to the historical and cultural forces that play upon and through them. For us, the more illuminating sources of such knowledge have been teachers' accounts, biographies, novels, poetry, plays, films, not the writings of social scientists. From our experience, and based on surveys in Britain and the US over the years, we know that teachers do not attribute their competence to courses taught by educationists. There are undoubtedly exceptions, but, in general, whatever may have been the content and method of such courses, the more theoretical courses are consistently viewed by teachers as irrelevant to practice – to their decisions about how to organize classroom life and intervene in the lives of children. However, it is not teachers' skepticism alone that raises questions about the value of teacher-education programs and educational disciplines generally. These questions have been raised in several reports by distinguished committees and individuals in both Britain and the US over the years.[17]

Questions remain unresolved about the nature of the educational disciplines as a whole and their relationship to the humanities and the established social sciences. Confusion is also reflected in the structure of faculties of education themselves – the separation into distinct divisions, areas or departments of persons devoted to curricular and practical studies, on the one hand, and those who view themselves as engaged in more basic or foundational research and teaching (historians, philosophers, psychologists, sociologists of education), on the other. We will confine ourselves to raising substantive and structural issues central to the development of more adequate teacher-education programs. In so doing, we clarify the implications of the broader argument we have made in this book, and briefly illustrate how the dilemma language may be used for penetrating a number of curricular and structural issues in both pre-service and in-service programs for teachers.

The purposes of the formal education of teachers

Our view of the primary function of formal training has been made explicit in our conception of critical inquiry for teachers which we illustrated and clarified above. To restate: the proper role of the formal education of teachers is to help persons develop their capacities to see their classroom behavior in the perspectives of culture and time, from the point of view of historical and contemporary others, thereby clarifying for themselves and others the alternatives for action. The structural features of institutions for the education of teachers, including the staffing policies, selection of knowledge, arrangement of learning environments and the pedagogical strategies of the instructors, are means towards this end. The entire program, all courses and practical experiences, should provide the aspiring or experienced teacher with access to persons (faculty members, teachers, colleagues and other persons) who can help *initiate and sustain a process of critical inquiry*.

Formulated in terms of the dilemma language, the purpose of teacher-education programs is to help teachers examine the political, cultural and moral choices and issues involved in their everyday patterns of resolution, and to initiate and/or encourage in teachers self-consciousness of how their own resolutions to the control, curriculum and societal dilemmas are joined to social continuity and change.[18] To do this, a formal program should provide opportunities for teachers to see their own resolutions in the perspectives of history and culture and to facilitate the development of craft. Most significant is the joining of public and personal knowledge of teachers, that is the connecting of knowing, and doing.[20]

The study of history, psychology and sociology could contribute greatly to critical inquiry by clarifying for teachers how social forces, past and contemporary, shape and have shaped particular patterns of resolutions. These disciplines are often seen by teachers as irrelevant to teaching since their connections to teachers' choices in the classroom are rarely drawn. It is, however, possible to organize 'foundations' courses to foster critical inquiry.[20] For example, a historical study of the teaching of reading could be structured to clarify for teachers how social, cultural and economic forces have affected the way they were taught to read and now affect their patterns of resolution as they teach reading. From this perspective the goal of teacher education cannot be said to be 'theoretical' or 'practical' – it is both, simultaneously.

This conception of education as critical inquiry is not a radical, or perhaps we should say not only a radical, view. It is a conception of education that is a familiar cornerstone of liberal constitutional, democratic as well as of democratic socialist theories of the state. James Madison expressed it as a basic tenet of liberal constitutional democracy as follows: 'People who mean to be their own governors must arm themselves with the power knowledge gives.' Becoming educated is being 'liberated' from parochial localist perspectives on oneself and one's social and physical world, thus becoming better able to view one's interests – intellectual, economic, political, social or otherwise – in terms of the social and political life and welfare of others. The idea of democracy or 'popular sovereignty' then includes the idea that it is legitimate and necessary for citizens to possess the inclination and capacity to question the status quo.

What clearly follows is that all formal schooling from nursery to college or university is implicated in the education of teachers, and *all* schooling, whatever the content or organization, however fragmented or unified it may be, including all programs for educating teachers, is political. It is political in that it either encourages or does not encourage persons to develop and use their critical capacities to examine the prevailing political, social and cultural arrangements, and the part their own acts (as teachers or non-teachers) play in sustaining or changing these arrangements. If the curriculum and faculty of teacher-education programs or courses fail to encourage critical inquiry into everyday problems of teaching and learning, a *de facto* political position has been taken. The continued separation of practical and theoretical knowledge in the education of teachers is a political act. And if it is true (as we argue in the last section of this book) that many pedagogical researchers fail to recognize the political and moral assumptions in their empirical research, then the transmission of their research to teachers discourages rather than encourages critical inquiry, deepening confusions over the separation of matters of fact from questions of value in the minds of their students, future teachers and teachers of teachers.

We will not attempt here to capture for the uninitiated the many and diverse ways that education faculties have been structured over the years. We must, however, note that it is not only conceivable but likely that persons who teach history, psychology, philosophy, sociology of education, those who teach curriculum and methods courses, and those who are the supervisors or tutors of practice teachers talk little if at all with one another about their educational efforts, virtually foreclosing the possibility of developing programs that foster critical inquiry. This fact is, in part, a reflection of the way hierarchies of knowledge have become ossified into particular structural arrangements making communication among educational specialists not impossible but a remarkable political feat nevertheless.

The failures of teacher-education programs to fulfill their promises are legion, but it is surely not the failure of schools and departments of education faculties alone. University and college academics in the arts, sciences and humanities have generally forsaken responsibility for the quality of the intellectual life of the common school. Inquiry into craft knowledge of teaching young persons, and the relationship of such knowledge to other realms of inquiry is generally seen as an inferior preoccupation to the academics' own special areas of inquiry. Whatever may be the benefits to the advancement of knowledge (and in some fields, it may be considerable), increased specialization within the university at large, as well as within faculties of education, makes it extraordinarily difficult to establish programs which foster the joining of practical situational problems that face teachers to broader cultural, social and political issues. The problem of specialization is compounded by the fact that one's place in the status hierarchy within universities and colleges correlates highly and inversely with a person's closeness to the practical realities of classroom life.

Any teacher-education program that attempts to join craft with the broader issues must contend with the fragmented structure and the hierarchical organization of higher education. These structures are creations of human effort and can be undone or modified, but not without great difficulties. That there are persons, working alone or with others, who have managed to transcend the problems presented by specialization and hierarchy, we do not doubt. But the question is not whether it is possible, but whether it is very likely, given the present divisions among faculties and the inability of the sub-traditions, even within the field of education itself, to cross the barriers of their own language systems, let alone communicate with, and learn on the basis of parity from teachers and other practitioners whom they generally consider their intellectual inferiors. The promise of teacher education is the promise of the university itself that such divisions can be overcome.

If there is to be serious effort to unify the theoretical and practical, teacher-education programs must be staffed by persons who themselves are committed to the clarification of the interconnections of culture, history and schooling practice. Persons who are expert in the craft of teaching and who have and continue to search for a broader understanding of schooling practice must participate in the design of such programs as full colleagues. The development and sustenance of such programs also requires persons who are well read in traditional disciplines but who do not presume that any tradition has any self-evident claim to superior status[21] and who view teacher knowledge as having equal status and merit to their own. Educational researchers are not excluded, but their contributions must be justified as all others', in terms of helping teachers make intelligent choices. And it is teachers and the people schools serve, not the researchers, who in the final analysis must make judgments of usefulness. There can be no presumption that persons in 'foundations' departments are the chief providers and carriers of knowledge, definers of theory and developers of technology, while those in the curricular and practical fields are the utilizers of their knowledge.

To put our point more directly, if a form of teacher education that unifies the realms of the practical and theoretical is to become a possibility within a college or university, a structure must be created that permits persons with these competencies and interests to work together without jeopardizing their careers, and that provides the same possibilities for job security that are available to others. Without such structures it is unlikely that such programs can develop or long survive. The difficulty, particularly at the present time, of obtaining regular appointments at universities and colleges in the UK and the US and the importance for advancement of approval by those whose work in the higher-status academic disciplines of psychology, sociology, history and philosophy are not politically nor morally neutral facts. These pressures push faculty members to pursue lines of inquiry that satisfy their peers within the sub-specialities rather than to focus on the joining of theory and practice. Whatever may be the merits of inquiries in the traditional academic disciplines, they divert persons from the difficult work of developing programs for teachers that bridge these sub-specialities and explore the relationships between the theoretical and empirical contributions of these specialized areas and the problems of educating children in schools. The specialized job of the professional teacher educator is to transcend the boundaries among fields of knowledge without prejudgment about the superior status or merit of any attempts to clarify these connections.

Because of the severe competition for jobs within the field of education, and because tenure and appointment depend upon performing according to certain assumed criteria for appointment, it is likely that the structural fragmentation of teacher education will remain, the divisions within faculties of education will continue to be taken as normal and the pressures toward further compartmentalization will increase. The difficulty of sustaining practice-oriented programs in the years ahead will undoubtedly lead some higher-status institutions to withdraw completely from the education of teachers, as once happened at Harvard,[22] leaving the mundane job of educating practitioners to lower-prestige and state institutions.

This withdrawal may, however, turn out to be myopic. Schools and departments of education have had a short and, in some cases, uneasy history in many institutions of higher education, and the present stresses serve to raise more questions about the usefulness of the educationalists. Whether the study of education as a field can survive in higher education without being nurtured by its connections to the daily lives of persons in schools will be put to the test. It is conceivable that the uncertain power of the educationists may disintegrate, some of it perhaps being passed to teacher organizations and/or to the traditional academic disciplines and schooling organizations. It is possible that – as difficult and complex as it may be – such an evolution may, in time, improve the prospects of breaking the barriers between theory and practice, knowing and acting, that prevail in teacher education as the decade of the 1980s begins.

What we are proposing is an approach to educational change grounded in an image of persons as intelligent human beings who are capable of reflecting on themselves and their behavior and revising their behavior in the light of reflection. We are arguing that the dilemmas can be used to structure curriculum and cultivate critical inquiry among teachers and between teachers, academics and the public, a process we call thinking when undertaken by ourselves and debate when it occurs in public among partisans of different views, opinions and interests.[23]

XI EDUCATIONAL RESEARCHERS AS CRITICAL INQUIRERS

What can the dilemma language contribute to social science inquiries, and to the clarification and formulation of schooling policy? Our argument throughout has been that research into schooling processes (as into the social process in other institutional forms) seeks to unite the 'micro' and the 'macro'; that is, to penetrate the connections between the circumstances and events of daily life in schools, and the moral, social and political decisions we face as teachers, administrators, parents, scholars, citizens – individually or collectively. Such research, we have argued, is simultaneously theoretical and practical. The distinction between 'basic' and 'applied' research, therefore, dissolves. Although often the practical import of social theories is left obscure and the theoretical assumptions of practice left unstated, both have the same moral burden of contributing to the making of intelligent choices in the realities we confront.

In the final pages of the book we will suggest how the dilemma language may be used to overcome some of the problems implicit in common forms of research that, formulated either from a macro or a micro perspective, fail to come to terms with the interconnections of these orientations.[1]

'MACRO' RESEARCH: JENCKS'S 'INEQUALITY', AND AN ALTERNATIVE FORMULATION

How does schooling experience contribute to the acceptance or questioning by the next generation of the accepted social relations and institutional structures of our social world, its conceptions of beauty, truth, justice, its way of looking and seeing? This is a restatement of the familiar social/cultural reproduction issue discus-

258

sed by social philosophers over the centuries and posed as a social scientific question in terms of schooling institutions in modern times by Emile Durkheim and other lesser known sociologists and social theorists. It is also the ultimate practical question since a position on what schools do and do not contribute to the maintenance and transformation of the political and social life of the community is presumed in the priority given to educational expenditures, and in the ways expenditures are used to influence schooling processes and structures.

The question of what schooling contributes to a person's life chances of becoming socially and economically successful is only a piece of this broader question. The narrower question, sometimes referred to by sociologists as the 'social selection' or 'social mobility' question, has preoccupied social scientific research for more than a half-century.[2] Put negatively, it is the question of how the structures and processes of schooling contribute to the maintenance of existing social and economic inequalities. As we noted in Chapter II, a number of sociological studies conducted through the 1960s, by showing empirically that educational opportunities were highly class- and region-related, buttressed the arguments of progressive educational reformers that the existing system of education was not only unfair but inefficient, and that structural changes in school (for example, a comprehensive system of secondary education) were necessary to halt the monumental waste of our greatest national asset, human talent. As we also noted in Chapter II, in the 1970s this inefficiency argument was turned on its head by Professor Christopher Jencks and others. At the time Jencks's *Inequality* provided what for many was the 'state of the art' study of multivariate social science survey research, a meticulous attempt to determine empirically schools' contributions to a person's life chances. He included in his calculations virtually all factors that he could conceivably relate statistically to a person's future income – intelligence, father's income, years at school, school expenditures, etc. By asking how much of the variation in persons' incomes could be accounted for by any factor (or combinations of factors) he was able to make a statistical statement about the schools' contributions to persons' economic success. The conclusion he drew from his calculations (in 1972) is by now well-known – the contribution of schooling was negligible. What was presumed by some to be the significant social policy implication of his study was widely repeated in academic circles and national political journals, raising the ire of some, but acclaimed by many: school reform may make John and Jane happier children, but in terms of hard economic and social realities, it is an ineffective (that is, inefficient) means of achieving social equality. Though Jencks, a socialist, argued for the need for more basic social reforms, this appeal was none too difficult to dismiss in practical politics. His work had vindicated the familiar arguments of both the strident 'New Left' and radical right, putting the scientific cap on the case that the social reforms of the Labour and Democratic Parties in the late 1960s and early 1970s were a waste of money and human effort.

We find no fault in the attempts by social scientists to calculate as best they can the contribution of schooling to future economic success. Indeed, taking the population as a whole, there is certainly nothing implausible in Jencks's conclusion that school attendance itself contributes relatively little to equalization of wealth or persons' opportunities for advancement. It may be, as Karabel and Halsey suggest after a devastating analysis of the limitations of Jencks's study, that Jencks 'brilliantly demolished the peculiarly American myth that school reform can serve as a substitute for more fundamental social change . . . [and] may unfortunately have replaced it with another equally destructive myth: that a viable strategy for social equality can afford to ignore the schools.' [3] Our view is that Jencks's and his colleagues' calculations were no surprise except perhaps to a few academics and political leaders who took too seriously the exorbitant political rhetoric used to sell to the public that progressive reforms (for example structural changes in schools – in the US, desegregation, in England, comprehensive schools) would bring about social and economic transformations.

An equally serious consequence of *Inequality* (and of Jencks's 1979 study) was that it was taken as relevant not only to the narrower political question of whether schools were wise social investments in terms of equalizing economic opportunity, but left the impression, or did little to dissuade us from thinking, that it had settled once and for all the question of what schools do – whether they have and can have *any* significant social, political and cultural effects upon the lives of individuals and on society at large – other than merely reproducing existing inequalities. Thus, *Inequality* made a significant contribution to confusing the debates over educational policies and programs – over what schools could and should do. What is significant is that such conclusions were drawn from a study in which no information had been gathered about what goes on inside the 'black box' of schools; without any inquiries into the process of daily life in classrooms, or into the consciousness of the actors (students, teachers, administrators – except through questionnaires, whose answers could be converted to numbers). The criticism that the Jencks sort of sociological study trivialized the question of social and cultural reproduction has been made repeatedly. Indeed, a year prior to the publication of *Inequality*, Basil Bernstein, in the widely known (in the UK) *Knowledge and Social Control*, leveled this same criticism at the entire tradition of social research wherein the complex questions of the consequences of schooling in social, cultural and political terms is reduced to 'a series of input–output problems'.[4]

We have attempted to show, in Chapter IX how studies that purport to make a statement on the social and political significance of the schooling process, including input–output studies as exemplified by *Inequality* (and Bowles and Gintis's *Schooling in Capitalist America*) can be reformulated in terms of the dilemma language and orientation. As we have argued, an analysis of schooling in terms of the dilemma language captures both the constraints on teachers' behavior and the opportunities open to them to engage in reflective action. It also points the way towards examining the complex and contradictory meanings that are being transmitted in classrooms. The approach to studying the relationship of teaching activity to social reproduction and change we have offered in this book therefore makes it possible to identify how people act in ways that 'contribute however minutely to the shaping of society'. Thus, in contrast to research such as Jencks's, ours is one way to frame studies that could help teachers and others make intelligent choices by illuminating the contribution their activities may make to the process of social transformation.

CURRICULUM INQUIRY: READING AND LANGUAGE

In 1967 Jean Chall, among the more widely known experts in North America on the teaching of reading, published *Learning to Read: The Great Debate*,[5] a report of a three-year study sponsored by the Carnegie Foundation. It was intended to still a stormy dispute over approaches to teaching reading that was thrust into public notice more than a decade earlier by Rudolf Flesch's *Why Johnny Can't Read*,[6] a book that remained on the best-seller list for thirty weeks and was widely serialized in newspapers across the continent. Mr Flesch claimed that the primary cause of Johnny's problem, the 'sight' method, was demonstrably inferior to the 'phonics' approach.

His book was attacked as a polemic by many of the experts of the time, while Professor Chall's book had about it the aura of a scientific document, one that provided a dispassionate reading of virtually all of the relevant available research on the teaching of reading. She concluded, in spite of the fact that the research evidence was 'shockingly inconclusive',[7] that Mr Flesch was almost right, that what she called the 'code emphasis' was, without doubt, superior to the 'meaning emphasis' – at least for beginning readers, particularly for children of 'average and below average intelligence and from lower socio-economic backgrounds'.[8] According to Chall, research from 1912 to 1965 indicated that a 'code-emphasis' method – that is, 'one that views beginning reading as essentially different from mature reading and emphasizes learning the printed code for the spoken language – produces better results, at least up to the point where sufficient evidence seems to be available, the end of the third grade'.[9] She went on to recommend, among other things, that publishers of 'basal' reading programs, the most widely used materials for the teaching of reading in the US, should heed her findings and shift the emphasis in reading texts and workbooks from 'look–say' to some systematic 'phonics' approach, a recommendation that appears to have had considerable influence. Put in terms of the dilemma language, Chall argued that a molecular emphasis in the teaching of beginning reading was superior to a more holistic approach. Writing in 1979, Professor Chall remained convinced;[10] nevertheless, the underlying philosophical differences that lurk behind the 'code' v. 'meaning' controversy continue to be as intensely debated today in similar and in quite different guises – embedded in the disputes over testing, formal v. informal methods, as well as in the continuing debate about the relative merits of phonics drills in 'basal' reading programs v. more holistic (for example, language experience) approaches.[11] Why, despite the fact that, according to Chall, the superiority of the phonics emphasis has been consistently proved, does controversy persist? Are the unconvinced unresponsive to scientific facts?

Continued skepticism of her conclusions can be explained in part by examining the nature of the scientific evidence Chall used to support her case. The question for which Chall and others wanted an answer seemed quite straightforward: 'What is the best way to teach a young child to read?'[12] Teaching (of reading or any other subject) can be conceived of as an ongoing process of behavior (or a set of 'interactions') that occur in a setting, often (but not always) a schoolroom. By the late 1960s, various social psychologists and educational researchers had developed a number of 'category systems' that enabled classroom 'interactions' to be classified, counted and compared.[13] However, given the assumptions of positivist pedagogical science, there was probably no way that such schemes could have been used or adapted to describe the sorts of differences in the process of teaching reading required to answer Chall's initial question. What Professor Chall did was to *transform* the initial question into a form that was considered acceptable in terms of positivist social science standards. Thus, rather than comparing the consequences of *methods in use*, she compared the effects on children of teachers who reported that they used instructional materials that emphasized either a code or a meaning approach. The relative effects of teachers' use of materials type A v. B upon children were determined by comparing their scores on standardized reading achievement tests (and sometimes on other questionnaires or rating scales whose results could be expressed as scores). Complications such as social, cultural and intellectual differences among children were handled by statistical controls. 'Mental age', which depends upon IQ test scores for its calculation, was taken as equivalent to 'ability', and social and cultural differences were 'controlled' by using numerical indices for 'SES' (socio-economic status), generally based on family income and/or father's occupation. A question which began its career as a puzzle over the consequences upon children of differing approaches to teaching reading, in order to meet the methodological rigors of empirical social science, was transformed into comparisons of the effects upon standardized reading test scores of types of teaching materials classified by the researchers primarily in terms of their relative emphasis on drill and repetition of sounds.

The problems in such transformations are enormous and have been raised by numbers of others. They go directly to the heart of the matter of whether Professor Chall's answers are at all relevant to her initial question. First, there are the problems that result from transforming the teaching process into 'materials used'; second, those that arise from transforming reading competence to performance on reading achievement tests. We discuss each in turn.

Professor Chall's transformation of the teaching process to type of material used requires that one take as fact a dubious assumption that the behavioral differences among persons using the same materials are less significant than the behavioral variations among teachers who reportedly use different teaching materials (either code or meaning emphasis). But in the study of how the materials are actually used, Chall ignores what may be the *most* significant factors for answering her initial question ('What is the best way to teach a child to read?'). For example, what Lillian Weber suggests may be the most significant factor in teaching – the adaptiveness and responsiveness of teachers to children and context – is ignored altogether in such research.[14] In our terms, researchers do not attend to how teachers shift their patterns of resolution in response to differences in children and context.

Another difficulty is that, in bypassing the process of teaching, Professor Chall reduces differences in methods to a single dimension: in terms of the dilemma language, to differences in emphasis in the resolution to *one* curriculum dilemma – learning is molecular v. holistic.

As we have shown, to conceive of teaching in terms of a resolution to a single dilemma is distorting because, with or without the teachers' or researchers' awareness, a whole range of dilemmas that deal with social and knowledge control are simultaneously being resolved. As a consequence of transforming 'method A' and 'method B' into the single dimension molecular–holistic one tends to look only at the more likely consequences of this resolution (for example, performance on reading tests), while the effects of resolutions to other teaching, learning and social dilemmas (implicit or explicit in the 'methods') upon children's critical intellectual, aesthetic, social, moral and emotional development remain unexplored. The practical implication of this transformation is of no small consequence. It can easily mislead us into accepting standardized test results as a reasonable, if not fully adequate, index of whether teachers and school heads are doing a good job, and whether children are learning.

The problems raised by transforming reading competence to performance on reading tests can be shown with reference to the Bullock Report, a volume published in 1975 in Britain, the product of a committee of twenty appointed by the then Education Secretary in the Conservative government, Margaret Thatcher. The committee was given the charge 'to inquire into the teaching in the schools of reading and the other uses of English'. The report, like Chall's, attempts to clarify the conflicting scientific claims and to offer guidance in formulating national and local policy. The contrast between the Chall and Bullock studies is interesting on a number of grounds; two are particularly relevant to this discussion. First, is the relative importance accorded to teachers' knowledge in Bullock. Unlike Chall's study the Bullock Report was not primarily the work of educational scientists but of a committee, the majority of whom were teachers, ex-teachers and school heads. Second, is the difference in underlying political orientations of the two reports. Though, like the Chall study, the Bullock Report was conceived as 'apolitical' or 'non-partisan', the latter acknowledged that there were basic philosophical (that is, political) differences that underlie alternative approaches to teaching reading and language. Though eschewing politics, Bullock announced its political position and its general conclusions in its title, *A Language for Life*. Chall, of course, also represents a particular political and moral view, but her political position is obscured by the presumption that hers is a value-free scientific analysis of the reading problem that transcended morals and politics.

The Bullock Report we think clearly identifies the political issue that lurks behind the different ways of assessing basic literacy and defining reading competency. The committee outlines the three basic definitions of reading as follows:[15]

Definition A

One can read in so far as he can respond to the language skills represented by graphic shapes as fully as he has learned to respond to the same language signals of his code represented by patterns of auditory shapes. [Quotation taken by the report writers from Fries]

Reading from this point of view is the child's *'ability to respond to letters and spelling patterns'*. The ability to call words and to define them presumably is the index of success.

Definition B

The purpose of reading is the reconstruction of meaning. Meaning is not in print, but it is meaning that the author begins with when he writes. Somehow the reader strives to reconstruct this meaning as he reads.

Thus, to read is to be able to take meaning from print accurately and success is demonstrated by the ability to summarize what one reads cogently and accurately. This is the definition implicit in reading comprehension tests in which presumably persons read passages and select from an array of statements the one which best represents what each passage means. Virtually all paper and pencil reading tests, standardized or 'minimal competency', employ this technique, thereby presumably taking this definition of reading as accepted.

Definition C

A good reader understands not only the meanings of a passage, but its related meaning as well, which includes all the reader knows that enriches or illuminates the literal meaning. Such knowledge may have been acquired through direct experience, through wide reading or through listening to others.

This, according to the Bullock Report, means that 'reading is more than a *reconstruction of the author's meanings*. It is the perception of those meanings within *the total context of the relevant experiences of the reader* — a much more active and demanding process.' [16]

The differences between these definitions, particularly between A and B v. C, are of obvious political significance. The third definition implies that proficiency in reading involves an active and critical process. A critical reader *not only* is able to decode and take the writer's meaning, but is able to take the reading material itself as problematical. This concept of 'critical literacy' has been enunciated in one form or another over the years by liberals and radicals alike. It is consistent with Paulo Freire's concept of 'critical consciousness', [17] it is the view expressly stated or implicit in writings of a number of so-called 'romantic' critics of the 1960s and early 1970s. [18] It is also the educational ideal embedded in American and English conceptions of constitutional democracy.

What the advocates of the meaning emphasis claim as its advantage is that it promotes in children the ability to relate verbal and written language to the children's own language and experience; in other words, Bullock's third definition, what we have called 'critical literacy'. The promise is that children will eventually become persons who *enjoy reading, and use it for increasing their understanding of self, culture and society*. Our concern here is not whether the promise is sheer romanticism (as some critics claim) but whether the advantages claimed by its proponents could show up on studies that measure results by short item reading tests. It is our view that reading tests can, at best, only assess children's abilities to read short paragraphs and to choose correctly from an array of answers under pressure of time. If one accepts as an imperfect but nevertheless adequate measure of students' reading ability their performance on reading tests then one has, in effect, tacitly accepted as adequate the underlying definition of reading literacy that is built into the tests, a passive conception of the reading process. Children who, for whatever reason, take more easily to the school game of quickly responding to teachers' questions without questioning either the questions or the answers will likely find the tests less troublesome than those who are resistant or indifferent to the school's assumed views of knowledge and learning. Use of such tests allows the test technologists (who have a vested interest in test use) to determine for the rest of us the patterns of resolution that are most valued and the conception of literacy that the schools take as a priority. We do not here dismiss the accountability question. We believe that professional educators *at all levels* including primary-school teachers, should be held accountable for their performance in the teaching of reading (and other subjects) but the means must be consistent with our professed ends. We do not think it is beyond the capacities of teachers, working together with school officials, parents, academics, writers and ordinary citizens to devise ways of approaching the task of assessing reading competence. It is far too important to be left to the educational scientists and psychometricians.

An alternative way to pose the question of the effects of differing approaches to teaching reading is to ask what are the meanings about control, knowledge and society children (or different groups of children) take from differing patterns of resolution used by teachers in the teaching of reading and language. By posing the question in this way, the range of dilemmas implicit in a given method is acknowledged and we are alerted to the range of possible meanings that may be taken from a given method, including children's awareness of the problematic nature of the reading material itself.[19] This formulation, by calling attention to the degree and form of reflexivity (or responsiveness of teachers to children and their experience), which is probably the most crucial in the development of critical literacy, will contribute a better understanding of how teachers can encourage development of critical reading – the 'perception of the author's meanings in the total context of the relevant experiences of the reader'.

THEORY-BASED RESEARCH

Studies that attempt to compare methods of teaching have been dubbed 'curriculum' or 'action' research to distinguish them from theory-based or theoretical research.[20] The logic of the case for the latter is that if there were adequate theory (and/or a set of empirically derived principles of language acquisition) then reading instruction, based on these principles, would be maximally effective.

An enormous corpus of 'theory-based' research has been produced over the years in the area of reading and language curriculum, probably more than any other single area of educational research[21] and, as one would expect, there are wide differences over what such 'theory' entails, how it is developed, and what is the relationship of theory (or principles) to practice. Whatever the orientation, all make assumptions (implicit or explicit) about the nature of language and its inter-relationship of culture and society, and about human psycho-social and intellectual development and learning. One class of such theories is behaviorist in orientation. Although there are many variants of a 'behaviorist' view of language acquisition, the basic notion is that words acquire their meaning by occurring together with the things which they stand for. 'Language is conceived as a vast network of associative links between separate elements: individual words and individual things.' [22] From this perspective what researchers seek to discover are a finite number of generally applicable principles similar to 'laws' of the natural sciences[23] which may be applied by practitioners as they teach children. This orientation has its roots in the positivism of Anglo-American experimental psychology, and in the 1930s, 1940s and 1950s it went almost unchallenged[24] until Noam Chomsky's seminal work on linguistics in the 1960s.[25] There are also significant variants among the competitors to behaviorist linguistic theories, but they have in common a rejection of the passivity of persons in the process of acquiring language. Persons are, in other words, creators of their culture, not passive culture-absorbing objects. What is also primary in such theories is the concept of meaning – 'the ability to make sense of things and, above all to make sense of what people do which, of course, includes what people say'.[26]

The intellectual divisions between these two warring traditions are deep. They are not only conceptual and methodological, but political. They represent contrasting world views that are as significant as the differences between Skinnerian reinforcement theory, which has no place for intentional action, and Meadian social behaviorism and Marxism, where the reflexive relationship between social context and intended action is central. But there is a persistent theme one finds in the literature on theory-based research on reading regardless of orientation: concern about the gap between theory and practice. It was noted repeatedly by many of the writers in a series of articles in the Canadian educational journal *Curriculum Inquiry*[27] in 1979, devoted to assessing the current state of reading research in North America, that teachers are largely indifferent, if not openly antagonistic, toward scientific research on reading.[28] There are numbers of reasons given for this antipathy. In our view a significant part of the explanation resides in the researchers' lack of respect for teachers' knowledge and intelligence which we noted earlier. For example, one of the contributors to the aforementioned series of articles attributes teachers' failure to use the principles of science to their 'intuitive' rather than rational turn of mind, with citations to Professors Lortie's and Jackson's work to buttress her view.

But what is probably more significant, as others have pointed out, is that researchers generate their problems out of their theoretical orientations, interests and concern for how scholars will assess their contributions to the research field. Teachers' problems arise out of their daily concern with teaching children to read. Whatever may be said in defense of the rigors of carefully-controlled laboratory studies of language acquisition, laboratories differ in fundamental ways from classrooms. To conceive, as do many researchers, of classrooms as places where teachers can apply 'theory' derived in controlled settings is to ignore the fact that classrooms are ongoing social language environments[29] where teachers (who are merely privileged members) are expected to intervene in the ongoing process of language acquisition. Their patterns of behavior in classrooms are likely different from patterns researchers play out in controlled situations, and children are unlikely to take the same meaning from classroom patterns as they would take from patterns in laboratory settings. It is, therefore, probably more important to understand how experience in classrooms influences their acquisition of language and the part teachers play in the process, than it is to understand how children react to 'stimuli' in controlled situations. Teachers' indifference to the fruits of theory-based research may not represent a rejection of rationality and scientific thinking but a basic grasp of the fundamental differences between the classroom and the laboratory contexts. It is by now quite clear, we think, that no theory, or set of empirical principles derived from such studies is adequate for guiding teachers' classroom behavior. And there is certainly at present as much reason to believe that what teachers have learned over the years from teaching children is as significant to development of an adequate theory of language acquisition (within the schooling situation) as are the contributions of the linguists, psychologists and curriculum researchers.

The goal of educational inquiry is to improve schooling practice. Collaborative research is not only desirable but a necessity if this promise is not to remain cant. The practical problems of conducting systematic inquiry in school settings are great. Many, including many reading researchers, have made similar pleas for studies of language in use in classrooms but few major changes have occurred. Some assign a limited role to classroom study – as sources of researchers' hypotheses which must then be validated in controlled situations or in large-scale surveys. Other voices call for intensive study of the schooling process itself, including teachers' efforts to help children learn to read. Such studies, however, if they are to fulfill their promise of improving the quality of life in classrooms and ultimately in society, must be cast in language and written in ways that are comprehensible to teachers and to lay persons, and must clarify the alternatives that are open to them, or that they may create.

The schooling dilemmas and the general orientation they represent, as we have attempted to show, hold some promise for portraying the ongoing process of teaching in classrooms, understanding its origins and clarifying the meanings children take from schooling experiences. Such knowledge will, we believe, contribute not only to the solution of practical problems, but also to the development of more adequate theories of human social behavior.

NOTES TO PART FIVE

Introduction

1 C. Wright Mills, *The Sociological Imagination* (London: Oxford University Press, 1959), 6.
2 The writings of the 'Frankfurt School' are relevant to this entire discussion, particularly the work of Jürgen Habermas. For a dependable introduction to critical theory and Habermasian thought see Richard J. Bernstein, *The Restructuring of Social and Political Theory* (London: Methuen, 1979, pt IV, 171–236). For a comprehensive interpretative study and bibliography see Thomas McCarthy, *The Critical Theory of Jürgen Habermas* (Cambridge, Mass.; London: MIT Press, 1978). We deal with the issues touched upon here in a forthcoming article available in manuscript from the authors.
3 Anthony Giddens, *New Rules of Sociological Method* (New York: Basic Books, 1976), 60.
4 Mills, 1959, op. cit., 186.
5 Giddens, op. cit., 157.
6 Mills, 1959, op. cit., 7.

Chapter X

1 Dan C. Lortie, *Schoolteacher* (Chicago: University of Chicago Press, 1975), 231.
2 ibid., 73.
3 Philip Jackson, *Life in Classrooms* (New York: Holt, 1968), 144. Jackson also writes that dramatic student growth 'sometimes seems to happen despite rather than as a result of, what anyone has done to the student. . . . Nevertheless, their unpredictability [does not discourage] . . . him [the teacher] from taking at least partial credit' (p. 138). 'Logically, at least, the conscientious teacher ought to point with pride or disappointment to the gains or losses of students as measured

by test performance. But as is often true in human affairs, the logical did not occur' (p. 123).
4 ibid., 144.
5 ibid., 145.
6 If teachers are held in low regard by the educationalists, teachers return the compliment. Lortie's study confirms what we know from our discussions with teachers over the years, that they hold their professional training in low regard except for their practice teaching. Most have been convinced from their own experience with their professional education courses that the fruits of educational science are few. Teachers, as a number of researchers have noted with some dismay, rarely look to educational researchers for answers to their practical problems. (See discussion of reading research in Chapter XI.) However, researchers' criticism of teachers' capacities is more likely to be accepted as fact than teachers' criticisms of researchers, in part because of the presumption that the researchers' views are scientifically derived, and the views of the professors, who control teacher-training programs and who are often hired as experts by government or local education authorities, have far greater impact on teachers than teachers' negative views of university educationalists have on the latter.

We note in passing that professors of education in the United States and the United Kingdom occupy low status within the higher education hierarchy and are themselves frequently viewed by their colleagues in the humanities and sciences as possessing the same deficiencies that they attribute to teachers. It is not irrelevant, also, to point out that the only persons who generally hold lower status in universities than educational researchers are the teacher educators.
7 There is, of course, no reason to suppose that classroom researchers are less vulnerable than other social scientists to the charge that they read their own biases into social reality. See Alvin Gouldner, *The Dialectic of Ideology and Technology* (New York: Seabury, 1976).
8 Lortie, op. cit., 107.
9 A teacher may use these questions to examine resolutions implicit in classroom encounters that occur more or less spontaneously throughout the day. These same questions can also be raised about resolutions implicit in daily plans, not only plans in the conventional sense of formal written lesson plans, but plans teachers carry in their minds, vague or explicit, about what they want to happen during a particular time period, and various forms of monitoring (tests, quizzes and other demonstrations of performance) they plan to use. These questions may also be used to focus an examination of resolutions implicit in an entire program or course of study. In the case of primary schools this might include an analysis of the child's school-arranged education over the course of a semester or year (or longer). For the secondary-school teacher, this might include examination of the content and method of a particular course or portion of a course.
10 Video-tapes, tape-recordings and photographs may also be usefully employed, although the special assets and problems of each must be recognized. See Robert Walker and Clem Adelman, *A Guide to Classroom Observation* (London: Methuen, 1975), for an excellent treatment of the issues, substantive and procedural, of teachers and others observing teachers' and students' schooling behaviors.
11 Quoted in Charles P. Curtis, Jr and Ferris Greenslet (eds), *The Practical Cogitator* (Boston: Houghton Mifflin, 1953), 107–8 (source given as follows: 'Bertrand Russell from a Haldeman-Julius pamphlet, *How to Become A Mathematician*, 1942').
12 We could extend this argument to include industries and professionals who sell their products and/or services to individual schools or to educational authorities –

architects, suppliers of furniture, textbooks and school equipment, etc. Each is an aspect of the schooling environment.

13 On the other hand, unless there was a basic difference over resolutions, Mrs Hollins respected the teachers' terrain, never issued mandates or directives regarding them. One teacher, whom Mrs Hollins saw as 'set in her ways', was not confronted. Yet as the patterns fostered by Mrs Hollins became increasingly taken for granted as the norm of the school, that teacher gradually modified her patterns of resolutions in the direction of the emergent norms. Mrs Hollins also had no compunctions about rearranging the classroom environments, sometimes without a teacher's prior consent.

14 Several teachers reported that the agreement to reorganize 'commitment' (the afternoon elective system) was arrived at collectively. Although everyone acknowledged that Mr Bolton set the bounds, the staff believed that discussion resulted in changes that he did not always fully endorse.

15 See, for example, James Lynch and John Pimlott, *Parents and Teachers* (London: Schools Council/Macmillan, 1976), *passim*; Cyril Poster, *The School and the Community* (London: Macmillan, 1971), *passim*; Judith Stone and Felicity Taylor, *The Parents' Schoolbook* (Harmondsworth, Middlesex: Penguin, 1976), *passim*; Robert Thornbury, *The Changing Urban School* (London: Methuen, 1978), ch. 16.

The professionals are, of course, not always successful. Obvious exceptions include the influence of proponents of community control in the US in the 1960s on professionals' resolutions to the *sub-group consciousness* dilemma.

16 Henry Adams, *The Education of Henry Adams* (Boston: Houghton Mifflin, 1961), 60.

17 See Board of Education, *Report on the Departmental Committee on the Training of Teachers for Public Elementary Schools* (London: HMSO, 1925), *passim*; *Teacher Education and Teacher Training* (the James Report) (London: HMSO, 1972). Burgess Tyrrell (ed.), *Dear Lord James, A Critique of Teacher Education* (Harmondsworth: Penguin, 1971).

In the US the most widely quoted report for many years was James B. Conant's *The Education of American Teachers* (New York: McGraw Hill, 1963); written with the assistance of the Carnegie Foundation, it denigrated the value of professional educational courses. Published the same year was James D. Koerner's *The Miseducation of American Teachers* (Boston: Houghton Mifflin, 1963); he placed virtually all the blame on the inferior intellectual quality of the educationalists.

18 For a discussion of the discontinuities and problems of teacher education see Marilyn Cohn, 'Linkage between campus research and classroom activity', paper presented to Missouri Association of Teacher Education, Washington University (mimeo, 1980).

19 We should point out that the issues and problems of such joining are different for the novice and the experienced teacher, thus for in-service and pre-service programs.

20 See, for example, David C. Bricker, 'Helping teachers appreciate the socal context of their teaching dilemmas', undated manuscript, Oakland University, Rochester, Minnesota.

21 Though we do not imply a relativity of knowledge, we do not undertake this discussion here. See earlier discussion, Chapter VII, n. 17.

22 As this is being written, we have learned of the appointment of a committee, under the chairmanship of Roland Barth, to re-examine the relationship of the Harvard Graduate School of Education's programs and priorities to the schools.

23 See Mills, *The Sociological Imagination* (London: Oxford University Press,

1959), 187. We are not, of course, proposing that teachers should engage continuously in reflective action, a practice that might well lead to inaction, but that, as all human beings, they should periodically subject their own acts to critical analysis.

Chapter XI

1 Naida Tushnet (Bagenstos) completed the earliest study of the schooling process using the dilemma language. She conducted an analysis of two elementary-school teachers' resolutions to the distributive and corrective justice dilemmas ('A participant observation study of four elementary classrooms: focus on issues of justice', unpublished dissertation, Washington University, 1975). Dane Manis used several dilemma terms in his case study of a single teacher's mode of adaptation to the mandated implementation of an 'early childhood' curriculum ('A case study of a teacher's implementation of a kindergarten program developed at a university research and development center', unpublished dissertation, Washington University, 1979). Other studies are underway. Edward R. Mikel is studying the operational curriculum decisions of three secondary-school social studies teachers focusing upon personal v. public knowledge resolutions. Rita Roth is investigating the differences in patterns of resolution of two first-grade teachers in their reading and language curriculum, and the differential meanings ten children take from these patterns. Rebecca Glenn is studying differences in resolutions experienced by boys and girls in three third-grade classrooms and the meanings related to gender taken from these differences. David Dodge is studying the resolutions of male pre-school teachers. Finally, Michael Silver is conducting an interview study of teachers in order to determine how their views of the schooling process changed as a consequence of their participation in a moral education in-service program.
2 See Chapter II, nn. 2, 3, 4 and 5.
3 Karabel and Halsey, *Power and Ideology in Education* (New York: Oxford University Press, 1977), 26.
4 Bernstein, *Class, Codes and Control* (London: Routledge & Kegan Paul, 1971), 47.
5 Jean Chall, *Learning to Read: The Great Debate* (New York: McGraw-Hill, 1967).
6 Rudolf Flesch, *Why Johnny Can't Read and What You Can Do About It* (New York: Harper, 1956).
7 Chall, op. cit., 88.
8 ibid., 138.
9 ibid.
10 Jean Chall, 'Reading research, for whom', *Curriculum Inquiry*, 9:1 (1979), 1.
11 There is a voluminous theoretical, empirical and practically-oriented literature on the subject of reading with, as one might expect, a rather confusing array of language used to describe differing approaches. The discussion in the Bullock Report, *A Language for Life* (London: HMSO, 1975), is a good entry into the morass. For those familiar with the general issue see Mary Anne Wolf, Mark K. McQuillan and Eugene Radwin (eds), *Thought and Language/Language and Reading* (*Harvard Educational Review*, reprint no. 14). It includes reprints of articles of sixty writers which appeared in the *Harvard Educational Review* over the last twenty years. Among them are many of the more widely known North American experts in the field.

'Language experience' approach is used in this context to refer to an orientation to and organization of curriculum that emphasizes an integration of reading, writing, speaking, and language acquisition and understanding always or virtually always in context. For an effort to set out this approach for use by teachers, see James Moffett, *A Student-Centered Language Arts Curriculum* (Boston: Houghton Mifflin, 1973).

12 Chall, 1967, op. cit., 1.

13 Sara Delamont, *Interaction in the Classroom* (London: Methuen, 1976).

14 Lillian Weber, 'Comments on Neville Bennett's book: *Teaching Styles and Pupil Progress*', mimeo, undated manuscript.

15 *A Language for Life* (op. cit.), Report of the Committee of Inquiry appointed by the Secretary of State for Education and Science under the Chairmanship of Sir Alan Bullock; 79.

There is here a parallel between these three definitions of reading and three distinctions made by Brian Fay (op. cit.) about approaches to social scientific research and their relationship to political practice: positivist, interpretive and critical. We do not want to suggest here that either of these sets of categories defines differences that are readily observable in the real world. They do, however, represent a way of distinguishing background assumptions. We will not attempt here to reconstruct Professor Fay's argument. In the positivist category he includes much of what is taken for granted in social, psychological and pedagogical research over the last twenty years in the US and the UK. It is this view that undergirds Chall's case. It depends heavily (but not necessarily) upon uses of standardized measures of educational performance, category systems and uses of quasi-experimental designs. The second, is the interpretive approach which includes traditions that focus on persons as conscious actors. The third, critical, does not deny the facts collected by the first (only their interpretations). It acknowledges and includes the broader social and political context of the situation and of the researchers. Fay shows that empirical questions and value questions are not separable and that all research 'paradigms' have political implications. This brief characterization does not do justice to the argument in the book. This analysis sharpens our argument that reading achievement monitored by instruments and approaches that ignore the situation and the broader social context, cannot be used to assess the success of reading and language curricula that emphasize contextual definitions of literacy.

16 Bullock Report, op. cit., 79.

17 See Paolo Freire, *Pedagogy of the Oppressed* (New York: Seabury Press, 1974); *Education: The Practice of Freedom*, (London: Readers' and Writers' Cooperative, 1976); J. Moffett, op. cit.

18 See Chapter III, n. 1.

19 Rosabeth Kanter, in *Men and Women of the Corporation* (New York: Basic Books, 1977), makes a parallel point with respect to the study of leadership styles. '[R]esearch attempts to distinguish more effective and less effective leadership styles . . . have generally failed in part because there are trade offs associated with one or another form of supervision' (p. 167).

20 Margaret Richek, 'Spiteful tracts compete against bloodless surveys: the use of reading research', *Curriculum Inquiry* 9:1 (1979).

21 Chall, 1967, op. cit.

22 Margaret Donaldson, *Children's Minds* (London: Fontana, 1978), 35–6.

23 Margaret Richek, op. cit., 52.

24 Donaldson, op. cit., 32.

25 Noam Chomsky, *Aspects of the Theory of Syntax* (Cambridge, Massachusetts: MIT Press, 1965).

26 Donaldson, op. cit., 38.
27 *Curriculum Inquiry*, 8:3–4 and 9:1.
28 Chall, 1967, op. cit.; Albert J. Harris, 'Practical applications of reading research', *Reading Teacher*, 29:6 (March 1976); Harry Singer, 'Research that should have made a difference', *Elementary English*, 49:1 (January 1970).
29 See Michael Stubbs, *Language, Schools and Classrooms* (London: Methuen, 1976).

BIBLIOGRAPHY

Adams, Henry (1961), *The Education of Henry Adams*, Boston, Houghton Mifflin; originally published Massachusetts Historical Society, 1918.

Anderson, Richard C. (1959), 'Learning in discussions: a resume of the authoritarian-democratic studies', *Harvard Educational Review (HER)* 29:4 201–15.

Andreski, Stanislaw (1972), *Social Science as Sorcery*, New York, St Martin's Press.

Apple, Michael, a review of G. Bernbaum, *Knowledge and Ideology in the Sociology of Education*, London, Macmillan Press, 1977, and P. Woods and M. Hammersley (eds), *School Experience: Explorations in the Sociology of Education*, New York, St Martin's Press, 1977, in *HER* 48:4, November 1978.

Apple, Michael, 'Curriculum and Reproduction', *Curriculum Inquiry*, 1979.

Apple, Michael (1979), *Ideology and the Curriculum*, London and Boston, Routledge & Kegan Paul.

Applebaum, Richard P. and Chotiner, Harry (1979), 'Science, critique and praxis in Marxist method', *Socialist Review* July/August, 46.

Aronowitz, Stanley (1973), *False Promises*, New York, McGraw Hill.

Avineri, Scholomo (1968), *The Social and Political Thought of Karl Marx*, Cambridge, Cambridge University Press.

Bagenstos, Naida T. (1975), *A Participant Observation Study of Four Elementary Classrooms: Focus on Issues of Justice*, unpublished doctoral dissertation, Washington University.

Banks, O. (1978), 'School and Society' in L. Barton and R. Meighan

276

(eds), *Sociological Interpretations of Schooling*, Driffield, Yorks., Nafferton Books.

Baratz, Joan and Stephen (1970), 'Early childhood intervention: the social scientific basis of institutionalized racism', *HER* 40:1 29–50.

Barth, Roland (1971), 'So you want to change to an open classroom', *Phi Delta Kappan*, October 1971, 46.

Barth, Roland (1972), *Open Education and the American School*, New York, Agathon Press.

Barton, Len and Meighan, Roland (eds) (1978), *Sociological Interpretations of Schooling and Classrooms: A Reappraisal*, Nafferton, Driffield, Nafferton Books.

Baters, Richard J. (1980), 'Educational administration, the sociology of science and the management of knowledge', *Education Administration Quarterly* 16:2.

Baters, Richard J. (1978), 'The new sociology of education: directions for theory and research', *NZJ Educ. Studies* 13 3–22.

Behn, H. (1974), 'School is bad, work is worse', *School Review (SR)* 83:1.

Benjamin, Harold (1937), *The Sabre Tooth Curriculum*, London and New York, McGraw Hill.

Benn, S.I. and Peters R.S. (1959), *Social Principles and the Democratic State*, London, George Allen & Unwin.

Bennett, Neville (1976), *Teaching Styles and Pupil Progress*, London, Open Books and Cambridge, Mass., Harvard University Press.

Bereiter, Carl and Engelmann, Siegfried (1966), *Teaching Disadvantaged Children in the Pre-School*, Englewood Cliffs, N.J., Prentice-Hall.

Berlak, Ann and Harold, Bagenstos, N.T. and Mikel, E.R. (1975), 'Teaching and learning in the English primary schools', *SR* 83:2.

Berlak, Ann and Harold (August 1977), 'On the uses of social psychological research on schooling', essay review of *Beyond Surface Curriculum: An Interview Study of Teachers' Understandings* (Anne M. Bussis, Edward A. Chittenden, and Marianne Amerel, Boulder, Col.: Westview, 1976) in *SR* 85:4.

Bernbaum, Gerald (1977), *Knowledge and Ideology in the Sociology of Education*, London, Macmillan.

Bernstein, Basil (1973), 'A brief account of the theory of codes' in Open University, *Social Relationships and Language: Some Aspects of the Work of Basil Bernstein*, Milton Keynes, Open University Press.

Bernstein, Basil (1973), *Class, Codes and Control*, vol. 1, *Theoretical Studies Towards a Sociology of Language*, London, Routledge & Kegan Paul.

Bernstein, Basil (1975), *Class, Codes and Control*, vol. 3, *Towards a Theory of Educational Transmissions* (2nd edn), London, Routledge & Kegan Paul.

Blackie, John (1967), *Inside the Primary School*, London, HMSO.

Blauner, Robert (1964), *Alienation and Freedom: The Factory Worker and His Industry*, Chicago, University of Chicago Press.

Blum, Jeffrey M. (1980), a review of L.S. Hearnshaw, *Cyril Burt, Psychologist*, New York, Cornell University Press, 1979, in *HER*.

Blumer, Herbert (1964), *Symbolic Interactionism: Perspective and Method*, Englewood Cliffs, N.J., Prentice-Hall.

Boggs, Carl (1976), *Gramsci's Marxism*, London, Writers' and Readers' Cooperative.

Boggs, Carl (Fall/Winter 1979–80), 'Marxism and the role of intellectuals', *New Political Science* 1:213.

Bowles, Samuel (1972), 'Unequal education and the reproduction of the social division of labor' in M. Carnoy (ed.), *Schooling in a Corporate Society: The Political Economy of Education in America*, New York, David McKay.

Bowles, Samuel and Gintis, Herbert (1974), 'IQ in the United States Class structure', in A. Gartner, C. Greer and F. Riessman (eds), *The New Assault on Equality*, New York and London, Harper & Row.

Bowles, Samuel and Gintis, Herbert (1976), *Schooling in Capitalist America*, New York, Basic Books.

Boyson, Rhodes (1975), *The Crisis in Education*, London, Woburn Press.

Braverman, Harry (1974), *Labor and Monopoly Capital*, New York, Monthly Review Press.

Bricker, David C. 'Helping teachers appreciate the social context of their teaching dilemmas', undated manuscript, Oakland University, Rochester, Minnesota.

Brodbeck, May (ed.) (1968), *Readings in the Philosophy of the Social Sciences*, New York, Macmillan and London, Collier Macmillan.

Brodersew, A. (ed.) (1964), *Studies in Social Theory*, The Hague, Martinus Nijhoff.

Bullock Report, *A Language for Life* (1975), London, HMSO.

Cagan, Elizabeth (May 1978), 'Individualism, collectivism, and radical educational reform', *HER* 42:2.

Callahan, Raymond, C. (1962), *Education and the Cult of Efficiency*, Chicago, University of Chicago Press.

Carini, P.F. (1975), *Observation and Description: An Alternative Methodology for Investigation of Human Phenomena*, North Dakota Study Group on Evaluation Monograph Series, Grand Forks, University of North Dakota Press.

Caspary, William (1976), *Contradiction and Synthesis, Theory and Practice in the Relation of Depth Psychology to Critical Theory*, mimeo available from author, Washington University Dept. of Political Science, St Louis 63130.

Chall, Jean (1967), *Learning to Read: The Great Debate*, New York, McGraw Hill.

Chall, Jean (1979), 'Reading research, for whom', *Curriculum Inquiry* 9:1 1.

Cherkaoui, Mohamed (1977), 'Basil Bernstein and Emile Durkheim', *HER* 47:4.

Children and Their Primary Schools, A Report of the Central Advisory Council for Education (the Plowden Report, 1967), London, HMSO.

Chomsky, Noam (1965), *Aspects of the Theory of Syntax*, Cambridge, Massachusetts, MIT Press.

Cicourel, Aaron V. *et al.* (1974), *Language Use and School Performance*, New York, Academic Press.

Clark, Kenneth (1950), 'Effects of prejudice and discrimination on personality development', prepared for the Mid-Century White House Conference on Children and Youth.

Clark, Kenneth (1955), *Prejudice and Your Child*, Boston, Beacon.

Cohen, David K. and Lazerson, Marvin (1971), 'Education and the corporate order' in J. Karabel and A. H. Halsey (eds), *Power and Ideology in Education*, New York, Oxford University Press.

Cohn, Marilyn (1980), 'Linkage between campus research and classroom activity', mimeo, paper presented to Missouri Association of Teacher Education, Washington University.

Coleman, James *et al.* (1966), *Equality of Educational Opportunity*, Washington, DC, US Government Printing Office.

Coleman, James S., Kelley, Sara D. and Moore, John A. (1975), *Trends in School Segregation 1968–73*, Washington DC, The Urban Institute.

Conant, James B. (1963), *The Education of American Teachers*, New York, McGraw Hill.

Copperman, Paul (1978), *The Literacy Hoax*, New York, William Morrow.

279

Coser, Lewis (1956), *The Functions of Social Conflict*, New York, Free Press and London, Collier Macmillan.

Cosin, B.R. *et al.* (1971), *School and Society*, London, Routledge & Kegan Paul with The Open University.

Counts, George S. (1932), 'Dare progressive education be progressive', *Progressive Education* 9:4.

Cox, C.B. and Dyson, A.E. (1971), *The Black Papers on Education*, London, Davis Poynter.

Curtis, Charles P. Jr and Greenslet, Ferris (eds) (1953), *The Practical Cogitator*, Boston, Houghton Mifflin.

Dale, Roger *et al.* (eds) (1976), *Schooling and Capitalism*, London, Routledge & Kegan Paul.

Davies, Brian (1976), *Social Control and Education*, London, Methuen.

Delamont, Sara (1976), *Interaction in the Classroom*, London, Methuen.

Dennison, George (1969), *The Lives of Children*, New York, Random House.

Desmonde, William H. (1957), 'G.H. Mead and Freud: American social psychology and psychoanalysis' in B. Nelson (ed.), *Psychoanalysis and the Future*, New York, National Psychological Association for Psychoanalysis Inc.

Deutsch, Martin (1963), 'The disadvantaged child and the learning process', in A.H. Passow, *Education in Depressed Areas*, New York, Teacher's College Press.

Dewey, John (1956), *The Child and the Curriculum*, Chicago, University of Chicago Press.

Dewey, John (1966), *Democracy and Education*, New York, Free Press and London, Collier Macmillan.

Dewey, John (1963), *Experience and Education*, New York, Free Press and London, Collier Macmillan.

Dockrell, W.B. and Hamilton, David (eds) (1979), *Rethinking Educational Research*, London, Sydney, Auckland and Toronto, Hodder & Stoughton.

Donaldson, Margaret (1978), *Children's Minds*, London, Fontana.

Dreben, Robert (1967), 'The contribution of schooling to the learning of norms', *HER* 37:2.

Eames, S. Morris (1977), *Pragmatic Naturalism, An Introduction*, Carbondale, Southern Illinois University Press and London and Amsterdam, Feffer E. Simon.

Eggleston, John (1977), *The Sociology of the School Curriculum*, London, Henley and Boston, Routledge & Kegan Paul.

Ellis, T., McWhorter, J., McColgan, D. and Haddow, B. (1976), *William Tyndale, The Teachers' Story*, London, Writers' and Readers' Cooperative.

Erikson, Frederick (1978), 'On standards of descriptive validity in studies of classroom activity', paper delivered at AERA, Toronto.

Esland, Geoffrey (1971), 'Teaching and learning as the organization of knowledge' in Michael F.D. Young, *Knowledge and Control: New Directions in The Sociology of Education*, West Drayton, Collier Macmillan.

Farberman, Harvey A. and Stone, G. (eds) (1970), *Social Psychology Through Symbolic Interaction*, Waltham, Toronto and London, Ginn Blaisdell.

Fay, Brian (1975), *Social Theory and Political Practice*, London, Allen & Unwin.

Featherstone, Joseph (1963), 'Report analysis: children and their primary schools', *HER* 38:2.

Featherstone, Joseph (1971), *Schools Where Children Learn*, New York, Liverwright.

Featherstone, Joseph (1976), a review of S. Bowles and H. Gintis, *Schooling in Capitalist America, New Republic* 174:22.

Flesch, Rudolf (1966), *Why Johnny Can't Read and What you Can do About it*, New York, Harper.

Flude, Michael and Ahler, John (1974), *Educability, Schools and Ideology*, New York, Halstead Press.

Friere, Paolo (1974), *Education for Critical Consciousness*, New York, Seabury Press, published under the title *Education: The Practice of Freedom*, London, Writers' and Readers' Co-operative, 1976.

Friere, Paolo (1974), *Pedagogy of the Oppressed*, New York, Seabury Press.

Galbraith, J.K. (1979), 'Oil', *New York Review of Books* 27 September.

Galper, Jeffery (1975), *The Politics of Social Service*, Englewood Cliffs, N.J., Prentice-Hall.

Galton, Maurice, Simon, Brian and Croll, Paul (1980), *Inside the Primary Classroom*, London and Boston, Routledge & Kegan Paul.

Gartner, Allen, Greer, Colin and Reissman, Frank (eds) (1974), *The*

281

New Assault on Equality, New York and London, Harper & Row.

Gerth, H.H. and Wright Mills, C. (trs, eds) (1946), *From Max Weber*, New York, Oxford University Press.

Giroux, Henry and Penna, Anthony N. (1979), 'Social education in the classroom: the dynamics of the hidden curriculum', *Theory and Research in Social Education* VII:1.

Gorelick, Sherry (1977), 'Schooling problems in capitalist America', *Monthly Review*, 29:5.

Gould, Stephen Jay (1980), 'Jensen's last stand', *New York Review of Books* 1 May.

Gouldner, Alvin W. (1970), *The Coming Crisis in Western Sociology*, New York, Equinox.

Gouldner, Alvin W. (1976), *The Dialectic of Ideology and Technology*, New York, Seabury.

Grannis, Joseph C. (1967), 'The school as a model of society', *Harvard Graduate School of Education Bulletin* 12:2.

Graubard, Allen (1972), *Free the Children*, New York, Vintage.

Gretton, John and Jackson, Mark (1976), *William Tyndale: Collapse of a School or System?*, London, George Allen & Unwin.

Giddens, Anthony (ed.) (1974), *Positivism and Sociology*, London, Heinemann.

Giddens, Anthony (1976), *New Rules of Sociological Method*, New York, Basic Books.

Ginsberg, Herbert (1972), *The Myth of Cultural Deprivation*, Englewood Cliffs, N.J., Prentice-Hall.

Giroux, Henry A. (1979), 'Beyond the limits of radical education reform: toward a critical theory of education', *J. Curriculum Theorizing* 2:1.

Gladwin, Thomas (1973), 'Culture and logical process' in N. Keddie (ed.), *The Myth of Cultural Deprivation*, Harmondsworth, Middlesex, Penguin.

Goffman, I. (1959), *The Presentation of Self in Everyday Life*, New York, Doubleday.

Goodman, Paul, (1977), *Compulsory Miseducation*, New York, Random House.

Habermas, Jürgen (1972), *Knowledge and Human Interests*, London, Heinemann and Boston, Beacon Press.

Habermas, Jürgen (1975), *Legitimation Crisis*, Boston, Beacon Press.

Halsey, A.H. (ed.) (1972), *Educational Priority*, vol. 1, *Problems and Policies*, London, DES and SSRC, HMSO.

Hammersley, Martyn and Woods, Peter (eds) (1976), *The Process of Schooling*, London, Routledge & Kegan Paul.

Hammersley, Martyn and Woods, Peter (1977), *Ethnography and the Schools*, a part of the Open University Course, 'Schooling and society', Units 7–8, Milton Keynes, Open University Press.

Hammersley, Martyn and Woods, Peter (eds) (1977), *School Experience*, London, Croom Helm.

Hansen, Donald A. (1976), *An Invitation to Critical Sociology*, New York, Free Press and London, Collier Macmillan.

Hargreaves, Andy (1978), 'The significance of classroom coping strategies', in L. Barton and R. Meighan (eds), *Sociological Interpretations of Schooling and Classrooms: A Reappraisal*, Driffield, Yorks., Nafferton.

Hargreaves, Andy (1979), 'Synthesis and the study of strategies: a project for the sociological imagination' in P. Woods (ed.), *Pupil Strategies*, London, Croom Helm.

Hargreaves, David (1967), *Social Relations in a Secondary School*, London, Routledge & Kegan Paul.

Hargreaves, David (1978), 'Whatever happened to symbolic interactionism' in L. Barton and R. Meighan (eds), *Sociological Interpretations of Schooling and Classrooms: A Reappraisal*, Driffield, Yorks., Nafferton.

Harris, Albert J. (1976), 'Practical applications of reading research', *Reading Teacher* 29:6.

Harvard Educational Review (Winter 1968), a special issue expanded into the volume *Equal Educational Opportunity*, Cambridge, Mass., Harvard University Press, 1969.

Hechinger, Fred (1979), 'Frail sociology', *New York Times*, 5 November.

Heilbroner, Robert (1972), *The Worldly Philosophers*, 4th edn, New York, Simon & Schuster.

Heilbroner, Robert (1974), *An Inquiry into the Human Prospect*, New York, Norton.

Heilbroner, Robert (1976), a review of Bowles' and Gintis' *Schooling in Capitalist America*, *New York Review of Books* 15 April.

Heilbroner, Robert (1980), review of A.S. Eichner (ed.), *A guide to Post Keynesian Economics*, *New York Review of Books* 21 February.

Henderson, Jeff and Cohen, Robin (1979), 'Capital and the work ethic', *Monthly Review Press* November.

Henry, Jules (1963), *Culture Against Man*, New York, Random House.

Herndon, James (1977), *How to Survive in Your Native Land*, New York, Simon & Schuster.

Herrnstein, Richard (1971), 'IQ', *Atlantic Monthly* December.

Hoffman, Banesh (1962), *Tyranny of Testing*, New York, Crowell Collier.

Holt, John (1969), *How Children Fail*, London, Pitman, 1965 and Harmondsworth, Middlesex, Pelican, 1969.

Holt, John (1970), *The Underachieving School*, New York, Dell.

Hopkins, Adam (1978), *The School Debate*, Harmondsworth, Penguin.

Hoyles, Martin (ed.) (1977), *The Politics of Literacy*, London, Writers' and Readers' Publishing Cooperative.

Hoyles, Martin (ed.) (1979), *Changing Childhood*, London, Writers' and Readers' Publishing Cooperative.

Hurn, Christopher J. (1976), an essay review of Michael Flude and J. Ahier, *Educability, Schools and Ideology*, New York, Halstead Press, 1974, and several of the Open University course books, 'Recent trends in the sociology of education', *HER* 46:1 February.

Isaacs, Susan (1971), *The Children We Teach*, London, University of London Press, 1963, New York, Schocken Books Inc., 1971.

Jackson, Philip (1968), *Life in Classrooms*, New York, Holt.

'James Report' (1972), *Teacher Education and Teacher Training*, London, HMSO.

Jay, Martin (1973), *The Dialectical Imagination*, Boston and Toronto, Little, Brown.

Jencks, Christopher *et al.* (1972), *Inequality: A Reassessment of the Effects of Family and Schooling in America*, New York, Basic Books.

Jencks, Christopher *et al.* (1979), *The Determinants of Economic Success in America*, New York, Basic Books.

Jensen, Arthur (1969), 'How much can we boost IQ and scholastic achievement', *HER* 39:2 1–123.

Jensen, Arthur (1972), *Genetics and Education*, New York, Harper & Row and London, Methuen.

Jensen, Arthur (1979), *Bias in Mental Testing*, Glencoe, The Free Press.

Kamin, Leon J. (1974), *The Science and Politics of IQ*, New York, John Wiley.

Kanter, Rosabeth (1977), *Men and Women of the Corporation*, New York, Basic Books.

Kanter, Rosabeth (1979), 'A good job is hard to find', *Working Papers for a New Society* May/June.

Kantor, Harvey (1979), 'The great school warriors', a review of D. Ravitch, *The Revisionists Revised in Social Policy*, March/April 9:5.

Karabel, J. and Halsey, A.H. (1971), *Power and Ideology in Education*, New York, Oxford University Press.

Karier, Clarence J. (1975), *Shaping of the American Educational State*, New York, Free Press.

Keddie, Nell (1971), 'Classroom Knowledge', in M.F.D. Young, *Knowledge and Control*, West Drayton, Collier Macmillan.

Keddie, Nell (ed.) (1973), *The Myth of Cultural Deprivation*, Harmondsworth, Middlesex, Penguin.

King, Ronald (1978), *All Things Bright and Beautiful*, New York, Wiley.

Koerner, James D. (1963), *The Miseducation of American Teachers*, Boston, Houghton Mifflin.

Kohl, Daniel M. (1976), 'The IQ game: bait and switch', *SR* 84:4.

Kohl, Herbert (1967), *36 Children*, New York, New American Library.

Kozol, Jonathan (1967), *Death at an Early Age*, Boston, Houghton Mifflin.

Labov, William (1970), 'The logic of non standard English' in F. Williams (ed.), *Language and Poverty*, Chicago, Markham.

Lacey, C. (1970), *Hightown Grammar: The School as a Social System*, Manchester, Manchester University Press.

Langeveld, Willem (1979), *Political Education for Teenagers*, Strasbourg, Council of Europe.

A Language for Life (1975), Report of the Committee of Inquiry appointed by the Secretary of State for Education and Science under the Chairmanship of Sir Alan Bullock, London, HMSO.

Lasch, Christopher (1979), *The Culture of Narcissism*, New York, Warner Books.

Leacock, Eleanor Burke (1969), *Teaching and Learning in City Schools*, New York, Basic Books.

Leacock, Eleanor Burke (ed.) (1971), *The Culture of Poverty: A Critique*, New York, Simon & Schuster.

Lee, Patrick and Groper, Nancy B. (1974), 'Sex role culture and educational practice', *HER* 44:3.

Levitas, Maurice (1974), *Marxist Perspectives in the Sociology of Education*, London and Boston, Routledge & Kegan Paul.

Levy, Gerald E. (1970), *Ghetto School*, Indianapolis, Bobbs Merrill.

Lewontin, Richard (1979–80), 'Marxists and the university', *New Political Science* 1:213.

Lightfoot, Sara Lawrence (1973), 'Politics and reasoning: through the eyes of teachers and children', *HER* 43:2.

Lightfoot, Sara Lawrence (1977), 'Family-school interactions: the cultural image of mothers and teachers', *Signs* 3:2.

Litt, E. and Parkinson M. (1978), *US and UK Educational Policy*, New York, Praeger.

Loehin, John, Gardner, Linsey and Spuhler, J.N. (1975), *Race Differences in Intelligence*, San Francisco, W.H. Freeman.

Lortie, Dan C. (1975), *Schoolteacher*, Chicago, University of Chicago Press.

Lukàcs, Georg (1968), *History and Class Consciousness*, Cambridge, Mass., MIT Press.

Lukàcs, Georg (1973), *Marxism and Human Liberation*, New York, Dell.

Lynch, James and Pimlott, John (1976), *Parents and Teachers*, London, Schools Council/Macmillan.

Lynd, Robert (1939), *Knowledge for What? The place of social science in American Culture*, Princeton, Princeton University Press.

McCarthy, Thomas (1978), *The Critical Theory of Jürgen Habermas*, Cambridge, Mass., and London, MIT Press.

Manis, Dane (1979), 'A case study of a teacher's implementation of a kindergarten program developed at a university research and development center', unpublished doctoral dissertation, Washington University.

Manis, Jerome G. and Meltzer, Bernard N. (eds) (1972), *Symbolic Interaction* (rev. edn), Boston, Allyn Bacon.

Mannheim, K. (1936), *Ideology and Utopia: An Introduction to the Sociology of Knowledge*, London, Routledge & Kegan Paul.

Marcuse, Herbert (1964), *One Dimensional Man*, Boston, Beacon Press.

Marcuse, Herbert (1969), *An Essay on Liberation*, Boston, Beacon Press.

Marcuse, Herbert (1972), *Counter-revolution and Revolt*, Boston, Beacon Press.

Marx, Karl (1967), *Capital*, vol. 1, New York, International Publishers.

Marx, Karl (1972), *Critique of the Gotha Programme*, Peking, Foreign Languages Press.

Marx, Karl and Engels, Friedrich (1968), *The German Ideology*, Moscow.

Mead, George Herbert (1923), 'Scientific method and the moral sciences', *Int. J. Ethics* 33.

Mead, George Herbert (1932), *The Philosophy of the Present*, Chicago, Open Court Publishing Co.

Mead, George Herbert (1934), *The Works of George Herbert Mead*, vol. 1, *Mind, Self and Society*, Chicago, University of Chicago Press.

Mead, George Herbert (1936), *The Works of George Herbert Mead*, vol. 2, *Movements of Thought in the Nineteenth Century*, Chicago, University of Chicago Press.

Mead, George Herbert (1938), *The Works of George Herbert Mead*, vol. 3, *The Philosophy of the Act*, Chicago, University of Chicago Press.

Mead, George Herbert (1964), *On Social Psychology*, ed. Anselm Strauss, Chicago, University of Chicago Press.

Mehan, Hugh (1979), *Learning Lessons: Social Organization in the Classroom*, Cambridge, Mass., Harvard University Press.

Merton, R.K. (1957), *Social Theory and Social Structure*, Glencoe, Illinois, Free Press.

Mikel, Edward R. (in progress), *A Study of Social Studies Teachers' Conceptions of Knowledge and Knowing*, St Louis, Washington University.

Miller, D.I. (1973), *George Herbert Mead: Self, Language and the World*, Austin, University of Texas Press.

Miller, D.I. (1973), 'George Herbert Mead: symbolic interaction and social change', *Psychological Record* 23 294–304.

Miller, S.M. (1978), 'The recapitalization of capitalism', *Social Policy* 9:3.

Mills, C. Wright, (1939), 'Language, logic and culture', *American Sociological Review* 4:5.

Mills, C. Wright (1959), *The Sociological Imagination*, London, Oxford University Press.

Mills, C. Wright (1962), *The Marxists*, New York, Dell.

Mishler, Elliot G. (1979), 'Meaning in context: is there any other kind?', *HER* 49:1.

Moffett, James (1973), *A Student-Centered Language Arts Cur-*

riculum, Boston, Houghton Mifflin.

Murrow, Carey and Liza (1971), *Children Came First*, New York, American Heritage Press.

NAS (1975), *Violent and Disruptive Behavior in Schools.*

Nash, Roy (1971), 'Camouflage in the classroom', *New Society* 22 April 447.

National Institute of Education (1978), *Violent schools, safe schools: The Safe School Study Report*, Washington DC, US Department of Health, Education and Welfare.

Neill, A.S. (1950), *Summerhill: A Radical Approach to Childrearing*, New York, Hart and London, Gollancz, 1962.

Nelson, Benjamin (ed.) (1957), *Psychoanalysis and the Future*, New York, National Psychological Association for Psychoanalysis Inc.

New York Times Magazine, 'The threatening economy', 30 December 1979.

Passow, A.H. (1963), *Education in Depressed Areas*, New York, Teachers College Press.

Persell, Caroline Hodges (1980), a review of Rutter *et al.*, *Fifteen Thousand Hours*, Cambridge, Mass., Harvard University Press, 1979 and London, Open Books, *HER* May.

Peters, R.S. (1966), *Ethics and Education*, London, George Allen & Unwin.

Popkewitz, Thomas S. (1980), 'Paradigms in educational science', *Journal of Education* 192:1.

Poster, Cyril (1971), *The School and the Community*, London, Macmillan.

Rader, Melvin (1979), *Marx's Interpretation of History*, New York, Oxford University Press.

Rathbone, C. (1971), 'The implicit rationale of the open education classroom', in C. Rathbone (ed.), *Open Education*, New York, Citation Press, 106–71.

Rawls, John (1971), *A Theory of Justice*, Cambridge, Mass., Harvard University Press.

Reich, Charles (1970), *Greening of America*, New York, Random House.

Report on the Departmental Committee on the Training of Teachers for Public Elementary Schools, London, HMSO, 1925.

Richardson, Ken and Spears, David (eds) (1972), *Race and Intelligence*, Harmondsworth, Middlesex, Penguin.

288

Richek, Margaret (1979), 'Spiteful tracts compete against bloodless surveys: the use of reading research', *Curriculum Inquiry* 9:1.

Richmond, W. Kenneth (1979), *Education in Britain Since 1944*, London, Methuen.

Rist, Ray (1973), *The Urban School: A Factory for Failure*, Cambridge, Mass., MIT Press.

Roberts, G. (1977), 'G.H. Mead: the theory and practice of his social psychology', *Ideology and Consciousness* autumn.

Rogers, Carl (1969), *Freedom to Learn*, Columbus, Ohio, Charles Merrill.

Rosenfeld, Gerry (1971), *Shut Them Thick Lips*, New York, Holt.

Rutter, Michael *et al.* (1979), *Fifteen Thousand Hours*, Cambridge, Mass., Harvard University Press and London, Open Books.

Schwab, Joseph (1964), 'Structure of the disciplines: meanings and significances', in G.W. Ford and L. Pugno (eds), *The Structure of Knowledge and the Curriculum*, Chicago, Rand McNally.

Sealey, Leonard (1977), *Open Education: A Study*, New Haven, Hazen Foundation.

Sennett, Richard and Cobb, Jonathan (1972), *The Hidden Injuries of Class*, New York, Random House.

Sharp, Rachel and Green, Anthony (1975), *Education and Social Control; A Study in Progressive Primary Education*, London, Henley and Boston, Routledge & Kegan Paul.

Sheffler, I. (1974), *Four Pragmatists: A Critical Introduction to Pierce, James, Mead and Dewey*, New York, Humanities Press.

Silberman, Charles (1970), *Crisis in the Classroom*, New York, Random House.

Silver, Harold (1974), *Equal Opportunity in Education*, London, Methuen.

Silver, Harold (1978), 'Education and public opinion', *New Society* 7 December.

Silver, Harold (1980), *Education and the Social Condition*, London, Methuen.

Simon, Brian (1977), 'Intelligence testing – its validity and implications', *Communist University of London Papers*.

Singer, Harry (1970), 'Research that should have made a difference', *Elementary English* 49:1.

Smith, L.M. and Geoffrey, W. (1968), *Complexities of an Urban Classroom*, New York, Holt Reinhart & Winston.

Smith, L.M. (1977), 'Effective teaching: a qualitative inquiry in aesthetic education', *Anthropology and Education Quarterly* 2 127–39.

Smith, L.M. and Keith, P. (1971), *Anatomy of Educational Innovation*, New York, Wiley.

Spring, Joel (1976), *The Sorting Machine. National Education Policy since 1945*, New York, David McKay.

Steinfels, Peter (1979), 'What neo-conservatives believe', *Social Policy* 10:1.

Stone, Gregory P. and Farberman, Harvey A. (eds) (1970), *Social Psychology Through Symbolic Interaction*, Waltham, Toronto and London, Ginn Blaisdell.

Stone, Judith and Taylor, Felicity (1976), *The Parents' Schoolbook*, Harmondsworth, Middlesex, Penguin.

Strauss, Anselm (ed.) (1956), *George Herbert Mead: On Social Psychology*, Chicago, University of Chicago Press.

Stubbs, Michael (1976), *Language, Schools and Classrooms*, London, Methuen.

Swartz, David (1977), 'Pierre Bourdieu: the cultural transmission of social inequality', *HER* 47:4.

Thornbury, Robert (1978), *The Changing Urban School*, London, Methuen.

Tucker, Robert C. (ed.) (1978), *The Marx Engels Reader*, New York, W.W. Norton.

Tullock, John (1976), 'Gradgrind's heirs: the quiz and the presentation of "knowledge" by British television', in G. Whitty and M. Young (eds) *Explorations in the Politics of School Knowledge*, Driffield, Yorks., Nafferton.

Tyack, David (1974), *The One Best System*, Cambridge, Mass., Harvard University Press.

Tyack, David and Hansot, Elizabeth (forthcoming 1980), 'From social movement to professional management: an inquiry into the changing character of leadership in public education', *American Educational Journal* (formerly *SR*).

Tyrell, Burgess (ed.) (1971), *Dear Lord James, A Critique of Teacher Education*, Harmondsworth, Middlesex, Penguin.

Waddenton, C.H. (1975), a review of Edward O. Wilson, *Sociobiology*, *New York Review of Books* 7 August.

Walker, Alan (1980), 'A right turn for the welfare state', *Social Policy* 10:5.

Walker, Robert and Adelman, Clem (1971), 'Interaction analysis in informal classrooms: a critical comment on the Flanders system', *B.J.E.P.* 45:1.

Walker, Robert and Adelman, Clem (1975), *A Guide to Classroom Observation*, London, Methuen.

Wall Street Journal (5 February 1980), 'Blackboard jungle. In inner-city schools getting an education is often a difficult job'.

Wann, T.W. (ed.) (1964, 2nd edn 1974), *Behaviourism and Phenomenology*, Chicago, London.

Wax, Murray L. and Rosalie (1971), 'Cultural deprivation as an educational ideology', in E. Leacock, *The Culture of Poverty: A Critique*, New York, Simon and Schuster.

Weber, Lillian (1971), *The English Infant School and Informal Education*, New York, Prentice-Hall.

Weber, Lillian (undated manuscript), 'Comments on Neville Bennett's book: *Teaching Styles and Pupil Progress*', mimeo.

Westbury, Ian (1979), 'Schooling as an agency of education: some implications for curriculum theory' in W.B. Dockrell and D. Hamilton (eds), *Rethinking Educational Research*, London, Sydney, Hodder and Stoughton.

Whitty, Geoff (1977), *School Knowledge and Social Control*, Milton Keynes, Open University Press.

Whitty, Geoff and Young, Michael (1976), *Exploration in the Politics of School Knowledge*, Driffield, Yorks., Nafferton.

Williams, Frederick (ed.) (1970), *Language and Poverty*, Chicago, Markham.

Williams, Raymond (1973), 'Base and superstructure in Marxist cultural theory', *New Left Review* December, 82.

Williams, Raymond (1977), *Marxism and Literature*, Oxford, Oxford University Press.

Willis, Paul (1978), *Learning to Labour*, Westmead, Saxon House.

Wilson, Edward O. (1975), *Sociobiology, the New Synthesis*, Cambridge, Mass., Harvard University Press.

Wirth, Arthur (1978), *John Dewey as Educator*, Huntington, New York, Krieger.

Wolf, Mary Anne, McQuillan, Mark K. and Radwin, Eugene (eds), 'Thought and language/language and reading', *HER* reprint no. 14.

Woodring, Paul (1966), 'Are intelligence tests unfair?', *Saturday Review* 16 April.

Woods, Peter (ed.) (1980), *Teacher Strategies*, London, Croom Helm.

Woods, Peter (ed.) (1980), *Pupil Strategies*, London, Croom Helm.

Young, Michael F.D. (1971), *Knowledge and Control: New Directions in The Sociology of Education*, West Drayton, Collier Macmillan.

Zeitlin, Irving (1973), *Rethinking Sociology*, Englewood Cliffs, N.J., Prentice-Hall.

Zetterberg, H. (1965), *On Theory and Verification in Sociology*, Totowa, New Jersey, Bedminster Press.

NAME INDEX

SUBJECT INDEX

accountability, 11, 226, 233–4
act, concept of, 111–12, 115–17, 128–9, 133
adaptation, Mead's concept, 112–13, 118–20, 166n, 167n
administrators, *see* educational administrators
affirmative action, 7; common culture v. sub group consciousness, 163; each child unique v. shared characteristics, 155; equal allocation v. differential, 159; self reliance of disadvantage v. self reliance, 161
alienated work, *see* work
alternative schools, 19
autonomy and collectivism, meanings about, 210–13, 225n, 227n
authoritarian-democratic, studies of, 225n

background assumptions, 23–4, 30n, 36n; in positivist social research, 12–18
base–superstructure, 121–3, 169–70n; *see also* Williams, R.
basics, 2, 6, 9, 192–3, 207; compared to non basics, 210; *see also* patterns of resolution, curriculum dilemmas
Bell-Curve . . . IQ, 11
Black Papers, 8, 224n
blacks, 83–4; child as person v. client, 155; common culture v. sub group, 163–4; equal v. differential allocation, 159–63; self reliance v. special consideration, 161; *see also* affirmative action, patterns of resolution

budget reductions on school expenditures, 7
Bullock Report, 263–5, 272–3n

capitalism, 1, 166–70n, 220–5
childhood, concept of, 227n; childhood continuous v. unique, 156–9, 187, 194–6
citizens, 1–4, 6–9; parent, expert collaboration, 249–52; role in critical inquiry, 233–6
classification, concept of, 16, 33n; *see also* Bernstein, B.
code: concept of, 16, 33n; *see also* Bernstein, B.; emphasis in reading instruction, 261–2
collectivist values, 213, 227n; common culture v. sub group, 163–4; learning is social v. individual, 154–5
comprehensive school, 1, 5, 26n, 259
consciousness, 14–16; and hegemony, 226n; and social research, 111; critical, 227n; false, 123; self, 132, 230–1 and Mead, 114, 118–9, 128; raising, 123–4; *see also* critical inquiry
Conservative policies, 1, 5–9, 28–9n
contradictions, 122, 124–5, 128, 202–3, 225–8n, 239–44; in educational policies, 5–9, 28n; in pedagogical research, 260–9; in teacher education, 251–6; in uses of educational research, 12, 17–18
crisis in the classroom, 20
critical inquiry, 49, 125, 229, 232–3; and Mead's concept of reflective action, 113–15, 119, 122; and

296